THAT WASN'T THE PLAN

REG SHERREN

That Wasn't the Plan

A Memoir

Douglas & McIntyre

DOUGLAS AND MCINTYRE (2013) LTD.
P.O. Box 219, Madeira Park, BC, V0N 2H0
www.douglas-mcintyre.com

Edited by Arlene Prunkl
Cover design by Anna Comfort O'Keeffe
Text design by Shed Simas / Onça Design
Printed and bound in Canada
Printed on paper certified by the Forest Stewardship Council

Douglas and McIntyre (2013) Ltd. acknowledges the support of the Canada Council for the Arts, the Government of Canada, and the Province of British Columbia through the BC Arts Council.

LIBRARY AND ARCHIVES CANADA CATALOGUING IN PUBLICATION
Title: That wasn't the plan : a memoir / Reg Sherren.
Other titles: That was not the plan.
Names: Sherren, Reg, 1959- author.
Identifiers: Canadiana (print) 20200200410 | Canadiana (ebook) 20200200429 | ISBN 9781771622547 (softcover) | ISBN 9781771622554 (HTML)
Subjects: LCSH: Sherren, Reg, 1959- | LCSH: Television journalists—Canada—Biography.
Classification: LCC PN4913.S47 A3 2020 | DDC 070.4/3092—dc23

To my family ... my dear wife Pamela, and my great source of joy and pride, our children Mitchell and Emma.

And for my dad, Nelson, who passed away while I was writing this book. Dad loved books, loved reading and absorbing what they had to offer. I wish he was here to read this one. Love you, Dad.

Contents

Introduction

Does anybody really have a plan? I don't think most people do. I certainly didn't. You can never really predict what life will throw at you. I didn't even try—much.

But when you find yourself on a Canadian warship less than a hundred kilometres off the coast of Kuwait, and the Navy kid lying in the bunk next to you says, "Jeez, there's twice as many Iraqi planes in the air today, and we don't know where they're coming from ..."

Or you're riding on the back of a humpback whale in a small rubber boat, through no fault of your own, and the beast nearly knocks you into the North Atlantic ...

Or when you and your camera operator are stuck in the middle of several hundred angry, protesting crab plant workers, and one of them turns on you both and says, "Let's throw these two in the harbour!"

At moments like those, you can't help but find yourself thinking, *"That wasn't the plan!"*

How did I go from a freckle-faced, red-headed kid growing up in small-town Western Labrador to a journalist travelling the world and telling stories for the CBC's flagship news program, *The*

I was barely three when I got the inkling that a career in television might be in my future!

National? That path certainly wasn't part of any plan I was aware of. As the middle child, in my early years, the plan was simply survival. And with two older brothers and two younger sisters, I had to be quick on my feet, and I became something of an artful dodger. Acting out, pulling pranks, performing, goofing off—anything to get attention—yes, that became my strategy, every day.

But the truth about how I became a journalist—well, that's another story altogether.

I am one of those increasingly rare journalists who began in the era of film, worked through the age of video, and then evolved into using the digital platforms that have become such a big part of our lives. Each offered its own challenges and opportunities.

These days, the brain sometimes creaks, just like my knees. But in the pages that follow, to the best of my memory, here are some of my most interesting stories from the road, and it is a great honour and pleasure to share them with you.

CHAPTER 1

And So It Begins

GROWING UP IN WABUSH

I grew up in the wilds of Labrador, in remote Wabush, where the idea of becoming a journalist was probably the furthest thing from my mind. As the middle child of five, I found myself constantly competing for attention.

Although remote, Wabush was the land of plenty. Yet the image most folks have of Labrador is of a frozen wasteland with polar bears and long cold winters. I remember visiting Montreal once with my mother, and she was asked if we lived in igloos. But in the land of rich iron-ore deposits, the only igloo was the Igloo Restaurant.

Everyone who wanted a job had one. The townsite—offering cheap, sturdy houses to anyone who ventured north—was built even before the people got there. The mine took care of everything. If a window broke, the mine fixed it. If the furnace failed, the mine installed another one. You worked for them, and they took care of you.

The modern all-grades school had everything a kid could ask for. Music, sports, art and my personal favourite, theatre. The local recreation centre had another huge gymnasium and stage, plus a bowling alley, a library and a darn near Olympic-sized swimming pool. Right next door was the ice rink, where you could also roller skate in the summer. All for fewer than five thousand people.

The land of plenty indeed—*if* you didn't mind freezing to death eight months of the year. It often snowed the first week of school, and it stayed. I can remember going trick-or-treating on a Ski-Doo. In the Labrador Trough, as it was known, four metres of snow was not unusual in winter. We would tunnel under it like moles, creating a whole other world beneath the surface of the snow. You had to. Wind chills approaching −70°C were not uncommon. Even with a block heater or two, sometimes you had to take the battery out of your car at night and bring it into the house if you wanted the engine to start in the morning.

We didn't seem to mind—we always had something to do. I loved to perform, whether in front of Dad's eight-millimetre-film camera or as one of the designated class clowns. I was in the Christmas play nearly every year, starting with kindergarten. One year I was chief snowbird, the next an elf. Every chance I got to "act," I did. On my report card one year the teacher had written, "Reg is an attention seeker," and I thought with amusement, "That's true!" I also came by my willingness to tell stories or act them out honestly. My mother wrote and told many stories, as did my aunt and my grandmother.

My father, who was one of the iron-ore mine managers, was ahead of his time. He had purchased a reel-to-reel tape recorder— well, it was more than that. It was one of those big polished-wood consoles many people had in their living rooms. Ours had the usual speakers, an AM/FM radio and a record player with space to store the LPs, plus the large reel-to-reel tape recorder, complete with two microphones.

Dad would record us, coaxing us to sing songs or recite poems like "The Cremation of Sam McGee" by Robert Service. It was my first introduction to a microphone, the first time I heard what I sounded like. Little pie-faced Reggie finds his voice.

Dad was also was a damn fine cameraman, recording pictures, if not sound, that chronicled our lives in the Big Land or on vacation across Atlantic Canada. He filmed us tobogganing in the bush, taking family road trips to New Brunswick, loading haystacks on a wagon or digging clams in Prince Edward Island. And usually in there somewhere was footage of Reg acting like a goof for the camera. I guess, in hindsight, Dad was inspiring my imagination. It would take me much further than I ever dreamed of going.

And Wabush, Labrador, was a great place to explore your imagination. It wasn't as if we were distracted by television—at least not much. In the early days, television consisted of one channel that started at 3:45 in the afternoon with the soap opera *The Edge of Night* and ended around 11:00 at night. Half the programming was French and everything was black and white. Most programming was a week old with the exception of news and hockey games. They were flown in on rolls of film and broadcast the next day. Radio usually broke the final score of the hockey game the day before you watched it.

We had some American programming, such as *Bonanza* and *The Wonderful World of Disney*, but most of it was pure Canadiana—*Chez Hélène* from CBC TV and *Bobino* from Radio-Canada (CBC's French-language service) or good old CBC Television programming like *Country Canada* or *The Forest Rangers*. That *Forest Rangers* theme song still plays in my head. I remember coming home for lunch one day to watch Stompin' Tom Connors get married on *Elwood Glover's Luncheon Date*. I thought that was pretty cool. It doesn't get any more Canadian than that!

When I was in Grade 7, I badly broke my arm. Then they discovered a cyst was eating through the bone and whisked me off to Montreal for surgery, where I was on a ward with three adult men at the Royal Victoria Hospital. One fellow was in traction, the result of being sideswiped by a transport truck while riding his motorcycle; the second had had both his legs crushed while loading a giant roll of newsprint down at the docks. The third, an elderly gentleman, had cataracts. He and I would watch westerns together on a twelve-inch black-and-white portable TV. He couldn't see the picture, so I would describe the action for him. It was my first gig as a commentator.

When I was in Grade 8, I entered a contest at our local radio station, CFLW. The idea was for contestants to sketch their version of the troglodyte, a caveman-type character from a hit song by a group called the Jimmy Castor Bunch. I drew this primitive-looking fellow in a tattered tuxedo with a bone through his nose and somehow managed to win an album by Three Dog Night called *Golden Biscuits*.

I still remember walking into the radio station, tucked into the basement of what was essentially a bungalow (the manager lived upstairs), to pick up my very first record album. I was twelve years old. The cramped space had posters on the walls from different performers, tiny studios with microphones, control boards, and panelling with little holes that the fellow showing me around said was something called "soundproofing."

Banging away in a small room by itself was a big green metal monster called a teletype. The teletype was like an extremely early mechanical version of the internet, used to deliver news wire services to various radio, TV and newspaper organizations through a dedicated telephone line. Not that I knew any of that then. That machine hammered out stories from around the world twenty-four hours a day. They rolled off the top, still warm from the ink-stained keys, in one long, continuous river of newsprint containing entire newscasts, sports, entertainment bulletins and weather forecasts. It was a wondrous thing.

At home at night, I would listen to different stations on my crystal radio set. The radio kit was a Christmas present that supplied the hardware to build your very own radio. It also offered the ability to escape. Sometimes stations from faraway places would find their way skipping across the Labrador sky: CFGO Ottawa, WOR New York or WBZ Boston.

Three years later, when I was fifteen, I landed my first job at that same Wabush radio station as an announcer—and I use the term loosely. How I got the job I'm not really sure. My best buddy, Larry Hennessey, was already working there and put in a good word, but I suspect my father's position may have also had something to do with it. Whatever the reason, I landed the noon-to-five time slot on Sunday afternoons.

I had absolutely zero training. For my first show I was given some very brief instruction by the fellow on the air before me, a guy who called himself Buffalo Bill Cody. He looked a little like Wild Bill Hickok with his long hair, moustache, cowboy hat and fringe jacket, and he wasn't a very good teacher. He showed me how to turn on the microphone and which controls delivered sound from the turntables or the reel-to-reel machine, and then he left. I sat there facing a baffling array of switches and dials. I spent the next five hours apologizing for being on the air—when I could get on the air—and my broadcasting career was born.

Being on the air was just one of my duties. I also had to make sure all the garbage cans were clean for Monday morning, and I had to change the paper—those big rolls of newsprint—on the teletype. Sometimes the big green monster would jam up. Once, I recall, all that balled-up friction caused it to almost catch fire. There was a lot of smoke. Some years later, after college, my first story with my very own byline would be hammered out on the big green machine in radio and TV stations across the system.

CFLW, that first station brave enough to hire me, was part of the Humber Valley Broadcasting chain, started by Dr. Noel Murphy, an obstetrician from Corner Brook, Newfoundland. His vision eventually stretched across the western part of the province, and then north. CFLW (Coming from Labrador West) had gone on the air in 1971.

There was no real music format. You could play pretty much whatever you liked, and I did. Sometimes I would play hard rockers like Led Zeppelin followed by a sketch from Monty Python (I had all their albums) before rolling the tape on *Back to the Bible*, a half-hour religious program sent from the United States. They paid Humber Valley Broadcasting good money for that half-hour, I was told, and programs like it could be the financial bread and butter of smaller stations.

Often you were the only person in the station. Going to the bathroom meant rolling an extended version of Glen Campbell's rendition of "Classical Gas." For bigger jobs—say, if you needed to step out to pick up a pizza— "Alice's Restaurant" was the song to use. It was over eighteen minutes long and the Hudson Restaurant was just a few minutes away. You got anything you wanted, thanks to "Alice's Restaurant"!

Playing Glen Campbell or a new ABBA hit on the radio was fun for a while, but after a couple of years, even I had to admit it was time to develop some version of a career strategy. My interest in theatre continued. I had a blast acting alongside Labrador greats like the Doyle clan and Kevin Lewis, an immense talent, in the Carol Players theatre troupe. I was giving some serious thought to that possibility but didn't have a clue how to go about it.

The big money in Labrador was made working in construction or in the local mine. I worked in both. Money was no problem. I made a *lot* of money for someone my age. The summer after I graduated from high school, 1976, I was making close to $2,500 every two weeks. So after I managed to save some of it, I decided I would travel.

The mine had a company plane that flew regularly to Montreal. Back then you could often hitch a ride and go on an adventure for a few days. I used to stay in a small tourist home on Sherbrooke Street just up from the Voyageur bus terminal. Now that I think about it, I can't imagine my son or daughter doing things like that at the age of sixteen or seventeen, but I was already living on my own and thought nothing of it.

In 1977, I flew alone from Montreal to the Canary Islands, just because it was the most exotic-looking place I could find at the travel agency. I flew out of the old Mirabel airport and landed in Tenerife in January, just two months before the largest air accident in the history of aviation took place there. A KLM aircraft collided with a Pan Am flight on the runway, and 583 people died.

On another trip to Montreal, I found myself in the lounge in the hotel across from where I was staying (no, I was not legally old enough to be in that lounge) when a gentleman came in with his wife. I was sitting at the bar with empty seats on either side of me. I saw he was looking around and the place was full, so I said, "Would you like me to move over so you can sit together?" He appreciated the gesture and we struck up a conversation.

Turned out he was a journalist with the *Montreal Star*. I told him I was from Newfoundland and Labrador, and he told me he had travelled across Newfoundland covering the last passenger train. It was called the *Newfie Bullet*, which was kind of an ironic joke: the *Bullet* was being discontinued because it was too slow. I told him the joke about the fellow who decided to commit suicide by lying down on the tracks but died of starvation waiting for the train to show up. He laughed and laughed. I also told him I had a little radio gig at our local station. He said, "Well then, you should come to the Press Club with us!" We grabbed a cab over to the Sheraton Mount Royal Hotel on Peel Street.

The Press Club was around the back, in the basement of the hotel. I remember the heavy wood panelling and all these serious-looking people in suits, and thinking, "I'm way out of my depth here." In one corner I saw Peter Kent, who just the year before had become the main anchor of *The National* on CBC Television. I had watched him introduce the stories about the air disaster in Tenerife. At that moment I didn't have enough nerve to introduce myself, but I remember thinking, "That fellow is a big deal." Did it leave an impression? Absolutely. So when I got back to Labrador and learned about a new college radio and television broadcasting program opening in North Bay, Ontario, I decided to check it out.

Canadore College had state-of-the-art equipment and, as part of the program, students operated a radio station and even broadcasted a nightly TV newscast on cable. It was a perfect fit, but I was honestly scared to death at the prospect. Wabush was familiar and comfortable. I could go off on adventures, but I could always come home. Somehow, I knew making this change would change everything—forever.

As things turned out, the decision was made for me. I didn't leave home, home left me. My family, the only family I knew, was going up in flames. Divorce was in the air for my parents, and change seemed inevitable.

But because I was from outside Ontario, getting into Canadore College was not going to be easy. I had to write several essays and complete manual dexterity tests. I guess I didn't put any square pegs into round holes, though, because I landed one of the four available first-year positions for non-Ontario residents.

Then something happened that has stayed with me ever since. Two weeks before I was to leave for school, I was walking behind the Sir Wilfred Grenfell Hotel in Wabush when I saw a wallet lying on the ground outside the entrance to the hotel's pub. Inside it was one piece of ID from the University of Toronto and $800 in cash.

I didn't recognize the face on the card, so I thought, "He must be staying at the hotel." I checked at the front desk and sure enough, he was. I went upstairs and knocked on his door. He proved to be an engineering student working for the summer at the mine. He couldn't thank me enough and wanted to give me a reward. "No thanks," I said. "It's your wallet and I'm just glad I could get it back to you."

Two weeks later, I was on a train out of Montreal bound for North Bay, Ontario. Everything I owned was in half a dozen cardboard boxes in baggage. I was staring out the window—miles away really, worrying about the future—when a fellow tapped me on the arm and said, "Are you Reg Sherren, by any chance?"

I said yes, wondering what sort of trouble was headed my way now, when he said, "I just found your wallet in the bathroom and thought you might want it back." I had $2,000 in cash and even more in traveller's cheques in that wallet, as well as all my ID and a credit card. I did not even know I had lost it. It must have fallen out from the motion of the train while I was fumbling around in the confined space of the washroom.

If you believe in such things, good karma found me that day and paid me back. It was a lesson I have never forgotten. It has been said many ways: "Do unto others as you would have them do unto you," or "What goes around, comes around," or "Kindness begets kindness." They are all true.

GETTING EDUCATED

For two years, I trained at Canadore College, which was nestled on top of a hill amid silver birch trees just outside North Bay. It was a fabulous place to learn. I worked as a DJ at the college's radio station, participated in the nightly newscast and did some semi-professional acting on the side (that dream was still alive). During school breaks I managed to get gigs as an announcer/operator back home at CBNLT, broadcasting on television across Western Labrador.

But my first work placement had more to do with selling than broadcasting. It was down in Toronto, where I apprenticed at a national advertising agency. It was all demographics and data spit out by a cool, brand-new tool in radio advertising, something called a "computer program." It was fascinating that a machine into which you typed simple facts and figures could then analyze the ratings in the ten largest radio markets in the country. In mere moments, it would do its magic and spit out the most cost-effective way to reach between one and two million eighteen-year-olds across Canada. It was the very beginning of a new form of technology that would change the world forever. But to me, it was about selling advertising, not making radio. I was fascinated by it and perhaps a little afraid of it, but I did know one thing: it wasn't for me.

When I returned to North Bay some months later, I was close to broke. College was ending and my future was looking rather hopeless. Then I heard they were looking for a television news anchor in Thunder Bay, Ontario. I hadn't done any television in months, and at twenty-two, I was pretty sure this job possibility was a long shot at best.

But I went into the studio, wrote up a newscast, set up a camera in front of the old news desk and played one of the most important acting roles of my young life, that of a television news anchor. I fired the tape off. Three days later I got a call telling me I had landed the role—I mean the position—of main television news anchor at CKPR-TV. I didn't know whether to laugh or cry. I was still almost broke and a long way from Thunder Bay. I was even farther from Labrador, and apparently heading west.

That same morning a good college buddy of mine, who for various reasons was unable to finish the course, dropped by to see if I'd gotten the job. I told him I was now a television news anchor—if I could figure out how to get to Thunder Bay. "Do you have any money?" he asked. "I have a hundred and fifty bucks to my name," I replied. "Give it to me," said Bob, and I did. Later that evening he returned with almost $400. How he had accomplished this feat I was afraid to ask. "Go, man, and do your thing. You're going to make it," he said. Bob had a lot more faith in me than I did. He went on to a career in computers and raised a fine family. I have never forgotten his support and kindness. It was that good karma again.

A FULL-TIME PROFESSIONAL

Just about everything I owned could still fit into several cardboard boxes. They were loaded into the storage compartments beneath me as I rode a Greyhound bus across the top of Lake Superior. By sheer coincidence, my best buddy, Larry Hennessey from Labrador, had also just taken a job in Thunder Bay, on the radio, with the same company that had hired me. It was a wonderful thing. A best friend for support and someone to help pay the rent. I would need it.

Thunder Bay wasn't a big market in the Canadian scheme of things, but it wasn't small either. The station broadcast across Northwestern Ontario, and in 1981, the place was booming. Huge grain-handling operations and the forest industry employed thousands, and Mini Queen's Park provided hundreds of government jobs.

The city had two daily newspapers, a morning and afternoon edition, and I was soon meeting some of the characters in the business. One of them was Howard Reid, who wrote a popular local social/gossip column and didn't pull any punches. A portly little fellow with a shock of white hair, he would march into a news conference and look around. If there wasn't a complimentary and completely outfitted bar in the room, Howard could be heard exclaiming, "No drinkie-poo, no interview. No booze, no news!" before turning on his heel and marching out of the room.

Newspapers were still a huge influence and dominated the news market. Gathering information for television was still cumbersome but changing quickly. Of course, there was no internet. We did have the news wire, with a slightly more sophisticated contraption spitting out the information than the big old green machine, and when I first started, video cameras were not used. All news events were shot on film, brought back to the basement and developed using a chemical process. The film was physically cut and taped together into a news reel. Some nights you didn't even know whether you had pictures until almost six o'clock. It could be a delicate dance, adding stories on the fly to fill time if the pictures did not appear. Within months videotape arrived, and the speed at which you could turn pictures around for broadcast now seemed practically instantaneous.

I was the main anchor from 6:00 to 7:00 p.m. I wrote and lined up the show. I also assembled and hosted the late news and did radio and television news reports. If that wasn't enough, I also organized, wrote and hosted a weekly half-hour public affairs program. My starting salary was $900 a month gross. It was barely enough to live on, but who cared? I certainly didn't. I was working so much I hardly had time to spend the money I didn't have anyway. To survive, I shared a house with my buddy Larry and another friend, Gord McLaughlin, a fellow I'd met in college who had since been hired to write at the *Chronicle-Journal*, one of the two local newspapers. Besides covering city hall, Gord was also a talented young playwright, making a name for himself in local theatre. We had it all covered: radio, TV and the newspapers. Heady times for three young men, and good friendships that continue to this day.

There were no cellphones. No computers or internet. We banged out the scripts on five-part paper using manual typewriters. You had to bang away hard to make those keys impact five copies, thanks to the carbon in between each sheet of paper. One for your script, one for the director, one for radio, one for the producer, and one for the files.

The CKPR station itself was a unique beast. It was what was called a twin stick, meaning the owner, Fraser Dougall, had both the CBC and CTV affiliates, technically competitors, under one roof. It was the first place in Canada where such a broadcast licence had been granted. The master control rooms were side by side. All newscasts were first aired on CBC (CKPR), recorded and then replayed on the CTV channel (CHFD) during the following hour. It was an arrangement eventually adopted in other markets too, places that were not big enough to support two separate stations. It meant that each night you might see CBC News stories on CTV and vice versa. To add to the confusion, we chopped off the reporter sign-offs. Dougall also owned two radio stations, AM and FM, with all of it broadcasting under the same roof.

What this meant was that I was on the air somewhere on a television in Thunder Bay, and across Northwestern Ontario, three hours a day. You might say I saturated the market. It was also my first experience with celebrity, and the feeling that folks were watching me all the time. I remember being mobbed by a crowd of high school girls outside a Cow Palace once (Thunder Bay's version of a 7-Eleven). Instead of exciting, it was a somewhat unnerving experience. They pushed me into a corner, and some even demanded I autograph their cigarette packs.

I like to think it didn't go to my head ... much. The fact that I never seemed to have more than $5 in my pocket helped. The good people of Thunder Bay adopted me. One older woman who worked in the corner shop near me always asked if I was eating well enough. Sometimes I would walk into the store and she would have a big pan of homemade lasagna waiting for me behind the counter, and she'd insist I take it back home. Once, after a trip to Vegas, she presented me with one of the silver dollars she had won, "for luck." I still have it to this day. My neighbours had become my family.

Decades later former viewers from Thunder Bay would approach me in an airport or on a street somewhere in the country to say, "We remember when you started out with us in Thunder Bay. We've been following your career." It was always gratifying and very much appreciated, as if they had been cheering me on.

There were some interesting characters working at the "station on the hill," as it was sometimes known. Ray Dee programmed radio. Early in his radio career he brought a new band into the station's studio to record a couple of songs. They had wandered into town from Winnipeg to play a few gigs and Ray thought they

My CKPR production team, a great bunch who did their best to teach me all they could. Back left to right: Me, Jon Ogden, Bill Kallio. Front: Bill McKirdy.

sounded pretty damn good. The band leader was a guy named Neil Young. Decades later Neil came looking for those original recordings and used several of them on his *Anthology* CD collection.

Rick Smith was a broadcasting icon in the city. Rick told me he had gotten the first North American interview with the Beatles. Apparently he was working in Montreal back in 1964 when his buddy at Trans World Airlines told him the Beatles' plane would stop there to refuel on its way to New York, where they had a date with *The Ed Sullivan Show*. Rick borrowed his buddy's TWA overalls, walked out to the plane and snagged a quick interview as John, Paul, George and Ringo stepped off for a breath of fresh air. That's how the story goes, anyway.

Weatherman Bob MacDonald was another character. Bob's claim to fame was his ability to stand behind a Plexiglas weather map and, using grease pencils in both hands, write the temperatures while doing the forecast. Of course, he had to write them backwards so they appeared normal on camera, while at the same time drawing a little figure up in one corner. I have never seen anything like it, before or since.

Mostly I anchored the news, but sometimes I stepped into news reporting, and I also did the weather segment on the late news. It resulted in an interesting relationship with some of the folks of Thunder Bay, especially my neighbours.

Thunder Bay was a diverse city with people from around the world. There was a large population from Finland, and then there were the Italians. They too had a large, vibrant community. In the fall some made wine the traditional way—barefoot, stomping around in large wooden barrels. In addition to growing their own, sometimes tractor-trailer loads of grapes would arrive from California. They loved to garden. Their greatest pride was their output of produce: the tomatoes, peppers, zucchini and of course their grapes. I lived in a very Italian neighbourhood.

In the fall, I would arrive home after the late news, close to midnight. When I pulled into the driveway, sometimes a crowd would have gathered just down the lane. The first time I saw them I didn't know what to think. Was it an unruly mob? Was it something I'd read on the news? After a few days, I grew used to them and would get out of my car and greet them. Then the designated spokesperson would shuffle toward me shyly, hands in pockets, kicking at the ground. Eventually he would look up and say, "You think maybe frost tonight?" Depending on what forecast I had received from Environment Canada, I would give him my opinion, which seemed to carry a great deal of weight. (I guess he needed an update from my last forecast on TV!) He would nod and return to the others to deliver the wisdom of a fellow who probably knew far less about it than they did. A short discussion would ensue before they dispersed. Later in the fall I would be presented with fresh produce and some of their fabulous homemade wine. I suppose my forecasts weren't too far off. Lovely people.

A CANTANKEROUS LITTLE FELLOW

Some individuals you never forget. Mayor Walter Assef was one of them. He was a small man with a larger-than-life personality, one that often came with a growl and some bite. An interview with Walter was always more like a lecture, delivered by him.

Former professional boxer and long-time Member of Provincial Parliament Mickey Hennessy once told me, "Never underestimate Assef," as he once had in an election. Back in the 1950s, he said, Walter created what he figured was one of the first political TV ads, certainly the first in Thunder Bay. It was a simple approach with a direct appeal to the voters. Walter stood in front of a curtain, speaking directly to the camera. At the end he said, "Now remember, vote Assef!" while taking a bow. Written on the top of his bald head in large black print were the words VOTE ASSEF! That was one political match where Mickey was out-boxed. Assef beat him by a landslide. Mickey eventually figured out how to win, and he went on to a long career both as a city councillor and as an MPP in Queen's Park.

And they were still talking about Walter Assef's shenanigans during the Queen's visit back in 1973 when I arrived almost ten years later. As the story goes, when Queen Elizabeth and Prince Philip first stepped off the plane, the jolly little mayor walked right past Her Majesty, grabbed Prince Philip to shake his hand and said, "Great to see you! Glad to see you could bring the missus."

But that was nothing. Later in the tour, reporters supposedly caught Walter patting Queen Elizabeth on her backside while showing her around. The British press went wild. Had the little mayor really patted the Queen's derrière? I've never seen a picture, but that doesn't mean it didn't happen.

Assef certainly cared about ruling council meetings. They could be a bit of a gong show, with the mayor telling people to shut up, threatening to punch other members of council, or verbally tearing apart civil servants who appeared before him to give presentations. You could always count on Walter Assef for a story.

LEARNING LESSONS

Four years flew by as I honed my craft, even eventually making a little more money, and I landed my first byline—my name on a network radio report on forest fires in Northwestern Ontario, pounding out on teletypes across the system.

The business was changing. In private broadcasting, someone was always looking for another way to make money. The sales department came to me one day with an idea: they wanted to sell a *news* break that would be paid for by a large beer company. Now, you would think a beer company—let's call this one SUDS—would want to attach itself to its traditional sportscast sponsorship. But some clever fellow thought that if SUDS could get their brand attached to a newscast, some of the news's credibility just might rub off on them.

The plan was to air a one-minute commercial spot and call it the SUDS News Break. I was still new to the game, but I did have strong opinions about "selling" the news. Without independence and objectivity, credibility was non-existent. You didn't have to look far to see that. Just across the border in Duluth, Minnesota, a local TV news operation that was sponsored by the Piggly Wiggly supermarket chain changed its name to the *Piggly Wiggly Newshour*. It even had the Piggly Wiggly Pig's image on the front of the anchor desk. It was like a skit from the Second City comedy troupe—you couldn't take anything that came out of their mouths seriously.

So I asked our salespeople, "What if SUDS has a problem with its product—say, twenty thousand cases of bad beer were accidentally released into the Thunder Bay market? Would that get reported on the news carrying the SUDS News Break?" *Silence.* "I will not do it," I stated emphatically. "I'll quit first." And I meant it. As I said, I did not know much, but I knew enough to know that without credibility in this business, you have nothing. They decided to change it to the SUDS Sports Break instead.

Those airwaves were not always smooth sailing. It was in Thunder Bay that I learned the real horror of not being able to control laughter. It's hard to explain unless you have experienced it. It's something about knowing you are broadcasting live, and this little image in your head grows into a hysterical monster that unleashes itself and leaves you more or less helpless—in my case, on live TV.

It couldn't have happened at a more unfortunate time. We had a story about three young men who had lost their lives at a local shipyard some months before. We were covering the inquiry into the cause of their deaths, and I was reading the scripted introduction to the taped report. A floor director in the studio was responsible for moving the massive old Marconi studio cameras to different positions around the set. They were huge, each on a three-wheeled pedestal. The poor woman tried to duck under the long lens of one of these beasts, but she didn't quite make it. Instead she clipped it with her forehead, and the whole camera shot shifted.

While she lay on the cement floor rubbing her head, out of the corner of my eye I could see the studio television monitor. It showed what was being broadcast over the air. Now, instead of a normal head-and-shoulders shot only my head was visible, with a lot of space above it. To the entire Thunder Bay audience, my body had disappeared. In her haste to rectify the situation, the person switching in the control room started pushing buttons and pulling levers. Now my face was gone and replaced with colour bars. Then a silhouette of black, then *poof!*—I was back on the screen.

I tried to continue, but the image of the technical carnage that had just unfolded was still dancing in my head. I started to snigger, fought to get control, then burst out with a big guffaw. Laughing out loud and horrified at the same time, there I was, the main television news anchor, live on the air, stumbling into a very serious story with uncontrollable hilarity.

When I got off the air, I was told there was a call waiting for me in master control. It was what I had dreaded most. An older gentleman, the father of one of the dead young men, was on the line. He said, "Son, I just wanted to let you know that I saw what happened to you tonight. It was obvious to me that much more than we could see was going on. Try not to be too hard on yourself." I could have kissed him. That he would take time, in his grief, to try and make a young broadcaster feel a little bit better about a horrible situation—a screw-up, really—taught me to have faith in my audience. I should never underestimate their ability to figure out when something isn't right—and their ability to forgive.

Some months later I had another phone call waiting in master control. A gentleman asked if I was related to Reverend John Sherren from Curling, Newfoundland. I was pleased to tell him I was his grandson. Grandfather Sherren had been a United Church minister. The gentleman on the phone said he was in the congregation the Sunday my grandfather collapsed in the pulpit. He died some months later of cancer. This had happened over twenty years before I was born, and I had rarely heard anyone outside the family refer to Grandfather. I was so stunned to hear this story that I didn't have the presence of mind to ask the caller his name. It was a powerful lesson on just how far you can reach as a broadcaster.

Those small-to-medium markets were critical learning grounds for many people who went on to report nationally and even internationally. CKPR Television has managed to survive, but sadly, many others have not. As broadcasters continue to consolidate and ownership dwindles to barely a handful of big players, opportunities like I had to learn every aspect of the news system have all but disappeared. How can having fewer sources of independent news, fewer diverse voices, be a good thing? It just isn't.

After four and a half years, I was feeling relatively steady on my news legs, and I was itchy to try bigger things. Farther west was calling me, but not entirely for career reasons.

In Thunder Bay I had met my beautiful future wife, Pamela Tennant; she was the weekend anchor at CKPR and a daily reporter. We had to keep it quiet because having a personal relationship in the newsroom was something management frowned on. Can you imagine them trying to do that today? But Pam was also pursuing a career path of her own.

She left before me, taking a reporting gig with CITV Edmonton. Not long afterward, I chased her west, landing a job at CBC Calgary.

CHAPTER 2

Alberta Bound

I have frequently said that Reg Sherren the journalist was much braver than Reg Sherren the human being. The journalist would put on his cape and attempt feats never imagined by the mere mortal. I like to think it was just part of my personal evolution, but in truth it was probably a combination of circumstance, naïveté and stupid, blind luck. Thats how I wound up with that job even farther west. I'd somehow managed to persuade the decision makers at CBC-TV's *Calgary Newshour* to give me a chance. It was 1984, and I would go from relatively small Thunder Bay to the fourth-largest city and market in the country. This was the big leagues, and I would have many opportunities to put on my journalistic cape over the next few years.

I had been hired on a one-year contract to create feature stories for the six o'clock show. Admittedly, I had limited experience in doing this kind of TV, but I was perfectly prepared to bluff my way through. In Thunder Bay I was predominantly a television news anchor. As luck would have it (it certainly wasn't the plan), I was also involved in the half-hour municipal affairs program with characters like Walter Assef. It made for an entertaining resumé reel, and the folks running CBC Calgary must have seen something they liked.

Calgary was a big city with big-city problems. It was also booming. The newsroom was full of talented people determined to make the show a success, so there was lots of competition but also lots of opportunity. I was now part of the CBC network, with a chance to get national exposure. Daily news assignments were thrown at me—city hall, traffic accidents, crimes and school board meetings—but the short features are what really gave me a chance to explore the craft and learn.

News items ran like a commuter train. B-roll (footage over which the reporter speaks), clip, B-roll, clip, stand-up closer. Most news items were around a minute and a half long—we called those "buck and a halfs." But features could be up to five minutes long. Features gave you a chance to set the scene using beautiful shots, music and pacing, and great camera people and editors helped you turn the scripts into appealing television.

I now had more time and support to develop a story than ever before, and this had a power all its own. Especially with the right characters.

PLOWING NEW GROUND

I first learned that early in 1985. I was assigned to tell a story about the spring planting. Many farmers were having a tough time of it and some were on the brink of going under. I had been asked to find a family in exactly that situation. I quickly discovered that people in the farming community were a lot like people in the fishing community. Coming from Newfoundland, where many of my relatives fished, I found that these were my people—fiercely proud, down-to-earth, honest and hard-working.

Eventually I found myself on the phone, talking to a family near Vulcan, Alberta. They had farmed for generations, but each season in recent years they hadn't quite been able to break even and were always losing a little more money. It was becoming a slow and painful demise for this family's farm. Even so, they invited me to come for a visit.

I could feel the financial strain the family was under just to get the ground seeded. I felt bad that Mom had cooked a big roast beef dinner for us, spending money they probably couldn't afford. But they were determined to be good hosts. As we sat around the kitchen table eating, Mom was polite, but somewhat quiet and withdrawn. She had also steadfastly refused to do an interview—that big imposing camera was just too intimidating.

Like many kitchens, it held a table, a kitchen counter island with cabinets above, and on the opposite side, with a big window over it, the kitchen sink. I knew that she had spent a lot of time at that sink, just like my own mother, washing dishes, looking out the window—and thinking.

We set up the camera where the kitchen table was. I asked my cameraman to shoot through the space between the counter and the hanging cabinets; I wanted a profile shot of Mom at the sink with the window included. Then I asked her if I could help do the dishes, where we could talk without that big camera in her face. She agreed, and while she washed and I dried, we began talking about the good old days.

Every time she looked up and out that window, she was seeing another time, a much happier time. As she talked about preparing a big lunch and driving out in the family station wagon to the fields where the men were harvesting, you could see her emotion building. "Everybody sat around the tailgate enjoying their dinner," she said. Then she paused, looked down into the sink and began to cry. "Nowadays everything is so different," she sobbed. "You try to keep everybody happy and you can't."

I was choking back tears myself. Her words would have moved anyone. I could feel them. I knew if it was half as powerful on videotape as it was in that kitchen, it would do more to illustrate what this farm family was going through than anything else we had taped that day.

Writing the script, I realized everything had to build to that moment. In the edit suite, the magical talents of editor Annie Churka helped bring it to life. She created pauses in the script, allowing time for viewers to absorb the story, which gave the actual moment even more impact. And she added music to squeeze every ounce of emotion from the videotape.

Would it work? I got my answer back in the newsroom. We were all young, career-addicted journalists, working stories right to deadline, and we'd sit around the newsroom yakking and watching as the show went to air. It could be a hard room. If your peers didn't like what they saw, they had no problem pointing it out.

My piece came on. It grew quieter in that newsroom as the story progressed. When the emotional mother began crying at the sink, there wasn't a sound. Some of the people watching had tears in their eyes. The piece had moved even these jaded journalists.

It was one of the most valuable lessons in my young career. Really, it was about two things. People—characters—are critical in any great story. Do everything you can to make them comfortable enough to tell you how they really feel, even if it means perhaps not having the best shot or the right lighting. Do everything possible to make the camera seem invisible.

Second, emotion is the most powerful thing television can deliver. Anger, fear, sadness, joy—the camera will show it all if you do it right. Television is not like a newspaper or magazine. You can't pick it up and read it again. It goes by so quickly that you have only one chance to capture viewers' attention, and if you can deliver real emotion, the story can have a lasting impression.

Learning those lessons served me well many times during my time in Alberta. A one-year contract stretched into two.

THE SHUTTLE

On the morning of January 28, 1986, I was in a small office in the Calgary police building, interviewing an officer who wasn't much older than me. The day before, early in the morning out on the Deerfoot Trail, my cameraman and I had come upon a terrible scene. A fellow driving a yellow Chevy Malibu had lost control, jumped the guardrail and nose-dived down a steep embankment. Neither he nor and his female passenger had been wearing seatbelts and they were thrown from the vehicle. Both were killed. A truck driver had seen the wreckage and pulled over, and we pulled in behind him just as emergency responders arrived. I still dream sometimes about what we saw that morning. It was a horrible sight.

Now we were doing a follow-up interview, but just as we started, another officer burst through the door and said, "The space shuttle just blew up." We all rushed down the hall to watch the coverage on a small black-and-white TV in the lunchroom. Nobody said a word. I think this must have been our generation's biggest news event, before the tragedy of 9/11; our response was akin to the previous generation's horror when John F. Kennedy was killed. Most of them could tell you exactly where they were when they heard the president was shot, and most of the people I grew up with can tell you where they were when the *Challenger* space shuttle was lost. (I have another space shuttle story to tell, but you'll have to wait until later for that one.)

The tragic story of the car crash we had set out to tell that morning was unfortunately lost in the enormity of the coverage about the *Challenger* disaster.

IT'S A WILD WORLD

Lots of stories were waiting to be told, great stories, all over Southern Alberta. Outside the city rose those beautiful Rocky

Mountains, and whether it was ghosts at the Banff Springs Hotel or cougars in Kananaskis Country, there was a rarely a dull moment.

I had been talking with a good-natured big-game biologist, a fellow named Orval Pall, about a capture program he was running for the provincial wildlife department. He agreed that showing a capture would be a great way to help explain the pressure cougars were under because of urban sprawl. People were concerned about increased sightings. (Although we were the ones invading their territory, not the other way around.) Orval would capture the big cats and put radio collars on them to assess their movements. But in order to place a radio collar on a cougar, first you had to catch one—no small feat. I wanted to capture it all on camera. That proved to be much more difficult than I thought.

First we tried filming from the air as Orval attempted to pick up a radio-collar signal. Camera operator Morris Cruise, a Brit with a dry sense of humour, agreed to go up in the small Cessna. It had no room for me, which turned out to be a good thing. The wind was rough as they dipped and doodled in the hills, pitching the little plane nearly upside down as they tried to pick up the radio signal. It was far too rough for Morris to get a shot. When they landed, he did *not* look well. When I asked him how things went, with his dry wit he replied, "Well, I threw up twice, but I managed to swallow it." We moved on to Plan B.

Cougars are fast, elusive animals. You could spend months in the back country and never see one, much less catch one. But where there's a will, there's a way. Orval had hired a group of fellows who called themselves the Houndsmen. Their hounds would be released in an area where Orval had seen scat, a kill or a bedding place—something to indicate cougar activity—and the hounds would soon pick up the scent.

Cougars are also short-winded. Once hounds flush out a cat, it takes off. It sprints for about a kilometre before becoming winded, then it climbs a tree. The hounds hold it there until everyone else catches up. It's no trouble finding them because the dogs will not shut up. The howling and barking never stops.

No problem, I figured. This time I went with cameraman Mike Hunchak, a big bull of a guy with a great eye for television. We would just follow Orval and the huntsmen, and bingo! We'd have a great cougar capture story.

Our first attempt to record a big cat was up the side of Wind Mountain, not far from Mount Lougheed. It was early April 1986. We drove as close to the site as we could, but after that it was all legwork. We had a heavy Betacam camera, batteries, a tripod and other gear. We had stripped the kit down as much as we could, but we still had a good thirty kilograms of gear to carry.

The hounds picked up the scent down in the valley and soon the cat was on the run. But it decided to bolt straight up the side of the mountain. Its path was steeper than a forty-five-degree angle, and within moments our legs had turned to rubber. By the time we reached the top, where the hounds had pinned the big cat, it was too dark to film. Unfortunately we had left the camera light and its heavy battery belt behind. It was a magnificent male, easily eighty kilos, but we didn't have a shot. My first attempt at becoming Canada's Marlin Perkins was a dismal failure.

A week later we tried again. Spring was starting in the Kananaskis, with green growth sprouting forth. But the night before, it had snowed—a lot. That morning a good fifteen centimetres of wet, fluffy mush was lying atop slippery new growth as we picked our way along narrow mountain trails with drop-offs of a hundred metres or more to the valley below.

Fearless Mike, who again had drawn the short straw to go with me, didn't flinch; he even got an incredible shot of a bald eagle screaming down at some bighorn sheep far below. We carried on. Soon the hounds were on the scent and had a cat trapped far up in a pine tree. Orval waited until we arrived and prepared to tranquilize

Orval Pall examines a young male cougar captured in Alberta's
Kananaskis Country. I was feeling pretty cool about the whole thing,
until I saw the claw marks nearby, made by a grizzly. Then I felt a
little scared.

the animal. He was using a new drug that basically immobilized the
cat but left it partially awake, eyes open.

The cougar we trapped was quite young. Mike got great shots
of the dart going in, the cougar being lowered and Orval working
out measurements and putting the radio collar on. I knew these
were pictures few had seen before, certainly not on the nightly news.
Our story would be from a much different perspective than news
stories about people having their dogs taken by cougars or cougars
challenging people on walking trails.

To protect the cat, Orval and his team planned to wait until it
had fully regained its senses. Mike and I had to hike out on our own.
"Just follow the creek bed down to the road," Orval said. Easy enough.
A kilometre down the hill we came upon a tree where a grizzly had
marked its territory. Huge fresh claw marks three or four metres
up scarred the side of the tree. Deep, angry claw marks. We were
not long in getting the heck out of there and back to the relative

safety of our van. I had never seen a grizzly in the wild and I really didn't want to see one that day.

It all led to my first feature on a network newscast—*Saturday Report*, hosted by George McLean. The half-hour news show gave me almost four minutes of airtime to show Orval and the cougar to viewers across Canada. George smiled after the piece ended. I beamed.

Two months later Orval was dead.

It was June 6, 1986. Orval and pilot Kenneth Wolff were again up in the Cessna, trying to pick up another radio signal, when they disappeared. Later that evening, another small plane went up looking for them, and it also crashed. Three people died in that tragedy.

A sad, tense week of searching dragged on. In the middle of it all, I decided we needed to do a story about the dangers of flying in the mountains in small planes. The idea was to use two cameras in different small planes, shooting between the two. There were no GoPro action cameras in those days, so we had to break our camera in two, separating the recorder from the lens so we could interview the pilot from the cockpit as he was flying.

The gentleman who would be taking me up was one of the most experienced pilots around, with decades of successful time flying in the mountains. As we were taxiing down the runway, he said, "It feels good to be back behind the controls. I had a heart attack a while back and I've just been cleared to fly again."

I thought about this revelation as we lifted into the air. After a few minutes I replied, "Nothing personal, but after we level off, maybe you can give me some pointers on how to land this thing— just in case?" He laughed. I laughed too, but I was nervous. The impact those mountain winds could quickly have on a small plane was dramatic; still, we recorded it all and we survived. But a week later, a military Twin Otter trying to spot the first two planes also crashed. Now thirteen people were dead. Ground crews eventually got to all three crash sites.

I have often thought the crash that killed Orval and his pilot could easily have happened when the other cameraman who worked with me on this story, Morris Cruise, was flying with them trying to spot cougars. But dwelling on "what ifs" can drive you a little crazy. Orval was a professional. He had the opportunity to tell the whole country about Alberta's magnificent cougars and what he was trying to accomplish as a wildlife biologist. An unfortunate accident ended his life and the lives of twelve others, but at least he died doing what he loved best.

The more stories I got under my belt, the more I learned which ones had a real impact on audiences. And although that wasn't the plan, I started to search them out: wildlife or human-interest stories, stories driven by emotion and stories driven by controversy. By the time I had finished telling this story, Orval Pall and his cougars, sadly, had delivered all three.

THE NAZIS ARE COMING

Later in the summer of 1986, I turned my attention to the Canadian head of the Aryan Nations. The story of Terry Long was driven by controversy and, unfortunately, by the emotions of fear and hate. This white supremacist and his organization had long-term plans to turn parts of Alberta, British Columbia and several US states into their own all-white society.

Long, who had grown up north of Calgary in Caroline, Alberta, lived on land just outside the town, and he was attempting to build a compound. The rumour was that it was going to be a training facility for some of his Aryan brethren. He was attracting a lot of attention, and he certainly had mine.

The local minister, a young, earnest fellow in a corduroy blazer with suede elbow patches, was understandably concerned, but Terry Long had been in the community his whole life. People knew him. He looked like an average guy living in rural Alberta—average dress, no big swastika tattoos—and he was a well-spoken, university-educated man. The minister, though worried, said Mr. Long didn't project an image that gave the local community much to get worked up about. Not yet, anyway. Others I interviewed said, "What he does on his own property is his own business."

Then my research led me to a gentleman named Larry Ryckman. Ryckman was a young businessman who also dabbled in film. He was trying to develop a new way to record albums using something called QSound, and he had also shot some startling footage about the Aryan Nations down in Idaho.

Hayden Lake, Idaho, at the time was a hotbed for the white supremacist movement. Richard Girnt Butler from California had bought land near the tiny village of Hayden Lake and set up his own training compound. He registered it as a non-profit church, calling it the Church of Jesus Christ Christian, and began inviting like-minded people to the area. They came first by the dozens and soon the hundreds to listen to the vitriol delivered from his pulpit, with its swastika pierced by a sword on the front—the Aryan Nations symbol.

I was never sure why, but Ryckman passed himself off as one of them—a damn gutsy move—and managed to infiltrate this camp, camera in hand. He got shots of angry-looking young skinheads covered in racist tattoos, snarling at the camera. They were armed with rifles, standing outside barbed-wire compounds with signs reading WHITES ONLY. In an interview one of these people actually said, "To me, killing a black man is no different than killing a dog or a chicken." These were seriously dangerous people, but they looked nothing like Terry Long, the man people were talking about near Caroline, Alberta.

Ryckman allowed me to screen his tape, and you will never guess what he had captured during a ritual cross-burning inside that compound. People were standing around in the firelight dressed in what you might call traditional Ku Klux Klan attire: white sheets with pointy hoods. But not all of them were dressed that way.

There, in the inner circle, bathed in the golden light of the burning crosses, dressed in a suit and tie, no less, was Terry Long. He was standing next to his Aryan kin as they all gave a Nazi salute. Now I could make a direct visual connection between Long and what was already happening south of the border in Idaho. I had my story.

After the feature aired, two things happened.

Number one: I received my first threatening phone call, suggesting strongly that it might not be good for my health to continue pursuing this coverage.

Number two: the people in the Caroline area called an emergency public meeting to discuss what to do about this presence in their community. It was held in a school gymnasium in nearby Sundre, Alberta, where over five hundred upset people showed up. They now had a clear idea of what they were dealing with. But in the middle of the meeting something very strange happened.

A man jumped to his feet to say he was the imperial wizard of the Ku Klux Klan in Canada, and he too was upset with Terry Long and the Aryan Nations. The problem, it seemed, was that without permission, the Aryan Nations group was using symbols the KKK claimed it had copyright over. It was a dramatic and disturbing turn of events. Afterward, some local fellows tried to punch the Klansman's lights out while he fought to get away.

Terry Long did not get to establish his compound, but he didn't go away either. Long eventually went underground, moving to British Columbia, but as recently as a few years ago he crawled back into the light to support those who agreed with his views.

RENÉ LÉVESQUE

Later that summer one of the more controversial political figures of my generation, René Lévesque, was to appear on the CBC Calgary program *Crossfire*. Just beforehand, he was autographing books at a store downtown. I bought a copy and stood in line. After he signed it, I said to him, "Mr. Lévesque, I know you're going to CBC after this and I would be happy to give you a ride." A big fellow suddenly appeared, stepped between us, and declared, "Monsieur Lévesque will take a cab!" I realized the man was his bodyguard. Lévesque shrugged, turning his hands up in exasperation.

I returned to the CBC building and waited behind reception. When they arrived, I stretched out my hand and said, "I am so glad you managed to make it here safely!" He laughed and rolled his eyes. We chatted for a few minutes, and then he was off to makeup.

SHAKING THINGS UP

By now I was getting regular face time on the network, hunting down stories that had national appeal. One of the places I could always count on was the world-class Banff Springs Hotel. It was a storyteller's gold mine.

I told stories about ghosts and other interesting characters. There was the bride who broke her neck falling down the back stairwell on her wedding night and still haunted the stairs, and the piano in a back dining room that played the song "Canadian Sunset" all by itself. There was the reunion of former employees, some dating back to those heady days when the rich families would show up for the summer with a couple dozen steamer trunks in tow. I remember a still somewhat embarrassed former employee blurting out on camera, fifty years after the fact, that she used to try on the women's beautiful ball gowns when nobody was around. There was the story of Marilyn Monroe injuring herself while filming *River of No Return*, and famous baseball player Joe DiMaggio, who was wooing Monroe, showing up at the hotel with dozens of red roses to console her.

The manager of this beautiful, majestic castle at the time was Ivor Petrak. He knew the value of my national exposure, and we

Interviewing Robin Leach at the Banff Springs Hotel, with Dennis Genereux manning the old, massive Betacam. The celebrity ski weekend was part of the huge promotion leading up to the 1988 Winter Olympics in Calgary, Alberta.

developed a great relationship. When they were building their super-luxury suite in the mid-1980s, complete with lap pool and private elevator to accommodate the ultra-rich, I got a call to come and take an exclusive look. The going rate was over $2,000 a night.

As the 1988 Winter Olympics in Calgary approached, I covered celebrity ski weekends that included Robin Leach from *Lifestyles of the Rich and Famous*, Brooke Shields and Arnold Schwarzenegger. One night the rock group America played at dinner. These were amazing times for a young fellow from Labrador. I could get used to this.

DEADLY LICENCE

Early in 1987, I told one of my last stories for CBC Calgary, and it was a blockbuster.

It happened because I answered the phone. The call had been transferred from the main switchboard to the newsroom, and I was the one who pushed the glowing plastic button at the bottom of the phone and answered.

George (not his real name) spoke in a hesitant, soft voice, saying perhaps calling wasn't such a good idea after all. I suggested that he must be concerned about something important, and maybe I could help. Then he admitted he had been worried about it for some time and needed to clear his conscience. What he said next floored me.

George had been working as a bisexual prostitute in the Calgary escort business for several years. Now he was dying of AIDS, but he was still seeing clients—as many as a dozen a day—and having unprotected sex. George's employers knew some clients did not like condoms, so they frowned on it. He also knew of several others in the same situation.

Immediately I knew this story was huge, perhaps the biggest scoop of my career, but it would have to be handled carefully.

I asked for an interview with the chief of police to discuss the issue of the escort business in Calgary, without mentioning George. During the interview, he as much as admitted that as far as the police were concerned, escort agencies were doing nothing more than legalized prostitution behind closed doors. In Calgary at the time, the city licensed escort agencies. It was as if they were licensing prostitution and now it was making people sick, potentially infecting them with a deadly virus.

When I asked George to grant me an interview, he declined, saying his life wouldn't be worth five cents. I offered to shoot a silhouette interview and alter his voice. He could look at it afterward to reassure himself that he would not be identified. He agreed.

While chain-smoking cigarettes, he told the whole sordid tale. He talked about how he'd struggled in the business, how his bosses only cared about money, about how he'd become sicker and about the others he knew.

It was Monday morning. I knew the licensing committee at city hall was meeting at one o'clock; after that it would be a week before they met again. That was the dilemma of the scoop. Should I let that meeting pass without telling anyone what I knew so I could deliver an exclusive story during the big 6:00 p.m. newscast, the one with the highest audience? If I waited until six to reveal George's story, it could be days or even a week before anything was done about it. In the meantime, more clients could potentially become infected by sick escorts.

I couldn't do it.

Instead, I phoned the city councillor who was the chairperson of the licensing committee. I told him he needed to come to the CBC that morning to watch an interview I was going to air later that night on the *Calgary Newshour*. He came in and watched George's interview. He went very pale. The one o'clock licensing committee meeting became an emergency session. He told them what he'd seen. They decided to suspend the escort licences until they could get a handle on the situation; I suspected visions of potential liability were playing in their heads. Other reporters also got the story, but they did not have the interview with George.

Some said I was crazy for blowing my own scoop. The way I saw it, it wasn't about getting a "scoop"; it was about doing my part in helping people to be safer, or at least informed, as quickly as I could. My own conscience wouldn't let me wait. As it turned out, some news agencies gave CBC credit for the story anyway.

The escort agencies knew they had to do something about what, until now, they had resisted. They went to AIDS Calgary, asking for help in distributing condoms and in teaching safe-sex practices. But the people who ran the agencies were not happy. Again my life was threatened, and I didn't like it any better the second time around. But eventually licences were restored and things settled down.

It was a year from the 1988 Olympics. CBC Calgary, with its team of great journalists, was getting traction. And for the first time in its history, CBC-TV became the number one television newscast in the Calgary market.

BREAKING CAMP

I was now a regular contributor on the network, at least on *Saturday Report* and on the syndicated news feed, NSS. But I made a decision some thought was even crazier than blowing my own scoop.

I decided to leave.

Perhaps it was just another indication that I really did not have a plan, not a professional one anyway. Calgary was a large market in Canada. The show was number one. I was getting network airtime. But in 1987 I decided to take a job with *Here & Now*, the television supper-hour show in St. John's, Newfoundland and Labrador. It was a much smaller market, but the decision was a personal one. All my relatives were still back East and I wanted to be closer. It was as simple as that.

CHAPTER 3

Going Backward to Go Forward

We had been chasing each other around the country. In truth, I had been chasing her. Pam took a reporter position in Edmonton, and I moved to Calgary. While I was establishing myself there, she moved to Vancouver to do media relations at Expo 86 and then returned to reporting, this time at CKVU in Vancouver. She loved temperate Vancouver and lived in Kitsilano, not far from the beach, and now this fellow she had been hopscotching across the country with for close to five years wanted her to move to Newfoundland. In February.

I asked her to come with me, and to my amazement, she said yes. I went ahead and she would follow. She was supposed to arrive on Valentine's Day, 1987. But a huge blizzard in St. John's went on for close to three days and she was stuck in Halifax, no doubt trying to decide whether to just book a one-way ticket back to Vancouver.

When she finally did arrive, we were stuck in a third-rate hotel on Kenmount Road for months. With more snow than St. John's had seen in fifty years (and that's saying something), it was almost impossible to get out the door. I was ready to jump back on a plane myself. The parkways had so much of the white stuff piled up it was like driving in a huge luge, with snow walls on both sides. You couldn't see a thing, including cars approaching the intersection, until you were both practically *in* the intersection. It was nuts.

Eventually we found a house and moved in. There was a six-metre drift in the backyard, higher than the house itself. Not a great start.

But at the station I received a warm welcome from senior producer Paul Harrington, the fellow who had hired me, and it soon became apparent the good karma had followed me east. At work I met Donna Wicks, who worked in finance, and I soon realized we had met before. Donna had been in the same high school class as me one year when we lived in Prince Edward Island. Not only that, but she had married a St. John's Crown prosecutor named Brad Wicks—the same Brad Wicks who'd been my best buddy when we were both just five years old growing up in Labrador! They still like to joke that I am the one thing they have in common.

Then another fellow arrived from Montreal. Jonathan Crowe, the new sports anchor, sat right next to me. We shared the same sense of humour, and, as it turned out, we also had a connection. Our fathers knew each other and worked together, again up in Labrador. Quickly we all became a tight circle of friends. It more than compensated for the brutal winter.

MINING AN AUDIENCE

Within a month, I was on the road anyway. A huge strike back in Labrador, in my hometown, was threatening the future of the area. The companies were demanding concessions, saying the steel industry was changing. New players were more competitive and driving down prices. The workers and their union did not want to budge.

I was assigned to produce a documentary—to try and find out the truth, no matter where it took me. It would take me to Labrador, Montreal, Northern Minnesota, New York and Pennsylvania, all in barely a week. I would be travelling with Ed Coady, the executive producer at the time, and camera operator Al Crocker.

Those two men were inclined to enjoy a drink on the road. Or two. After travelling to Montreal and Toronto we eventually arrived in the Big Apple. By the time we reached New York City, where I was to interview a Wall Street broker about a huge new Brazilian ore deposit that was undercutting the iron-ore industry in North America, I was feeling more than a little bit desperate. Call it trial by fire—or firewater.

Ed was my new boss, and I was hardly in any position to tell him what to do. Al, a burly longshoreman type, was just happy to be along for the trip. We got to Manhattan early in the afternoon. I had never been to New York City in my life. It seemed to breathe menacingly—a dangerous place. We stayed in an older hotel not far off Broadway. On the street outside, I remember the doorman saying to someone as he was helping them into one of those famous yellow taxis, "New York, New York ... you know the best thing about New York? The road to the frickin' airport!"

Our interview wasn't scheduled until the next morning. Ed and Al found a nice bar downstairs in the hotel and we settled in. By five or six o'clock that evening, things were well along and we had moved to a small landing with a few tables at the top of a huge winding staircase that led down to the hotel lobby. Al said he wanted to change his pants and disappeared. Then Ed went off to the washroom.

After half an hour I went down to the washrooms, expecting to find Ed lying on the floor after being jumped by some New York ne'er-do-wells. He was nowhere to be found. I went back to my room, a gaudy shoebox with red-and-black-velvet wallpaper and about five deadbolts on the door.

At ten o'clock my hotel room phone rang. It was Ed. He was in a jazz bar in Greenwich Village and I had to come right down. He didn't say why, but he was the boss. I reluctantly grabbed a cab, climbed some stairs and walked into what could best be described as a "joint." The first thing I saw was a long bar down one side. I immediately spotted Ed at the corner of the bar. I also noticed that a) he was in a huge argument, and b) we were the only two white people in the entire room.

To say I was concerned would be more than an understatement. Yet by the time I had reached that bar, Ed had turned everything around and had everyone laughing and slapping each other on the back. It was one of his many talents.

I got him back to the hotel, and the next morning, as always, both Ed and Al were right on time. The interview confirmed my research. The iron-ore industry was indeed being turned upside down. We had one more stop. We had to drive out to Bethlehem, Pennsylvania, headquarters of Bethlehem Steel, a big player in the iron-ore industry in Labrador. Much of the iron ore mined there wound up in Bethlehem.

On the radio on the drive out, the news reports were full of the Gary Hart scandal. Hart was considered the frontrunner for the Democratic presidential nomination in 1988—that is, until he got caught having an extramarital affair with a woman named Donna Rice. Stories about his dalliances with the woman on a yacht named *Monkey Business* were everywhere. I didn't realize it at the time, but what we focused on in the business of "news" was already starting to shift.

The steel plant was massive, a flat steel rolling mill that stretched on for kilometres. It was in trouble, with huge layoffs and more coming as it struggled to compete with cheaper, offshore steel producers. The owners no longer felt obligated to buy from places like Labrador if they could get a better, more competitive price on iron ore somewhere else.

Over lunch, the fellow showing us around, a mountain of a guy named Bubba, said, "That's just the American way, survival of the fittest. Change or die." He also took the time to pass comment on the situation Gary Hart had found himself in. Said Bubba, "You know, I think the biggest mistake Gary Hart made with Donna Rice was he should have got Teddy Kennedy to give her a ride home." I wasn't sure if he was kidding or not. If he was, it was American political humour at its darkest. (If you don't get it, do an internet search on Teddy Kennedy and the Chappaquiddick incident.)

We flew out that afternoon and on the taxi ride to JFK, I remember thinking, "This *is* the best thing about New York—the road to the frickin' airport." It would not be the last time journalism would carry me there.

When the story aired, I was told both the iron-ore company and the steelworkers broke their negotiations to watch the documentary. It was almost nineteen minutes long, half the entire supper-hour show. Within a day they had settled.

FINDING MY SEA LEGS

Pam and I had settled in. There was a story around every corner and down on every wharf as it appeared the cod fishery, one of the largest food sources in the world, was also in trouble. Catch rates had plummeted with the Europeans, Russians and Japanese right on the edge of the two-hundred-mile limit, scooping up whatever they could.

The Russians had made a deal with Ottawa that even allowed them inside the limit, on the very spawning grounds of the Northern cod. As long as they were buying Canadian wheat, they could fish. Factory freezer trawlers fished relentlessly, twenty-four hours a day, and as the cod disappeared, the fishing community scrambled to adjust.

But that summer my first story on the network from Newfoundland came from another species entirely. Humpback whale activity was on the upswing in the waters around Newfoundland, and they were constantly coming into conflict with fishing gear—cod traps in particular. A cod trap was like a big box of fishing nets and rope, laid out in the ocean to trap schools of cod. One could cost as much as $8,000 to $10,000. Having a creature that weighed several tons plow through it, tear it up and drag away what was left wasn't a welcome prospect, and it was happening all the time.

World-renowned environmentalist and filmmaker Jacques Cousteau had travelled to Newfoundland earlier in the '80s, and his crew filmed while they released an entangled baby humpback. It was a touching scene with momma humpback circling nearby, but in the process of releasing the little fellow they cut all the fishing gear loose, letting it drop to the bottom of the ocean. It was a huge loss for the owners, and they were decidedly not happy about it.

There had to be a better way, and Memorial University professor Jon Lien thought he had found it. He wanted the fishing community to respect whales, not hate them, and he had developed a way to recover some of the damaged fishing gear the next time a whale was trapped. "This will make great television," I thought. "All we need to do is be there when he releases the whale and catch it all on videotape."

You would have thought I had learned my lesson with cougars, but no.

Jon was a great fellow and he agreed to let us tag along, but he would not wait for us. We had to be ready when he was. I was in bed when he called around midnight. A whale had been caught in fishing gear, just off St. Bride's, Placentia Bay, a good three hours away, and they were heading out. Camera operator Kevin Hanlon and I scrambled to meet Jon and his student assistant in the middle of the night, out by the edge of the city. Towing a small rubber Zodiac boat, our little convoy headed down the coast. The fog was so thick we could barely see the headlights coming toward us.

We crawled along and arrived just as the sun was rising, casting a shimmering golden hue on thankfully calm water. As Jon was preparing to launch the little Zodiac, we realized there was not enough room for all of us. Jon decided the assistant would stay behind and I would go along to help out. Right.

We followed the fishing crew who had called as they led us out to where a large humpback was entangled in about a hundred metres of line. Jon threw a line of his own with a grapple hook on the end—like one of those gizmos cat burglars or commandos use in movies when they have to scale a wall. He hooked the line trailing behind the whale and began pulling. We drew closer and closer—until suddenly we were literally on its back! Jon, who was wearing a diver's wetsuit, put on a snorkel and mask. "Hang on to the belt on my waist," he said. With that he bent over the side, right up to his waist—I thought we were going in the water—and cut the line as close to the whale's mouth as possible. A huge pectoral fin flew by my head, and just like that the whale, blowing and rolling, was free.

Jon still held on to the cut line and the fishing crew began gathering up as much of the damaged gear as possible. Over the side came two of the biggest lobster claws I had ever seen. No lobster, just the claws and arms, stuck in the rope. They were almost the size of footballs. I joked about this giant lobster, back on the ocean floor, telling his buddies, "Jeez, there I was minding my own business caught in this cod trapline, when this bloody whale came along and ripped my arms off!"

I did several more stories with Jon, and it was always fascinating. Years later I dove on a lobster conservation site, farther up in the head of Placentia Bay, with another expert from the Department of Fisheries and Oceans, Gerry Innes. Fishing at the site had been banned for the better part of twenty years, and lobsters there were the length of my leg.

The piece about rescuing humpbacks from the nets went over very well back in Toronto with the network crowd. It had definitely been worth the risk (as if I'd given the risk any thought). But it did confirm for me once again that stories that delivered unique pictures, wildlife, adventure or emotion would find their way onto the network. Riding on a whale's back—who wouldn't want to watch that, especially if it was combined with important issues around conservation and the fishery?

There would be many more fish stories in the days ahead. Things were heating up on the high seas. Many nations wanted the ocean's fish, and those fish were becoming scarce.

BEWARE LES BASQUES

The small French islands of St. Pierre and Miquelon off Newfoundland's south coast were still sovereign French territory, France's last toehold in the New World. These two islands claimed their own economic zone as well as the right to fish inside Canada's two-hundred-mile economic zone. For them too the fishery was about tradition—and survival. No fish, no jobs. The fact that millions in oil and gas might be lying beneath the ocean floor might also have been driving the French push for that economic zone.

But Canada maintained the French had no jurisdiction in Canadian waters and threatened to arrest anyone caught fishing illegally in them. So, to make a point, in late winter of 1988 the St. Pierre fishing vessel the *Croix de Lorraine*, with several politicians on board, sailed into Canadian waters to do exactly that—get themselves arrested.

The DFO responded by sending a ship to intervene with an armed boarding party. When word got out, the new national reporter in St. John's had visions of videotaping this confrontation on the high seas. You couldn't really blame him. It all sounded very dramatic. But to do it, you'd have to hire a ship to take you where the action was happening, then attempt a ship-to-ship transfer in ten-metre swells or worse. This would be no small feat, especially in winter on the North Atlantic.

It was suggested by some of the more experienced camera people that the reporter's best bet would be to grab some shots, from a vantage point high on Signal Hill, of the arrested vessel being escorted through a thin strip of water called the Narrows. From Signal Hill you could see out across the ocean for several kilometres. But undeterred, the reporter hired a small fishing vessel.

I wasn't there, but cameraman Sterling Snow was, and he told the tale of what happened. Now, Sterling is a larger-than-life character who tells one hell of a story, and he wasn't above a little, shall we say, embellishment—you know, just to help the story along.

According to Sterling, they were preparing to set sail from St. John's Harbour. Our national reporter friend and his Radio-Canada counterpart were down in the galley. The French journalist said, "It could get a little rough—you eat maybe a couple of pieces of dry toast to help keep your stomach settled." He was not going. He had been out in these boats before and learned his lesson.

Sterling picked up the story just as they were beginning to leave the harbour through the Narrows. Sterling, the captain, the first mate, our national reporter, and local reporter Rick Seaward were all standing on the bridge, looking out the front windows. A somewhat concerned Rick was clutching onto a support beam as though it contained the essence of life itself. (Thank God I was not assigned to go; I am no sailor.) The national guy was bundled into a heavy coat, sweater, hat and scarf as it was freezing outside.

Suddenly, off came his coat. A minute later, off came his sweater. The first mate looked at Sterling and said, in his best Newfoundland accent, "Yer buddy looks some queer colour." The poor reporter was now a greyish hue of green. He made an abrupt dash past Sterling to the door at the back of the bridge. "I've got to get some air!" he wailed.

After a moment or two, Sterling went out to check on him. The poor fellow was drenched with sea spray, shirt torn open almost to the waist, and he was now completely grey, just like the colour of the sea. Sterling said he grabbed him by the scruff of the neck, worried he might get washed overboard, and put him in the small head (bathroom) so he could throw up in the sink.

They still hadn't even cleared the Narrows. The captain said, "I think it's gonna get rough, but I can punch on through 'er for a few more miles if ye wants." Sterling said, "No, that's okay, bring her around and we'll head back in."

The next morning, sitting on the reporter's desk like a little pyramid was a stack of Gravol.

You can't beat local knowledge. Or listening closely to the people you are trying to talk to. Often, when sent down to the wharf to speak with fishermen about the state of the fishery, I would first ask the camera person to leave the gear in the van. If the folks on the dock were already busy doing something, say, hauling out a boat, we would join in and help out. Only afterward would we ask if they were okay with talking to us about whatever was going on. Those first few moments were always critical in establishing a connection.

DIRTY WATER

Not that it always worked. Sometimes circumstances took over and you just had to go with the flow, hoping it didn't mean swimming for your life.

One morning I was told to go down to a place called Witless Bay. There was nothing funny about Witless Bay. Over a hundred crab workers, upset with their employer, were off the job and in no mood to settle down. Just before we arrived, they had overturned a couple of pickup trucks.

We were down in the middle of the throng when one little fellow piped up to say, "Jesus byes, CBC is taking pictures of all we crowd! Let's throw 'em in the harbour!" As if that weren't bad enough, the water's surface was covered in rotting crab guts and oil. It did not look good. This was definitely *not* the plan.

At that very moment, I came to fully grasp the old saying, "Sometimes the best defence is a great offence." I decided to jump right into that little fellow's face. Shaking my fist, I yelled, "You son of a bitch. You call us up and ask us to come down here and represent your point of view and this is the way you want to treat us? Screw you!" To be honest, pretty much all of me was shaking. I was scared to death we were going into the water.

Then someone else yelled, "No byes, they're okay—leave 'em alone." I quickly suggested to the cameraman that we should beat it, and we scrambled up the bank to our van. The RCMP arrived only to have the skinny constable from Marystown pull out his megaphone. "All right ye crowd," he said. "CBC's got pictures of all ye, and we'll get their videotape and you'll all be charged!"

After yelling to the camera guy to fire up the van, I jumped up on the bumper and shouted, "We don't work for the RCMP—if they want our video they'll have to go to court to get it!" With that we jumped into the van and beat a hasty retreat. The RCMP never did come after our tape, and I never again waded into the middle of an angry mob. We were lucky it hadn't ended in a much worse fashion. We could easily have found ourselves swimming with the fishes that day!

HOOK, LINE AND SINKER

Overfishing was becoming a bigger and bigger issue, not just around Newfoundland but on the high seas. Tensions escalated. Spanish trawlers were arrested as Canada tried to assert some level of control over the amount of fish being hauled from the water. Stories of concern, outrage and desperation surrounded the state of the fishery. Eventually it would all lead to disaster.

Any fool could see it coming. John Crosbie, the federal minister of fisheries for Brian Mulroney, was dispatched to Spain to twist some arms. Both the Spaniards and the Portuguese were being accused of gross overfishing practices, but it was the former who appeared to possess the most efficient fish-killing technology.

I was chosen to try to figure it all out. Money did not seem to be an issue. I proposed we follow Crosbie and at the same time take a closer look at the fishing operations of Spain and Portugal.

Now, Portugal was (and still is) viewed with a certain affection by some Newfoundlanders, particularly in St. John's. For centuries the fishermen of its White Fleet worked the waters around the island, and they were a fixture in the capital, wandering the streets or playing soccer down on the docks while they resupplied. Fishing being what it was, many of those young men also reeled in local girls, marrying and carrying them back home. It was a relationship that stretched back close to five hundred years.

The earliest footage from out on the banks was shot in 1967 by cameraman John O'Brien on board a ship from the Portuguese White Fleet. John was a man of the deepest integrity, and he had a whip-smart mind. Every day he walked to work, no small distance, he always wore a tie, and when he walked into the camera room, he had a quiet but commanding presence.

John was now sixty years old if he was a day, still lugging around camera gear—the newfangled, bloody heavy three-tube Betacam cameras. They weighed twenty-five-plus kilos, and John was barely sixty kilos himself. His film footage from the Grand Banks had taken people to another world. Portuguese fishermen rowing away from the main schooner in their little dories, carrying tubs full of baited hooks, all alone on the North Atlantic hundreds of kilometres from shore, working from before sun-up until sundown to fish the cod, the *bacalhau*.

So John was the perfect choice to go to Spain and Portugal. The circle was complete. Kevin Norman was also along as producer. As it turned out, we never saw Crosbie—well, only briefly. Itineraries shuffled and telephone communication proved impossible with the language barrier.

Taking a break from filming in Aveiro, Portugal, to promote the
CBC with some beach art. We were shooting a piece on foreign
overfishing.

It didn't really matter. We had come to figure out whether the
Spanish and the Portuguese were the villains they were being made
out to be. Turned out the answer wasn't quite that simple. In Canada
back then, the average Canadian consumed under thirteen kilos of
fish a year. For the Spanish and Portuguese, the number was closer
to sixty kilos. To them, fishing was about feeding a nation.

At four in the morning we started taping, as the fishing boats
arriving on the docks in Lisbon. Fish was coming from the four corners of the world. It was an amazing sight that stretched out for
kilometres along the huge docks.

The Portuguese people were polite and friendly. In Aveiro,
the home of the White Fleet, when folks learned we were from
Newfoundland we were like long-lost cousins. There were grilled
fish dinners and shots of Portuguese almond liqueur toasting our
long-standing friendship and history.

In the harbour a few of the original White Fleet boats remained, rusting against the dock, but they were more about nostalgia than practicality. The White Fleet would never sail again. It was becoming increasingly harder to get young men to go to sea for months on end and work back-breaking hours far from home.

Of course, the Portuguese were still fishing: they had a nation to feed. But much of their equipment appeared old and dated. They also seemed genuinely upset that they had been lumped in with what the Spanish fishing fleets were doing. There is an old saying in Portugal: "From Espanha, no good wind blows, and no good marriage either!"

The Spaniards, I have to say, didn't appear as friendly. They were cagey. You could clearly see that their fleet in the harbour near San Sebastián was much more modern, more efficient than the Portuguese fleet. We saw them again in Vigo on the Atlantic coast. They were noncommittal about the state of the fish stocks and whether there was any need to cut back on fishing. Their nonchalant attitude toward overfishing was as profound as it was prophetic.

In the end, I wound up producing a three-part documentary focusing on why the fishery off Newfoundland was so important to the Spanish and the Portuguese. It was all about the politics of cod. As I said, any fool could see the end of the fishery coming.

CHAPTER 4

Playing Politics

As fishing catches continued to decline and the protests grew, the political will to do *something* slowly started to shift. It was a big story for me as a journalist, but it had personal implications as well. Although I had grown up in Labrador, I spent most of the summers of my young life on the Ramea Islands, just off Newfoundland's south coast. My mother's people were fishing people. Her father, my grandfather, was a fishing schooner captain at the age of sixteen.

For a fellow who was born and raised a Newfoundlander, it was sad to watch the demise unfolding in slow motion. The fishing industry had defined Newfoundland for centuries, either through policies exacted by the rich fish merchants, who mostly formed the government in St. John's, or later through policies set and enforced by the crowd in Ottawa.

Politics drove everything. Some would argue it drove the fishery under. Strangely enough for a young Newfoundland fellow born and raised on the west coast of the island and in Labrador, I had never seen the provincial seat of power up close. Never been to town. Now here I was, face first in codfish and politics. And a new wave was rising, preparing to wash in a completely new era.

When I arrived in 1987, the Liberal opposition leader at the time was Leo Barry. But the word was that Barry was on the way out and a new fellow, who was really an old fellow, was waiting in the wings. His name was Clyde Wells, and he had sat in the House of Assembly before. Back in the 1960s he had been a member of then-premier Joey Smallwood's cabinet. But he and another Liberal at the time, a fellow named John Crosbie (yes, *that* John Crosbie), were not happy campers.

They had suspected shenanigans around the financing of the Come By Chance oil refinery and left the government, choosing to sit as independent Liberals. John Crosbie went on to become a federal Conservative, eventually even making a run for the leadership. Wells left politics, went back to his law practice and was considered one of the finest constitutional minds in the country. Now he was coming back.

I was dispatched to the Confederation Building to try and sort it all out. The Liberals under Barry were having a hard go of it, and Brian Peckford's PCs weren't making it any more comfortable for them. The opposition offices were in disrepair. Water was drip-drip-dripping from the ceiling.

When I looked into their conference room, there, sitting among the water buckets on the table, was Rex Murphy (yes, *that* Rex Murphy). I remembered Rex from my high school days, when he had cohosted the very same CBC supper-hour show, *Here & Now*, that I was currently working for. I recalled watching him and thinking he was brilliant. Now that I reflect on it, he probably had an influence on me in one way or another.

I went in and introduced myself, telling him I'd been a fan of his work on the show some years before. Lately he had been working with the provincial Liberals—doing some research for them, as I recall. But he said he wasn't sure what the future would bring as this new fellow Wells was on his way back, and he didn't see eye to eye with him.

When I returned to the station, I mentioned to boss Ed Coady that I had seen Rex. I said, "Wouldn't it be great if we got Rex in here doing commentaries or something?" Ed wasn't too sure about that idea. "He's too close to the Liberals," he said. But not long after that, Ed Coady announced during a morning story meeting that Rex Murphy would be joining *Here & Now*, doing commentaries. Rex went on to become one of the country's top commentators.

And it was just as well. Clyde Wells did indeed become the leader of the opposition and Brian Peckford's government was beginning to wobble, in no small part because of make-work schemes like the Sprung Greenhouse.

Phil Sprung was a Calgary businessman and entrepreneur. He had quite a sales pitch. Combining his unique soft-sided buildings with some sort of hydroponic magic, Phil claimed he could grow healthy, fresh produce faster than almost anyone on the planet. And Brian Peckford believed him.

With the government's help, Phil set up shop in Mount Pearl outside of St. John's. The bills started to grow. Cucumbers grew too, but they were fewer and farther between than was ever promised, and the jobs, the export markets, the profits—they never materialized.

As I covered the whole debacle, I could sense it might be the rock to bring down Goliath. The Conservatives had been in power over a decade and a half, and Peckford was now increasingly being seen as arrogant and out of touch.

I remember interviewing a fellow from out around the bay about the state of the situation. He was a fisherman, spoke with a thick accent and didn't pull any punches. He summed it all up: "Lord Jesus bye, I suppose we could grow bananas at the North Pole if we wanted to, but what the frig would they cost?"

It got a little worse when word leaked that Peckford had ignored the advice of some senior civil servants, who had warned him the Sprung Greenhouse numbers just didn't add up.

I waited hours and hours in the lobby of the House of Assembly for the good premier to leave his bunker up on the eighth floor. I knew he was still up in his office and he had only two ways to leave: the main bank of elevators or the private elevator installed right next to the front door. I guessed which one he would eventually use—the one he thought would provide the quickest escape.

The elevator light went on, meaning someone was on the way down. The camera started rolling. The doors opened and it was quite the picture. There was Brian Peckford, wearing a huge, full-length fur coat and smoking a cigar. I said, "Mr. Premier, your senior people were telling you to back away from the Sprung Greenhouse because it was a bad deal. Why didn't you listen to them?" He looked right at me and replied, "If I listened to them, I would never get anything done!" Then he reached over to push the button. The elevator doors closed, and he went back up to his office. He was going up and his government was on the way down.

Shortly afterward, he resigned. In the end the final taxpayers' bill for growing cucumbers in Mount Pearl came in at over $22 million. I still wonder what it might cost to grow bananas at the North Pole.

THE WORLD IS CHANGING

After seventeen years of Tory rule, Clyde Wells swept to power, taking thirty-one of fifty-two seats in the House of Assembly. But his own seat wasn't one of them. Wells had decided to run for the seat in Humber East against another lawyer, Conservative Lynn Verge. Verge had been one of the first women elected in Newfoundland to become a cabinet minister, and she had survived Brian Peckford as his justice minister. She also survived Wells, defeating him in the election. Mr. Wells had to run again in a by-election in another district where a successful Liberal candidate agreed to resign to make room for him. This time he was unopposed and took his place in the

House of Assembly. The Clyde Wells era had begun, and it wouldn't be long before Newfoundland's premier was firmly in the spotlight of the entire country.

While all this was going on, another politician quietly came to town, one who would also play a large role on the national stage. His name was Jean Chrétien, and he showed up on the south coast of the island to pay back MHA Dave Gilbert. Gilbert, the member for Burgeo–Bay d'Espoir, was a huge supporter of Chrétien and helped him secure many delegates during Chrétien's federal leadership drive.

So for a couple days it was just me, Jean Chrétien, cameraman Lloyd Pennell and a chopper pilot flying right across the south coast from Burgeo to Ramea to François and eventually to Bay d'Espoir. On a personal level, Chrétien was a soft-spoken and engaging character. He praised and encouraged me for trying to speak French with him, told me the story about working to get Gros Morne designated as a UNESCO World Heritage Site and impressed me with what seemed a genuine affection for Newfoundland and its people.

But what really impressed me were his skills as a politician and the quick lesson he gave a young journalist. As we were flying into Bay d'Espoir I mentioned to him that it was kind of ironic. In French, Bay d'Espoir means the Bay of Hope. But here the unemployment rate under twenty-one years of age was close to 50 per cent. I mentioned there wasn't much hope in a number like that. Chrétien exited the chopper and walked into the community centre, where about 150 people were waiting. He got up on the platform and in his endearing Québécois accent began, "You know, in my language dis is Bay d'Espoir, da Bay of 'ope, but since the Mulroney government has come to power in Ottawa, dis is truly Bay Despair!"

His other favourite saying on that trip was, "You know, da biggest difference between me and Brian Mulroney, is dat I only talk out of one side of my mouth."

DON'T DO THAT!

It wasn't all politics. Sometimes there was crime, big crime. As the summer rolled on, another Quebecker flew in, this one a big player in the Montreal mafia's crime syndicate. There had been a huge hashish drug bust near Clarenville, Newfoundland, at a remote location called Ireland's Eye. Sixteen tons of hash were seized, at the time the largest drug bust in Canadian history.

The RCMP charged Vito Rizzuto, among others. Vito, also known as Montreal's Teflon Don, looked the part. At the time, he was considered the most powerful criminal in Montreal, if not Canada. It was said he came to power after participating in the assassination of some renegade mobsters associated with the Bonanno crime family of New York. He and two others, wearing ski masks, apparently shot three of them to death.

I was assigned to cover some preliminary court proceedings at the courthouse in Clarenville. Mr. Rizzuto and his colleagues had flown in for just that occasion. Cameraman Sterling Snow was again with me. Sterling is a tall, lanky fellow with a big walrus moustache. He is also tough as nails and afraid of nothing. We waited outside the court for some sign of action.

Vito and his gang soon arrived. Vito was an imposing, nasty presence, with slicked-back hair and a big hooked nose. He was also immaculately dressed in a long camel-hair coat, silk scarf and fine leather gloves. As he approached, I asked him if he would like to say anything. He smiled and said nothing. Then, as he was passing Sterling, he bent his shoulder into the camera, hitting it. Sterling said, "Jesus, buddy, watch it!"

"Sterling!" I hissed, "forget it." Thankfully, he did.

The court proceedings dragged on and were eventually adjourned until the afternoon. Nothing to do but eat lunch. With few options, we chose the restaurant at the Holiday Inn up by the highway. As we entered, Vito and his gang walked in right behind us. He nodded politely and there we sat, elbow to elbow, eating club sandwiches with the head of the Montreal mafia.

The charges against Montreal's Teflon Don eventually slipped right off him. They were dropped after the RCMP was caught trying to illegally wiretap another restaurant table, this one belonging to Rizzuto's lawyers.

I DO

Through it all, Pam was a real trooper. Her coming to Newfoundland was a big ask, a huge ask. She had put her own successful career on hold, not to mention that apartment by the beach in Kitsilano, Vancouver (I know if I don't mention it, she will).

Other friends were getting married, having children. I had stalled long enough. But I guess we both knew that if we were going to figure it out, we would have to be in the same province, same city, and yes, the same house.

We figured it out.

In the fall of 1989, we were married. October 7 was a beautiful day in Brigus, Newfoundland, almost as beautiful as the bride herself. Twenty-two degrees with barely a cloud in the sky. We were married in the Anglican Church down by the sea, and we never looked back.

Pam was now getting some part-time work at the CBC and things were rolling right along. At the CBC Christmas party that year, we won the big prize, a trip for two to South America. (They knew how to throw a party in Newfoundland!) Then in January we learned we were going to have a baby. It appeared that 1990 was going to be quite a year.

We decided, considering the pregnancy, South America wasn't a good idea, so we opted for Florida instead. There we were in February, lying on St. Pete Beach, when I heard on the radio that the space shuttle *Atlantis* was to be launched that evening. I said to Pam, "I think I'll go." She chose to stay on the beach and off I went.

What a beautiful day! What a lucky guy. Pam and I make a run for it after our lovely reception, with some delicious wedding cake in tow.

Driving to the Kennedy Space Center in our rental car, I realized I needed a plan (finally). I decided the plan should be not just to watch the launch, but to get up close and personal. I pulled into a Kmart and picked up a notepad as well as a small cassette tape recorder.

As I was nearing the Cape Canaveral Air Force Station, I spotted a local television van up ahead and decided to follow it. It took me right to the main security gate and media security. In I walked with my handy Kmart recorder and my driver's licence, announcing I was from the Canadian Broadcasting Corporation and I had arrived to cover the launch of the space shuttle. They said I would need some way to prove I was there for work. "What do you require?" I asked, and was told that a fax from my office confirming my assignment should do it. I went outside to the phone booth on the corner and called the St. John's newsroom collect. Producer Kevin Norman answered the phone. I said, "Kevin, can you get a piece of paper with our CBC logo on it and fax a message to this crowd here at the Kennedy Space Center saying I'm on assignment?"

"Lord Jesus, Reg, what are you up to now?" Kevin said.

"No big deal," I replied. "Can you do it?"

Twenty minutes later, the fax arrived, and I was in. Can you imagine attempting that today? No passport, no media ID, just a cassette recorder, a driver's licence and a fax from the newsroom. It was even more incredible when you consider it was also a highly secretive defence department flight mission. I guess I didn't come across as much of a threat. I drove into the compound. CBS, ABC and CBS all had buildings on site. F-18s were buzzing overhead as I stood down by the big digital clock, the one they always show on TV, with the shuttle lit up a few kilometres in the distance.

As I stood there with newspaper reporters from the *Wichita Eagle* and the *Tallahassee Democrat*, the digital clock started to count down. Then, at T minus 31 seconds, the mission was scrubbed because of weather.

After that, technicians drained liquid oxygen from the big bomb they didn't get to light up. All that manoeuvring and I didn't get to see the big show. When I got back to my vehicle, it and every other car in the lot was covered with a fine white powder. A paper under the windshield warned *not* to use water to get rid of it, but only to wipe it off with a dry cloth. Who knows what exactly that stuff was. Good thing it didn't rain. I did call the newsroom in Toronto and offered to file a report, but because the mission was scrubbed, they told me to forget it.

Several years later I did get to watch the shuttle *Atlantis* launch in all its glory. This time it was from the city of Titusville, Florida. I took my son, the same little fellow we were pregnant with back in 1990. It was quite a sight, standing along the shoreline with thousands of others. People were crying, singing and praying as *Atlantis* blasted through the sky and into space.

Decades after that I would be lucky enough to spend some time with Roberta Bondar, Canada's first woman in space. But more on that later.

MEECH LAKE AND THE WORLD ACCORDING TO CLYDE

That shuttle launch was, in fact, a little like the spectacle around Brian Mulroney in the spring of 1990. Mulroney's Meech Lake Accord negotiations were running into launch trouble too. All of the leaders of the provinces and territories were needed to achieve constitutional change, but there were holdouts. One of them was Newfoundland premier Clyde Wells.

The accord had been negotiated back in 1987, but it still had to be ratified. In theory, it was supposed to give the provinces greater control over Supreme Court appointments and immigration. It also afforded a veto over constitutional changes and gave the provinces increased power in federal funding decisions in areas such as education and health care.

But the big problem for Clyde Wells was that the accord also recognized Quebec as a distinct society within Canada. Wells argued that Quebec would wind up with greater legislative powers than other provinces, making future constitutional reform nearly impossible and possibly undermining federal funding to poorer provinces like Newfoundland and Labrador.

Mulroney argued that refusing to sign the accord would threaten national unity by possibly re-igniting separatist tensions in Quebec. Wells said, "Put it to a referendum." Mulroney refused. If the agreement wasn't ratified by Parliament and the provinces in 1990, it was dead. By the end of May all players converged on Ottawa for a few days to try to hammer out a deal. The stakes seemed astronomical.

I got the nod to shadow Mr. Wells, now a key player and under enormous pressure. We booked into the Château Laurier hotel and the games began.

The talks were being held right across the street in the conference centre. It was quite the spectacle. All the media cameras—dozens of them—were set up in a long line down one side of the entranceway. Don Newman from CBC Newsworld (now CBC News Network), itself less than a year old, was there to broadcast live to the entire country on the brand-new all-news channel. Newman had figured out a way to stand out. Rather than screaming to get his questions heard in a crowd with dozens of aggressive reporters, he had set up his own PA system with an amplifier for his microphone. He made it darn near impossible for the politicians to ignore him.

And you could tell when Mulroney was about to make an entrance. Just before he was to arrive, a school bus drove up full of immaculately dressed children, each with a little Canadian flag, who were placed on the far side across from the cameras. They would be in the prime minister's background, waving their little red-and-white flags whenever he walked in.

Before politics, Brian Mulroney was the head of the Iron Ore Company of Canada, which was owned, ironically, by three American companies that operated the mine in Labrador City. It was five kilometres away from where my father helped manage Wabush Mines. They knew each other. There were stories about infamous drinking parties at the Wabush Mines suite in the Sir Wilfred Grenfell Hotel, even one story about a member of the United Steelworkers Union who burst in one night and quickly "engaged" Mr. Mulroney, and not in a friendly way. My father said he had to haul the guy off Mulroney. A staunch Liberal at the time, my dad also joked that he should have let them finish their business.

Now, Mulroney was the prime minister, and he was determined to drive his Meech Lake Accord forward. I had managed to secure exclusive access to Premier Wells, away from the action, usually in his hotel suite. His communications director at the time was Judy Foote. She would go on to be a federal cabinet minister and lieutenant governor of Newfoundland and Labrador. But right now she was the voice on the other end of the phone. She would call without warning, and we would rush upstairs to get a few minutes to speak with the premier. These stories focused more on what was happening behind the scenes, and you could sense the tremendous pressure Mr. Wells was under.

We were under some pressure ourselves. We were a two-man team, no sound person, no producer, no big crew like the others had, just me and my sidekick Sterling Snow. He was the perfect man for the job. Strong and stubborn, he had no trouble getting the shots we needed. Late one evening after a long day of shooting, I was screening some tape Sterling had shot over by the Canadian Museum of History, across the river in Hull (now Gatineau). The premiers had gathered for dinner, and outside two gentlemen were arguing about the two solitudes, Quebec and Canada. Quite a crowd had gathered around them.

In Sterling's camera shot a head suddenly appeared, blocking his view. On the audio track you could hear Sterling say, "Hey buddy, you're in my shot." The head did not move. Again Sterling said, "Look, buddy, move—you're in my shot." Still no movement. Finally, Sterling said, "Hey buddy, you see this elbow? It's going right in the side of your head in a minute!" The head moved out of the shot. You didn't mess with Sterling.

This political roller coaster was becoming quite a ride. The gathering was supposed to last a couple of days, but it was stretching to five. We would videotape all day and sometimes late into the evening. Then I'd screen the tape and write a script, usually finishing at two or three in the morning. I would then wash my socks and underwear in the sink, grab maybe twenty winks, then go right back to taping in the morning. Just after lunch I would visit our mobile truck, edit the story, record a five-minute satellite debrief with the studio in St. John's, then go do it all over again. At one point I gave up the washing and took a small break to go buy more underwear.

In the middle of this constitutional crisis, I got a call from the hotel's manager. She had a crisis of her own. She politely informed me that we would have to leave the hotel—a convention had been booked in and they needed the space. Fair enough—we were now a day or two past our reservation. But I could not leave. I explained to her that I was a journalist covering Clyde Wells, the premier of Newfoundland, and at a moment's notice I needed to scramble up the back staircase to do an interview. I simply had to stay.

She said it was unfortunate, but she wasn't changing her mind. We would have to leave. I said, "Well, I'm not leaving and neither is my cameraman, so what are you going to do about it?" Somewhere in the back of my head I had this notion that if you were occupying a room and had done nothing wrong, they could not force you to leave.

"I'm going to call the police," she said. I invited her to go right ahead, saying I'd tape the whole thing, showing how she had treated the only news crew from Newfoundland during this historic debate. "You don't have to be like that," she said. I said again, "Look, I am not leaving, and neither is my cameraman. You call me back when you figure what you're going to do." Then I hung up.

Sterling turned to me and sighed. "My son, you got skin on you like a pig." All the other news teams were kicked out of the Château Laurier. We were not. But they moved us around—a lot. One evening I returned and picked up the key to my room, only to find myself in a huge corner suite, complete with a gourmet kitchen big enough for several chefs to cook in. Like we had time to eat.

After one particularly long day, when it looked as if Clyde Wells would indeed scuttle the deal, we were sitting at the bar downstairs, having a rare beer. Sterling was seated to my left, and to my right was this little fellow from *Le Devoir*, the big French-language newspaper. The room was full of politicians with their aides and consultants.

The little fellow kept going on about Clyde Wells and how he was ruining the country. I was tired of it all. Finally I said, "Look, I know everybody has their opinion about this, but I wish you would be quiet because I'm sick of listening to yours." With this, Sterling piped up and said, "Now, Reg bye, that's how we got into this mess in the first place. We have to talk things through." With that, our little French friend said, "As far as I am concerned, Newfoundland is nothing. It's like the Bangladesh of Canada."

Sterling stood bolt upright, reached across me, and grabbed this fellow by the collar. He also said a few choice words I will not repeat here before I managed to get him off the guy. People were turning to see what the fuss was about. Our French friend scurried away. We decided to scurry away too.

The next morning, I was down in the lobby by six o'clock. Sterling was already there, stomping around. "That little so-and-so," he said. "He put me right off my cornflakes. I just wanted to see if I could spot him." Oh, the fun we were having.

In the end they pretended there was a deal, when really there wasn't, and everyone defaulted to their respective legislatures for a final vote. Turned out it wasn't necessary. Before Newfoundland cast even one vote, former chief and member of the Manitoba legislature Elijah Harper rose in his place and torpedoed the good ship Meech Lake on behalf of an Aboriginal community that felt completely left out of the process. His explanation?

> Well, I was opposed to the Meech Lake Accord because we weren't included in the Constitution. We were to recognize Quebec as a distinct society, whereas we as Aboriginal people were completely left out. We were the First Peoples here—First Nations of Canada—we were the ones that made treaties with the settlers that came from Europe. These settler people and their governments didn't recognize us as a Nation, as a government, and that is why we opposed the Meech Lake Accord.

CHAPTER 5

Off to War

During the summer of 1990, our lives changed in the best of ways. In August our son Mitchell was born. I have often said I never really knew why I was on the planet until I became a father. Then it all made sense. It was a proud moment.

But other things were happening too, dark things on the world stage, and they would soon land much closer to home than I had ever imagined. Over in the powder keg known as the Middle East, Iraq, under the leadership of Saddam Hussein, had invaded nearby Kuwait. Now it looked very much like US president George Bush Sr. wanted to do something about it. Throughout the summer there was a lot of sabre rattling, but little public support for an American intervention.

Then a fifteen-year-old Kuwaiti girl, who was given the name Nayirah to protect her identity, appeared before the Congressional Human Rights Caucus in Washington. With tears in her eyes, she spoke about seeing little babies being ripped from their incubators in Kuwaiti hospitals by Iraqi soldiers who apparently then left them on the cold floor to die.

The president himself told the story over and over. By late September the public sentiment was now overwhelmingly in favour of military intervention to pull the Iraqis out of Kuwait.

Operation Desert Storm was born, a UN-sanctioned combat operation undertaken by a coalition of thirty-five countries led by the United States. Canadian forces would be part of this plan, with their component code-named Operation Friction and based in Bahrain. Initially three warships would be used to help form a blockade in the Persian Gulf and around Kuwait as coalition forces ramped up to attack.

Through research, I learned some interesting facts. Newfoundland's population represented less than 2 per cent of the population of Canada, yet Newfoundlanders made up over 30 per cent of the forces being sent to the Gulf. The province had a strong Sea Cadet program and going on to serve in the Navy was a career choice for many young Newfoundland men and women. To me, the fact that they were now about to get tangled up in this drama unfolding on the world stage—that was a story.

Don't forget, until then our armed forces had primarily been involved in peacekeeping missions. Many of those had been dangerous, but this was something else altogether. I pushed hard with our newsroom leaders, arguing that we/I should go and show those at home what that fellow from Carbonear or that young woman from Mount Pearl, now proud members of the Navy, had gotten themselves into.

I worked for weeks to get the Canadian military on side, and spent days—countless hours using a fax machine (my only available form of reliable international communication)—trying to persuade the government of Bahrain to let me in. The Canadian Navy, along with Americans and some Brits, would be based in Manama, the capital. That was the place to be.

Finally, I was able to secure permission to videotape in their country. I'm still not sure how exactly it happened, but one day the fax arrived, and the last obstacle had been removed. Well, almost the last obstacle. I still had to persuade my employers. I argued that this was a huge shift in the way our military operated—these were Newfoundlanders, clearly in harm's way. I promised that I would also do stories for other regions and produce a half-hour TV show, and all the material would be sent out through the syndicated news service. This would help pay for the trip.

Back in 1990, the CBC regions still had a great deal of autonomy and more control over their budgets. You could negotiate and find little pockets of money from other regions or programs to help make a project more viable. The bosses went for it. To be fair, the leadership in St. John's didn't take much convincing. They were always willing to find their own path to a story involving Newfoundlanders. I had just managed to talk myself into going to war, with a three-month-old son at home. My wife was not impressed.

But our team would travel there before the intervention was scheduled to begin, arriving in late October and staying for two weeks. We would have no way to feed tape back to Canada; instead, we would have to carry it back ourselves (feeding it by satellite was much too expensive, even if you could secure an uplink). We had only the fax machine for communication. There were phones, but you could rarely get them to work, certainly not for international calls, and if you could, the cost was astronomical.

The fax machine, for those who don't know or remember, gave you the ability to send a printed document through the phone system. You fed it into the machine, and on the other end the fax machine spat it out. It worked most of the time. We would make do.

Cameraman Mark Thompson and I would make the trip. With our many cases of gear we flew to Toronto, then on to London. The next day, we jumped on a British Airways jet that would take us down the Suez Canal, across Saudi Arabia and into Bahrain. The flight was twelve or thirteen hours, and the plane was practically empty, with fewer than a dozen passengers including us. At that point the Middle East was hardly a popular destination. Planes flew in to take people out, not the other way around.

The State of Bahrain was a very rich country. It also had a reputation of being somewhat lax in security, and we soon learned it was a reputation the country was trying to dispel. When we landed, there were soldiers everywhere with automatic weapons—and no sense of humour.

They went through everything in our big camera-gear cases. They went through everything in our luggage. They even squeezed some of my toothpaste out of the tube. It went on for hours. In the end they removed all our camera gear, left us our luggage and sent us on our way to our hotel, the Ramada Inn downtown.

As I walked out the front doors of the airport, I was hit by a wall of heat. Daytime highs were 40° to 45°C and the humidity was 100 per cent. I had never experienced heat like this; it took my breath away. The hotel had a cool-water pool. It was so hot outside they literally had to cool down the pool water. Here we were, in the Persian Gulf, as the coalition prepared for war. Without a camera.

It did show up the next day, but we were not allowed to shoot anything without our government escort. One day passed, then another. I was getting nervous. This was a big assignment, and so far I had zilch.

But I was learning a bit more about the country. The Bahraini currency was the most powerful I had ever seen. One Bahraini dinar was worth well over US$3. The economy was based on offshore banking and finance with some tourism, in better times, mixed in. For many years the British had control in the region, but in 1971 Bahrain had declared its independence.

That former British influence had an upside. Besides the roundabouts and even a fish-and-chip shop, you could buy beer there. It was the only one of the Arab Emirates that imported beer, *if* you could afford it. One beer, which you could find only in the hotel lounge or in the mini fridge in your room, was about $15 Canadian. That was one expensive frosty one.

The other thing about Bahrain was that most of the people working there were from somewhere else. They were from India or Pakistan or the Philippines, hired by the rich of Bahrain to do the jobs they did not want to do. Foreigners, who outnumbered Bahrainis by close to two to one, did most of the work.

Tipping was strictly forbidden. In lieu of tipping everything had a 15 per cent service charge. Once a month the hotel we were staying in named their "employee of the month," who received a bonus of two dinars. Somebody was making a lot of money and it wasn't the employees. In our hotel, the staff all lived in a compound out back that was surrounded by a fence with barbed wire. They would move from the compound to the hotel and back again. It did not take long to figure out this was not a democracy—or anything close to it. Here foreign workers had no real rights and not much of a life either, just work and a bed.

We had to take cabs everywhere. The cab from the airport was five dinars. I spoke with an American in the lobby who told us we paid too much. If the cabbies think they can get away with it, he said, they will charge you as much as they can, especially with all the foreign troops in town, but no cab ride should be more than half a dinar. He said if you do not barter with them, they will not respect you. Lesson learned.

I made contact with the Canadian Navy and needed to meet with them, so I called a taxi. Before we left I asked the driver, "How much?" "Five dinars," he replied. "That's not a fair price," I said, starting to get out of the cab. "But for you my friend, just half a dinar," came the quick response. I agreed, but he would have to wait and bring me back. Even getting a cab quickly was becoming a challenge. Hold 'em while you got 'em. Lesson number two.

The Navy was helping smooth things out with Bahraini authorities. We still didn't have permission to videotape on land. The Bahrainis had no control over what we taped on Canadian warships, but our Navy did. Back when I had first proposed going, Canadian military authorities wanted to dog-tag us—to essentially enlist us and fly us over on military aircraft. It meant they would have complete control over what we shot and what we said. We said, "No thanks."

I had no interest in becoming a propaganda arm of the Canadian military. We had maintained our independence, but between the military and the Bahraini Ministry of Information, there was precious little real information to be had. It was becoming a very frustrating, hot experience, enough to drive a man to drink. And that cold Bahraini beer was financially out of reach.

I was lamenting that very fact to my new friend the cab driver when, in a moment of mutual respect, he proposed I meet him outside the front of the hotel later that evening. When I did, he took me to the back of the hotel where another cab was waiting. In the trunk was a case of Löwenbräu beer. He asked for US$40. I countered with $30 and we settled on $35. Thanks to my new friends, I had finally accomplished something.

The next morning, more success. A young fellow dressed in traditional Arabic attire appeared and declared he was our escort. Standing there in his flowing white linen, he didn't appear to be more than sixteen years old. And he was driving a powerful two-door, super-charged Mustang, not exactly the perfect vehicle to be lugging around two big Canadian guys with half a ton of camera gear. I didn't care, though—we were shooting!

We took shots of the bustle of the city, and then, travelling at well over 160 kilometres an hour, our young friend zoomed us out to the desert, where we were surrounded by camels and oil derricks. In the city, nobody would speak on camera; off camera, Bahrainis told me they were nervous. A small island nation joined to Saudi Arabia by causeway, Bahrain's fear was that if Saddam Hussein could march into Kuwait, what or who would stop him if he decided Bahrain was next?

The Americans would stop him, of course, and the coalition. They had arrived with their fleet of warships, and it seemed

It was hard to believe, but there I was, having my picture taken in the middle of the biggest world conflict of the day. This was about as smooth as the Persian Gulf got. The *Protecteur* is behind me.

they had almost taken over the city. They were everywhere. The Canadian military was setting up shop too, but our ships weren't allowed in the harbour. We were told they had to anchor several kilometres offshore because they were carrying fuel and explosives. Why the Americans didn't have to do the same is another story, but I will save that for later. Our Canadian forces were where our real story was.

There were three Canadian ships: HMCS *Protecteur*, HMCS *Athabaskan* and HMCS *Terra Nova*. The *Terra Nova* and the *Athabaskan* were frigates, already out in the Gulf on patrol. To get to the supply ship *Protecteur*, which was anchored outside the harbour, we would have to take a water taxi, which was sort of like a gigantic cork rolling and bobbing on the water. It reminded me of those little one-man tugs you saw pushing logs around off the coast of British Columbia just like on *The Beachcombers* (if you are old enough to remember that great Canadian show!).

I am *not* a good sea person. This was *not* a seagoing vessel. It was designed to move people around the harbour, not for sailing a couple of kilometres offshore. The Persian Gulf can get rough—we learned that soon enough. Like an ant crawling through tall grass, we moved precariously through the fleet of warships tied up everywhere in the harbour.

On board were just me and Mark and two crew. The captain barely spoke. His assistant, who was from Bhopal, India, spoke English very well. During the ride out he told me he worked on the boat twenty-four hours a day, seven days a week. He slept on the small wooden bench in the cabin. He had one pair of flip-flops, two pairs of pants and two shirts. He cooked and ate on the boat, with just a couple of pots and pans. Twice a year they flew him back to India for a week to see his wife and six children. The rest of his life, he was on this boat. He seemed resigned to it all. These two gentlemen and their bobbing cork would become our only means of getting to and from HMCS *Protecteur*. Every trip would be an adventure.

And today it was rough. Once we'd cleared the harbour, the swells kept getting bigger and bigger. A floating dock was attached to the *Protecteur*, at the time our Navy's largest service and fuel resupply vessel, with a large flight hangar housing the Sikorsky Sea King helicopter on its stern.

As we approached in the swells, I could see getting on that dock was going to be more than a challenge. It would mean risking our lives. At one point the dock was a good three metres above our heads, then below us, then above. We had to time it perfectly to transfer the gear and then ourselves during that brief moment when both our boat and the dock were level. One slipped step and you could lose your leg—or worse. Slowly, slowly, we timed each transfer, then counted all our fingers and toes.

On board, the crew was excited for our arrival. Like a little piece of home, the boys from Newfoundland CBC's *Here & Now* had come all the way to the Persian Gulf to see them. They were a great bunch, eager for news from home, and whenever we were on board they couldn't do enough for us.

The plan was to lift off the back of the *Protecteur* and fly out to the *Athabaskan*, which was patrolling off the coast of Kuwait. We would land on the back of it and shoot them on patrol, perhaps even videotape a practice attack drill. No sweat. Well, as it turned out, a *lot* of sweat. It was hot enough on deck. In the chopper, where we wore flight suits, helmets and water-flotation gear, it was stifling at just shy of 50 °C.

The Sea King was well maintained but old. We did a little rehearsal drill about ditching in the water. I did not want that to happen. Earlier, looking over the side of the ship, I'd seen massive sea snakes, lots of them, swimming just under the surface.

When we lifted off there was a big swell, but nothing too serious. By the time HMCS *Athabaskan* came into sight, however, it had become extremely rough. It was so rough the Sea King couldn't get onto the deck without help. Our crew dropped a grapple cable with a claw on the end. Below us, the deck crew attached it to a large steel ball on the stern, and we were literally winched down to the surface of the ship, hitting it with a not insignificant thud. And there we were, on a Canadian warship a hundred kilometres off the coast of Kuwait.

My adrenaline was pumping and we were eager to get started, but there was a problem. The water was now so rough we could barely stand up. We attempted to do an interview, but it proved impossible. And I was starting to feel queasy. Everybody was. It was decided, as it was getting late, that we should bunk down for the night. We followed a crew member down a steep set of stairs then to the back. Again, down and to the back, and then again. I thought, "If this keeps up, we'll be underneath this damn ship."

Finally, he pointed to a row of bunks and said I was up on top. I rolled into the bunk, lying on my back, with a few centimetres between the tip of my nose and a big steam pipe. A curtain hung on my right. A voice on the other side said, "How's it going?" After I said hello. the voice continued. "Hey man, I'm from the operations room. I don't want to scare you or nothin', but there are twice as many Iraqi planes in the air today as yesterday, and we don't know where they're coming from."

For the first time on this surreal trip, I thought, "Okay, now you've really got yourself in the middle of something—something serious." It was a scary thought, one the crew was no doubt having every day.

By morning the seas had calmed down. We spoke with many members of the crew, and not only people from Newfoundland. I learned that the province with the second-highest number of people in the Navy was Saskatchewan, the one province or territory farthest from the ocean! It seemed those wide-open fields were not unlike looking out over the water. But most of the young people here, and many were very young, called Newfoundland home.

I remember interviewing one nineteen-year-old from Carbonear, Newfoundland, out on the deck. He said, "Mom always told me that as soon as I signed up, something was going to happen, and sure enough, it did." But mostly they seemed resigned to their situation, and happy to be part of it all. They did not seem to know a lot, or care, about what could be coming. I often heard, "I'm here on a need-to-know basis. What I don't need to know, I don't care about."

What they did care about was enforcing the blockade. Every day they contacted ships, everything from large tankers to small Arab fishing vessels called *dhows* moving through the zone. If they didn't like the radio response or if something seemed suspicious, an armed boarding team was dispatched.

And although it would still be close to two months before the coalition was ready to start pushing the Iraqi army out of Kuwait, the possibility of attack by Saddam Hussein's forces was very real. So they practised, defending against a mock attack. During one drill, the big ship was slicing through the water at better than twenty-five knots while crews scrambled to get to stations. It was very realistic and more than a little unnerving.

But on October 31, there was time for a little fun. On our way back to the *Protecteur* from the *Athabaskan*, a giant pumpkin shipped from Canada was loaded into the cargo bay of the Sea King, with dozens of glow sticks packed inside. It was massive and must have weighed at least a hundred kilos. With the cargo bay open and the giant pumpkin smiling out the door, we lifted off, just after dark. The idea was to give the crew of HMCS *Terra Nova* a little visual treat. As we circled the warship, that huge toothy grin was glowing for those on deck to see, as they waved back to us from the high seas of the Persian Gulf.

Over the next week or so we taped Christmas greetings to be used during the holidays and for families back home, greetings from cooks and officers alike, all serving their country. We shot a little music video for a song written by one Newfoundland crew member who sang about being so far away from home. I even met one fellow from my hometown—Rob Lawrence from Wabush, Labrador. Unbelievable.

The day before we left, a Canadian officer invited me for a drink in the hotel lounge. I sat next to a Saudi businessman who had driven over the causeway because he had an appetite for gin, strictly forbidden back in the kingdom. He seemed very relaxed about the whole Iraqi situation, even smug. He said the Americans would take care of it because they wanted Saudi oil. He drank three triple gins while I sat beside him.

Across the room a British soldier was making a lot of noise, even banging his head into the wall. Quite drunk, he told me he was a paratrooper. He kept saying over and over, "Mate, do you know what my life expectancy is when I hit the ground? About six bloody hours!" He wasn't much older than me. The whole experience left me sad and a little depressed.

Our time was up. Soon enough the coalition would be lighting up Baghdad "like a Christmas tree." I thought about that British soldier on my trip all the way home, which included an overnight stay in London.

Cue the "It's a Small World (After All)" theme again. I had just walked into a pub in Piccadilly Circus to get some supper and was waiting for a pint at the bar when I heard someone shout, "Hey Reg!" Standing at the bar just down from me was a fellow I knew from Brigus, Newfoundland, where Pam and I had married. Unbelievable.

We knew we had great material, and the network couldn't get enough of it. We rolled it out in the weeks leading up to Christmas, and I like to think it not only gave Newfoundlanders and Canadians a sense of what our young men and women were doing in the Persian Gulf, but helped bring them a little closer to home for the holidays.

By January 16, 1991, the American-led coalition began pounding Baghdad, live on television around the world. CNN had somehow managed to get a cable link hard-wired into the Iraqi capital. Once the ground campaign began, it did not take long—about a hundred hours in the desert—to push Saddam Hussein out of Kuwait, but the cost was enormous. Two years after the war a study put the cost at over US$670 billion, with Saudi Arabia, Kuwait and other Gulf states picking up some of the tab, but the Americans shouldering most of it. The coalition lost over 290 soldiers, the British 47. I have often wondered if that British paratrooper in Bahrain was one of them. Thirteen journalists also lost their lives covering Operation Desert Storm; two more were wounded and two are still listed as missing.

And here's the thing. Remember the young girl appearing before the US congressional committee, with tears in her eyes, to talk about seeing babies ripped from incubators by Iraqi troops? To conceal her identity, Nayirah was the only name they gave her. What they didn't say was that she was a member of Kuwaiti royalty. Her last name was al-Sabah. Her father, Saud al-Sabah, was the Kuwaiti ambassador to Washington. He sat unidentified in the room with her that morning as she wept for the cameras.

In 1992, after the war was over, Amnesty International, along with other organizations, conducted a thorough investigation. They interviewed doctors and nurses on the ground in Kuwaiti hospitals across the country. They could not document a single case of babies being ripped from incubators. It did not happen. The girl's entire testimony—and, depending on how you chose to look at it, the war that ensued—may have been orchestrated by an American public relations firm hired by the Kuwaiti government.

The truth may set you free, but in this case, a massive lie led to war. Talk about *Wag the Dog*. In the movie, released in 1997, a spin doctor and a Hollywood producer fake a war. In this case the war was real—it was just the motivation to get the American people on side that was faked.

CHAPTER 6

Boats and Bears

In less than four years at CBC Newfoundland and Labrador, I'd worked on stories that had taken me across North America and overseas. I had covered a looming fisheries disaster, a major constitutional crisis and the preparation for war in the Middle East. Maybe it hadn't been the plan, but the decision to move back East was working out pretty darn well.

Some of it was circumstance. A lot of it was the faith that the folks running the newsroom had in me to deliver the story, guys like executive producers Ed Coady and Bob Wakeham. They were determined to tell the story of Newfoundlanders quite literally anywhere in the world it took us. And back then, they always seemed to be able to find the money to make it happen. Current affairs was still a vibrant part of every regional television operation.

Did all this attention have me thinking I was headed for the big leagues? Maybe, just a little. But my first attempt at landing a job as a reporter for *The National* soon cleared that up. The network system that fed *The National* was looking for five journalists, and I thought I had a decent shot. I didn't even get an interview. It was a real eye-opener for me, and a painful brush with disappointment. But I dusted myself off and carried on.

In 1991, a gentleman from Toronto named Paul Lewis came to St. John's. He was starting a new television show for the CBC with a name that dated back to 1953, an old program called *CBC Newsmagazine*. It would air in the early evening and the content would be longer features, four or five minutes in length. He suggested to our news gang that we all gather at a local watering hole to hash it over. For some reason, I was one of the few who showed up. His enthusiasm for the new show was infectious. It was right in my wheelhouse, and I looked forward to the opportunity.

I would do many stories for Paul, stories about oiled seabirds, about polar bears, about forgotten Newfoundland shores and, of course, stories about the fishery. The Northern codfish, once considered one of the largest food sources on the planet, continued to disappear. And skirmishes with the foreign fishing fleets had started to ramp up.

THE LAST LIVING FATHER

But the biggest story in Newfoundland and Labrador in 1991 happened just before Christmas.

On December 17, the (self-named) last living father of Confederation, Joey Smallwood, died at the age of ninety. Smallwood had always been a force in Newfoundland, right from the time he brought the province into Confederation at midnight, March 31, 1949 (by a vote of just 52.3 per cent). Some called it a bad April Fool's joke. Those against Confederation and in favour of an economic union with the United States included Chesley Crosbie, John Crosbie's father.

Joey's skills as a speaker and a campaigner kept him on the top rung of the political ladder for the first twenty-three years of Newfoundland's membership in the Dominion of Canada. One of my favourite pieces of memorabilia from a Joey Smallwood campaign was a cookie-sized button with the slogan, GUESS WHO'S VOTING FOR

JOEY? When you turned it over, it was a vanity mirror that women could carry with them in their purses. He rarely missed a trick. And Lord help those below him who had the gall to oppose him.

There is a great political cartoon, originally published in Halifax's *Chronicle-Herald*, that depicts Joey up in the bow of a small fishing dory, all decked out in his fishing gear. A long rope leads from the bow of the dory up to the back of a big ocean liner named *Mainland*. Fellows in captain's hats are standing around the back rail where the rope is attached and staring down at Joey. As I recall, Joey has a big knife in his hand, and he's yelling to the crowd on the ship, "I'm warning you fellows—if I hear any more foolish talk, I'll cut you adrift!"

He may have possessed a distorted view of his importance in the bigger scheme of things, but he ruled like a king. Near the end of his rule, though, cracks appeared in his armour. Clyde Wells didn't mind opposing him. Neither did John Crosbie as—like father, like son—he and Smallwood clashed in the House of Assembly. Near the end of his life, in a cruel note of irony, the man known across Canada for his skill as an orator was left small and frail, unable to speak.

And now he was gone. A big snowstorm raged all afternoon and into the evening. I had been dispatched to travel out to Bay Roberts to the funeral home where, for the moment, Joey was being waked. As a young man he had taught school there. Later he would be moved into the House of Assembly.

To get to the funeral home, camera operator Gerry Davis from *The National* and I risked our lives, slipping down the Trans-Canada and across Roaches Line in a howling gale with snow coming down sideways. When we arrived, it was dead quiet. Of course the roads were almost impassable.

Gerry positioned himself out front, and for an inordinately long period of time inside the funeral home, there we were, just me—and Joey. As I've mentioned, my father and Joey knew each other. As a child, I remember the premier sending Dad a postcard during one of his visits to China. It didn't say much, just "Greetings, JRS." I'm sure hundreds were sent, but it was signed by hand. I still have it.

Years later, I attended a high school graduation dinner at JR Smallwood Collegiate in Wabush. Joey, the guest speaker, talked for what seemed like forever, delaying the graduation dance. The kids sat there, slumping lower and lower in their chairs, while Joey insisted that everyone say a prayer for Quebec.

And now here he was, not a metre from me, lying there in his trademark bow tie and his glasses. I had a sudden overwhelming urge to grab those iconic black horn-rimmed glasses right off his face. You never, ever saw a picture of Joey without them. Eventually I got over myself and my powerful, unexplainable urge.

Several people who had walked through the storm stomped their way in through the funeral parlour doors. I even recognized one woman, Greta Hussey. Over eighty, she had walked many kilometres from Port de Grave in the storm, just to say goodbye. By midnight the wind and snow had moved off to sea. We jumped in the van and crawled back to St. John's.

Now, I was not beyond playing the occasional practical joke and the next morning, during the story meeting, a plan was hatched in my admittedly twisted mind. The discussion centred on how exactly we were going to cover Joey, soon to be lying up at the House of Assembly, when I suddenly blurted out, "I have one of his fingers!" Many groans and comments ensued, with people saying, "That's sick!" I just thought of it as a sort of black humour. "No," I said, "it snapped off just like a twig!"

Through snorts of disgust, I wandered back out into the newsroom and found a small cardboard paper-clip box. I cut a hole in the bottom just big enough to get my middle finger through, surrounded it with tissue paper, used a little black marker on the nail and closed the lid. And then I waited outside the meeting.

Reporter Rick Seaward was the first through the door after the meeting ended. As usual he was deep in thought, probably organizing his assignment in his head. I said, "Rick, Rick, I'm not kidding—I have one of his fingers. Look!" I showed him the box, and as I lifted the top and he looked in, I wiggled that finger just a little bit.

Rick shrieked and jumped, then slid down the side of the wall. He went very pale. It was just a joke, but it worked better than expected. Almost too well.

Many jokes followed over the next few days. Joey was nothing if not controversial. He was one of those "love him or hate him" sort of leaders. Some folks joked they went to the House of Assembly just to make sure he was dead.

But the big joke of the day was that they had his "lying in state" all buggered up. As one fellow put it, "Jeez bye, that's no good, they should have him lying face down so everybody can kiss his arse one last time."

Poor Joey.

A COMMERCIAL EXTINCTION

In 1992 it all finally came to a head in the fishery. In June, an international dispute resolution tribunal granted St. Pierre and Miquelon their "corridor," a thin strip of territory jutting into Canadian waters, and control over all the resources in it. Not that there were many resources left—certainly not fish.

On July 2, federal Fisheries and Oceans Minister John Crosbie, still Newfoundland's representative in Mulroney's cabinet, announced the largest mass layoff in Canadian history. Twenty-seven thousand members of the fishing community were abruptly thrown out of work.

The great stocks of Northern cod had finally collapsed. It was the commercial extinction of a species. The question was, would it take down the province with it? Not if the people outside the news conference doors that day had anything to do with it.

In their wisdom, some geniuses at the Department of Fisheries and Oceans decided members of the fishing community should not be in the same room with Minister Crosbie. Instead, they were gathering around a television, viewing the event from another hotel room down the hall.

I was locked inside Crosbie's news conference room along with dozens of other reporters, government officials and security. It was a tense scene, especially when the angry crowd of fisherfolk, prompted by one of their leaders, Cabot Martin, decided they wanted inside. They pounded and kicked at the doors, seeming ready to riot. Inside, security had jammed the metal legs of a chair down inside the push bars on the doors so they would not open. Some of the side doors had been tied with rope. At one point I noticed a local photographer who was inside with us quietly trying to untie a rope. He failed. Maybe he thought a crowd of angry fishermen busting into the room to confront Mr. Crosbie would make for a better shot.

Crosbie said to the cameras that it was no good "going berserk," as he put it, trying to scare him, because he simply did not scare. But they were watching the news conference live in Ottawa, and you might say the Mulroney government blinked a few times. Years later Crosbie admitted to me that when the cabinet in Ottawa saw what was happening, they agreed to almost triple the compensation package, something that no doubt saved many families from undue hardship. I guess there are times when going berserk can work.

After the layoffs, Newfoundland's population began to decline. People were forced to simply walk away, their trap skiffs rotting in the grass, never to float again. A way of life for the inshore fishing community was gone forever. As one fellow from the Great Northern Peninsula put it, "Today there's a tear in my eye, and a knob in my throat, to look out there, where I once belonged, and to know I don't belong there anymore."

It hit me too. It was part of my heritage. My grandfather had carried salt cod to Jamaica and the Bahamas, exchanging it for hemp and molasses and Jamaican black rum, also known as Newfoundland screech. The national dish of Jamaica is ackee fruit and salt cod. The last time I was there, all the salt cod was from Iceland or Norway.

The collapse of the industry was a calamity that had struck deep, and it still reverberates today. Almost thirty years later, there is still no significant commercial fishery to speak of. There may not be again in our lifetime, not for the Northern cod anyway.

Those who chased the fish jumped to other species such as crab, shrimp and lobster. Now they too were coming under pressure, just like the politicians. The politicians, on the other hand, were hoping the massive offshore oil development known as Hibernia was going to save them. Construction was underway, and in addition to new jobs would come royalty revenues, money that would eventually take Newfoundland from being a have-not province to one that was finally putting more into Canada than it took out.

The same waters that had sustained the province for over five hundred years were again promising to lead to salvation, not because of what was in them, but because of what was *underneath* them.

THE BINGO BEAR OF THE BAYROCK LOUNGE

I was looking for salvation of my own in the form of new, interesting feature stories. I had been poking along, doing the occasional feature for the network or for regional current affairs programs like *Land and Sea*. I produced stories about kayaking and about forgotten shores, about historic ships and about those lost at sea.

Then came the story about the polar bear who wandered off the ice and into a fellow's house, down near a place called Trepassey. "Jeez, ol' man," the man told me. "I hears this racket in the middle of the night, goes into the living room and there's a polar bear in the bloody living room! So naturally, I throws the La-Z-Boy at 'im, and he jumps back out the living room window. Wicked, it was!" Now, polar bears wandering around on the island of Newfoundland was and is a fairly rare occurrence, but it does happen as the Arctic ice drifts south in the spring, and it can be, understandably, more then a little unnerving.

I decided to affectionately refer to this particular bear as the Bingo Bear of the Bayrock Lounge. Old Bingo kept following his nose along the coast until he came upon a place named the Bayrock Lounge near the community of St. Joseph's. A large group of women had congregated there for a game of bingo and supper, and they were just cooking up a big load of fish and chips. Then along came old Bingo. The smell coming out of the kitchen's exhaust fan was more than he could resist. As Bingo circled, looking for a way to get in, some women spotted him in the parking lot. As you can imagine, they pretty much freaked out. The women called Wildlife Services, who showed up with a big metal tube-like device, intent on trapping old Bingo. But they had no bait. No problem—the women did. They put some fish and chips in the trap, and in ten minutes flat, Bingo was jailed. I arrived to take pictures of it all, and that was when they discovered Bingo had managed to break off one of his impressive canine teeth.

So as they flew him back up North in a big net hanging beneath the helicopter, they landed in St. Anthony for a quick visit to the dentist. The good dentist was able to fix Bingo up very nicely (he was sedated, of course). I sometimes imagined, years later, an Inuit hunter bagging old Bingo, only to discover that "Jeez, this bear has had dental surgery!" The hunter would probably spend the rest of his life trying to figure out how the heck a bear had been to the dentist. Those irresistible fish and chips! That's how!

A BEAR OF A DIFFERENT COLOUR

Bear story number two. This time the colour was black, and the bears were unique to this planet: they were the only black bears in the world living above the treeline. Their home was Northern Labrador, in the subarctic Torngat Mountains, one of the most beautiful places I have ever been. The bears had moved into the territory about 150 years ago, after the giant Kodiak bears departed.

As you know, I grew up in Labrador, but that was deep in the interior, several hundred kilometres from the coast. The northern coastline was another world. It was a part of the Big Land I had never travelled to, but that was about to change.

I had heard through a biologist friend that a fellow from the University of Alberta was studying these unique black bears up in the Torngat Mountain range. Biologist Al Veitch was conducting an ongoing study of the bears, based out of a provincial government camp about 250 kilometres north of Nain. This was remote, unforgiving territory, ruled more by an Inuit deity known as Tuurngait than any human regulation. Tuurngait controlled the forces of nature and the animals and was ignored at your peril. We would soon learn that lesson.

It was late May and the black bears had not yet emerged from their snow dens. The average black bear can forage over about a hundred square kilometres, but these little creatures were forced to cover close to a thousand just to survive. As a result, they were quite small. A large male would barely reach 140 kilos.

The Torngat Mountain Range appears as if it launched itself right out of the Labrador Sea and straight up thousands of metres. Flying close, we spotted a mother polar bear and two cubs moving along the rocky shore. We nudged closer for a better shot. It was my first good look at a polar bear in the wild, and it was an impressive and humbling sight.

Taking my turn cooking on a Coleman stove in Hebron Fjord in Northern Labrador. We were there to film a study of the only black bears in the world that live above the treeline. The week before we arrived, the cabin was trashed by a polar bear!

As we approached the ice still choking the mouth of the bay, I saw little black specks—seals lying close to their breathing holes. I was stoked, adrenaline pumping, from the beauty of it all. We landed on a makeshift pad up behind the log cabin that would serve as our base and tossed out the gear, raring to go. I had visions of seal shots dancing in my head and they were just offshore, out on the ice.

Ty Evans was my camera operator, and there wasn't a better fellow for the job. An outdoor enthusiast all his life, Ty was a huge man with an easygoing personality and a wicked sense of humour.

Now here we were, staring out of the bay toward the Labrador Sea. At least a kilometre of thick sea ice stretched before us. We could see the seals out there, but even with the long lens, the image was too small. We decided to creep slowly out on the ice to see how much closer we could get.

The wind was picking up—first a gentle breeze, then Tuurngait decided to make a statement. It began to blow. We were now crawling on our hands and knees. Suddenly Tuurngait let loose with a howl. Now we were lying on our stomachs, jamming the toes of our boots down into cracks in the ice, in real danger of our spiritual Inuit friend blowing us across the polished ice and right into the Labrador Sea. The seals seemed to be laughing at us.

It took us close to an hour to slither our way back to the shore, defeated and humiliated. We did not get a shot. "I guess we showed them," said Ty sarcastically.

We trudged back to the camp, shoulders bent into Tuurngait's breath, and cracked the door on our home for the next week. The log cabin was a fairly solid-looking structure. Out front was a tangle of caribou antlers piled close to five metres high. Inside was one large room six of us would share. I was tucked into one corner. On my left was a window, and another was directly over my head. Great for reading, I thought. I lay down to test it out and noticed massive claw marks carved into the logs and Styrofoam across the inside of the ceiling. "A polar bear trashed the place just before we arrived," said biologist Veitch. I wondered whether it was Bingo. So much for sleep. A loaded pump-action shotgun stood menacingly by the door. It remained there for the duration of the trip.

The land was just waking up. The days were getting warmer but there was still lots of snow and ice, and our black bears were still asleep. But Al had a plan. We would use the chopper to fly up to the head of the fjord, hike nearly straight up the side of the mountain, dig our way into the bears' winter den, tranquilize them and fit them with radio collars. Nothing to it. At least it was not on the back of a humpback whale in the North Atlantic, right?

Mike, our pilot, flew low and fast, following the snaking river as if we were on patrol in the Mekong Delta of Vietnam. The sides grew narrower and higher the farther we went in. "Where exactly are we going to land?" I thought. The angle on the sides of those mountains was now approaching forty-five degrees. But Mike found a place to tuck in and we piled out with the gear. Way too much gear for climbing. We had a tough hike ahead of us, and the snow was hard-packed—and deep.

It was three or four hundred metres of hard slogging, straight up, occasionally punching through the outer crust and finding yourself up to your hips in snow. There wasn't even a tree or bush to grab hold of. Suddenly, thankfully, Al said, "This is the spot!" His radio antenna had picked up the signal from the collar he'd placed on a female the previous fall. Using a small shovel, he started digging.

Close to a metre in, Al broke through. After putting on his headlight, he dove in, just the soles of his boots sticking out of the snow hole. They were in there all right, a mom and two cubs, very groggy but not completely asleep. Al decided the best course of action was to tranquilize momma just so things didn't get too exciting. The dart was administered using a long expandable aluminum stick. After a few minutes he went back in and dragged her slowly and carefully out into the light. Momma had been in that den with her babies for darn near eight months. I was surprised at how small she was, probably not much bigger than a German shepherd.

Al worked quickly to replace her radio collar with a new battery so her movements could be tracked during her five months of active time roaming the fjords and eating berries and flowers and whatever she could find for her growing cubs. The radio collar evoked memories of biologist Orval Pall, and how he had lost his life doing similar work with cougars. We had great material, but we would have to return again in September, when the bears were active.

Summer flew by, and we choppered back in on September 3, my birthday. Black bears had been scarce, but the Inuit were on the land. Two families were camped out in canvas tents just on the other side of the creek, where they had been hunting and fishing. Sammy Flowers from Nain came by to say hello with his two girls, about ten and twelve years old. Near their big canvas tents were racks of caribou ribs and Arctic char, all split, hung and drying in the sun. Sammy admired the helicopter, but something else had attracted the girls' attention. Something they had never seen before. It was a kayak.

A university student named Dilip had joined Al for the summer. Dilip was born in Nova Scotia but his folks were from India. He had brought a collapsible kayak with him, complete with an outrigger. The girls were fascinated by it. Their world was all modern long-liners, speedboats, perhaps a canoe, but they had never laid eyes on the sailing vessel their ancestors had invented.

It was quite a birthday present—there, in the evening light, watching a young man of East Indian heritage teaching two Inuit girls paddling technique in a kayak in the Hebron Fjord. What a Canadian moment!

Just before dark we heard via the radio that an aggressive black bear had been shot in another Inuit camp not far away. We went by boat to see it. It would be the only bear we would see for days.

It was warm, actually hot for early September in Northern Labrador. For us, several days into the trip, food spoilage was becoming an issue. We didn't have enough fuel to power the generator 24/7. Al explained the problem to Sammy one evening over a cup of tea. Sammy listened quietly, then simply said, "Come with me." A small brook ran down beside the cabin from the top of the fjord. Sammy hiked up along the side about fifty metres, pulled out his hatchet, removed some muskeg brush and chopped a chunk of ice from the side of the hill the size of a refrigerator. Sammy's people had been on this land for thousands of years. Generator? Who needs a generator?

On our second-last day we got to see the elusive black bear of Northern Labrador running wild. We were using the chopper to try to spot at least one when suddenly, there he was—a male, sauntering along the riverbed, taking his time. When he saw us, he looked for a moment and then started to run. Fast. It was a beautiful sight. Al Veitch and his colleagues never did get a signal from our female's radio collar while we were visiting, but he assured me she was out there, and she and her cubs were doing well.

Far too quickly, it was time to leave. At least, I thought we were leaving. I had hired a bush pilot to pick us up from Goose Bay. But when I told Al the name of the person I had hired to come get us, he wasn't impressed. The man was known as a fly-by-the-arse-of-your-pants sort of bush pilot, not big on paying attention to weight, fuel or distance. Now he was on his way. Great.

Later in the afternoon we heard the steady drone of a single engine, and our Cessna 210 splashed down and motored up to the dock. Out jumped our pilot onto the pontoon, declaring, "It's a beautiful day! Let's get this bird loaded up and back in the air!" As I've mentioned, we had *a lot* of gear. "How much do you think all this weighs?" I asked. "Don't worry about it," was the reply. "How are you for fuel?" I asked. "Don't worry about it!" came the reply. Now I *was* worried about it.

If my sidekick Ty was worried, he wasn't showing it. He climbed into the back, sprawled himself across a ton of gear and was asleep before we left the dock. I became the unwilling co-pilot. "Going to be an interesting climb outta here," Fly-By-Your-Arse said. I said nothing. We skipped along the water for an inordinately long time before finally lifting off. The climb was slow, very slow. It was so slow I was beginning to think we would have to start throwing stuff out or we were not going to clear the top of the fjord.

But we did. Mr. Don't-Worry-About-It set a course for Goose Bay, flicked on the autopilot and then he too went to sleep. I pulled out my Nintendo Game Boy to settle my nerves. There I was, high above the Labrador wilderness, with one eye on the screen playing golf and the other fixed on the fuel gauge as it steadily dropped. When the engine coughed, Mr. Pilot woke up, switched to the other tank and on we went. We landed on Lake Melville and taxied up to the dock in Goose Bay on what must have been fumes.

"Nice flight," said Ty with a yawn.

I made a little promise to myself never to fly in a single-engine plane *ever* again.

DISASTER AT SEA

October of 1992 was the fiftieth anniversary of the sinking of the steamship *Caribou*. For many years its memorial poster hung on the wall in many Newfoundland homes: REMEMBER THE *CARIBOU* AND HER GALLANT CREW. The torpedoing of SS *Caribou* was the largest marine disaster in Canadian waters during World War II. It was the ferry running between Port aux Basques, Newfoundland, and North Sydney, Nova Scotia, at the time. Don't forget, Newfoundland was still a separate country during the war, but it had also become a strategic location in the war effort. Even though the *Caribou* was supposed to be a passenger ferry, the military was constantly using it to move troops. In the eyes of the Germans, that made it a legitimate target.

For the anniversary, I was determined to find as many people connected to the tragedy as possible, and to tell their stories. But first, if I may, a little history.

The *Caribou* left North Sydney on the northern tip of Cape Breton, Nova Scotia, around 9:30 on the evening of October 13, 1942. Captain Ben Tavernor was a nervous man that night, and he had every reason to be. German U-boats had been sinking ships up and down the St. Lawrence. On board were 237 passengers and crew, including a large contingent of troops mixed in with the civilians.

The *Caribou* had two things going for it. First, it was fast, travelling at thirteen knots, faster than any U-boat. Second, it had been given an escort for protection, a Bangor-class minesweeper equipped with depth charges called the *Grandmère*. I managed to find its captain, James Cuthbert, in Nova Scotia. He was not happy that night either. He had been ordered to escort the *Caribou* from behind, which was practically useless. He took his complaints all the way to Ottawa but was told to follow orders.

I also managed to find others who were attached to the disaster. Together they told one hell of a tale. When the torpedo hit, the ship's first mate, a man named Dominie, managed to get one lifeboat launched, but the plugs in its bottom had been removed to drain rainwater. It quickly capsized and rolled over. As people died all around him, Dominie told me he thought, "I guess it's God for us all." But determination kept him alive.

In North Sydney I found Tom Flemming. Tom was Newfoundland's immigration officer. He was on board to make sure everyone headed to Newfoundland had proper documentation. He was probably one of the last people to see Captain Tavernor alive. He met him on the main deck by the stairs leading up to the bridge, where the captain told Tom it was time to jump. Tavernor then turned and headed up the stairs to the bridge, climbed up on the railing and jumped.

Also on board were Gladys Shiers and her very young son Leonard. I found Leonard, who was only fourteen months old during the crossing, living in Ontario. He is believed to be the only child to survive. Their story was the most compelling of all.

Gladys had made the crossing before. Her husband, little Lennie's father, was a soldier stationed in St. John's. As it was a night crossing, many of the businessmen travelling gave up their cabins to the women and children on board. Gladys was nervous and left her door slightly ajar. Many women and children went to the bottom, and were later unable to get out of their cabins because the doors jammed when the torpedo wrenched the entire frame of the ship. Gladys and Leonard made it to the main deck, only to be blasted overboard by a second explosion.

A Navy man swimming on the surface suddenly saw this child floating in front of him. It was Leonard! The air trapped in the rubber pants over his diaper was keeping him afloat. The Navy man managed to swim to a nearby float, wrap the child in his coat and place him on it. His mother Gladys lay unconscious on another float nearby.

The captain of the escort ship, James Cuthbert, was forced, by Navy protocol, to hunt for the submarine. If he didn't, he risked being torpedoed himself. He told me eventually he couldn't take it anymore and stopped to pick up survivors anyway. The controversy and the trauma of seeing women and children dead in the water were the main reasons he suffered a nervous breakdown after the war. He had rarely spoken about that night, but he was dying of cancer and so decided to "set the record straight" through me.

Gladys Shiers and her son Leonard were reunited on Cuthbert's ship. Gladys went on to become a Girl Guide leader and swimming instructor. Amazingly, Leonard went on to a career in the Navy. When we met, he still had the little bracelet his mother had made specifically for the trip, with his name and address on it in the unlikely event they were separated.

I received a nice letter from the lieutenant-governor at the time, the Honourable Frederick William Russell, thanking me for telling the story and reminding people of this tragedy. It has been re-aired many times since.

These longer pieces foreshadowed what was to come later in my career. Of course, I did not know it at the time. To me, shooting these kinds of stories was much more satisfying than working for a living, so in addition to my duties on the local supper-hour show, I jumped at them every chance I got.

CHAPTER 7

Nosing Around the Network

I was quite content with the state of everything, but rumours started again about more CBC cutbacks. There had always been cutbacks, it seemed, but this was serious talk, talk of perhaps even station closures. In 1993 our beautiful little girl, Emma Kathleen, arrived. Now there were four of us. With a young family, my first and only priority was securing our future. Because I had no real career plan, I had delayed switching from being a contract employee to holding a full-time staff position. When I finally made the jump in 1989 I was relatively low on the seniority list, and the possibility of losing my job was no joke.

Back in 1990 the CBC had abruptly turned out the lights on my former employer, the *Calgary Newshour*. We had taken the show to number one in the market, the only time in its history, just in time for management to shut it down. If they could do something as stupid as that in Calgary, they could do it anywhere. It was on my mind—a lot.

THE TEST

In 1993 they wanted to take this fish out of his familiar waters and see how he swam in the big pond, and I was offered a summer replacement position in Toronto. At that point I thought, "What have I got to lose?" If they were thinking about shutting Newfoundland down, the offer could be a chance for better job security. They provided an apartment just off Jarvis Street near the old national TV newsroom, and there I was, Replacement Reg, trying to turn relatively boring summer stories into network television.

It wasn't easy. Deadlines could be tight, and it was a whole new way of working—new shooters, new editors, new producers. Big expectations. Nobody was interested in excuses, just results. I dug out stories about crime—scam artists robbing banks and high-speed cigarette-smuggling boats operating with night vision goggles near Cornwall, Ontario.

Then I turned to what I always knew was a sure bet: I managed to find a wildlife story in the heart of downtown Toronto. The estimated raccoon population in the city was over seven hundred thousand. There was a real concern that the rabies virus, which was rapidly increasing in the American raccoon just south of the border, was steadily creeping north. Authorities feared that an outbreak in that population could endanger domestic animals and pets, and of course, the raccoons themselves. These little guys were fearless. They would move in just about anywhere. We followed an exterminator to a well-to-do part of town where an entire masked family had taken up residence in the chimney of a large three-storey brick home. The human family had been on vacation. The raccoon squatters had managed to get inside and create an unbelievable mess. Through the chimney.

We arrived with the experts when they knew the raccoons would be fast asleep, holed up inside the chimney. To get the best pictures, we decided to get up on the roof as they were extracted.

In hindsight, that was probably not the best idea. The roof was ceramic tile. One slip, three floors up, and it would not be a pleasant ride down.

To get them out of their lair, the exterminator dropped an extension cord with a light on the end of it all the way down. Then he switched the light on. Raccoons do not like light, so as the light was pulled back up they scurried up ahead of it. As the little ones popped their heads out, another fellow grabbed them. Momma was the holdout. We knew she would be bigger, and the exterminator waited with a noose pole, essentially a long metal pole with a drawstring noose on one end. When she popped her head out, the noose would be dropped over it and tightened, and she would be hauled out. Easy.

There was the exterminator with the pole. My cameraman, Rick, was right behind him. I was behind Rick, holding on to his belt to try to help him balance. We were all perched on the peak of the roof with a steep drop-off on either side.

Out popped her head. Swoosh went the noose. Got her. The exterminator started pulling. Finally, this fifty-pound demon of fur, teeth and claws cleared the opening, writhing and bucking on the end of a two-metre pole. The expert was trying to hold it high above his head but couldn't maintain his balance. I had visions of the thing knocking all three of us over and into the hedge. He said, "Jesus, I can't hold it," and with that the raccoon, pole attached, disappeared over the side of the roof.

Now the poor exterminator had visions of appearing on national television killing one of God's little creatures. As luck would have it, a tall cedar broke its fall, and the raccoon, momentarily stunned and winded, just lay there. But by the time we had scrambled down the ladder and grabbed hold of the pole, the raccoon was ready to take up the fight again. It took some doing and more than a little swearing to get the monster into the holding cage. She continued to snarl and spit all the way into the van, but it all made for great television. I didn't know it at the time, but that not-so-little momma may have even helped secure a place for me on the network.

Things had gone very well in Toronto, but no national positions were available. I would have to keep trying to find great stories back in Newfoundland, hoping something would change.

REALITY HITS HOME

Growing up in Wabush, Labrador, had kept me insulated from the harsh realities going on in the rest of the country. In Wabush, everyone had a job. If you weren't working, it was because you chose not to. Everyone had nice, highly subsidized company homes. Everyone had a car, a couple of Ski-Doos, took vacations. There were no poor people. There were also no old people. They lived somewhere else.

And growing up in Western Labrador, believe it or not, was an international experience. Back then, the mining industry attracted people from around the world. I went to school with kids from England, Scotland, Germany, India, Pakistan, the Azores and Jamaica (I'm sure there were others I have missed). We also had a healthy Québécois population. But I don't remember going to school with any Indigenous kids. A woman who worked in the local Dominion grocery store was Inuit, from the Labrador coast, and I learned some years later that one family was an English-Inuit mix, but that was about it.

Sometimes during the winter carnival some Naskapi folks (Innu First Nation) might wander into town from the bush, and in my very early years there was a camp down by the lake near the float-plane base. All of which is to say my exposure to the situation many Indigenous people found themselves in was limited.

That changed for me one cold winter day in 1993 when six young children in the coastal Labrador community of Davis Inlet were caught on tape sniffing gasoline and screaming that they wanted to die. They had been sniffing gas in a small shed down by the shore. A rag had been soaked with gasoline usually used for snow machines, and the vapours offered a cheap high, perhaps a sort of escape from their lives.

We had chartered a plane to fly in, a twin-engine Navajo. A national news team was travelling with us. Not long after takeoff from St. John's, it became apparent we had a problem. The seal on the back door wasn't working and it was impossible to keep heat in the cabin. It was about −20°C inside, but we pushed on. Several hours later we arrived in Goose Bay to refuel. I remember taking off my Ski-Doo boots and putting my feet directly on the heaters in the airport.

We took off for the coast. The town was about three kilometres from the landing strip with only one way to get there. We had to pile the gear and ourselves into a large open plywood box on a sled, which was towed behind a Ski-Doo. It was easily −25°C. My teeth were chattering. We finally saw the first houses, only to discover that the entire village had no power.

This was not where the Mushuau Innu First Nation wanted to live; this was where the government had put them. They had been a nomadic people, following the caribou for hundreds of years. Now they had been placed here. The government's thinking, apparently, was that in poor caribou-hunting years, other food sources would be available here.

But the houses were tiny, poorly insulated and completely unsuited for multi-generational family living. And because the government, in its wisdom, had decided to locate the townsite on what was essentially a massive island of rock, the homes had no basements, and no water or sewer systems either. Not long after the site was constructed, it was discovered there was an insufficient water supply, and what was available quickly became contaminated. So, a shortage of drinking water, poor housing and terrible overcrowding. Who came up with this government plan in the first place? Soon tuberculosis, a disease once thought eradicated, reappeared there.

It had all been a disaster unfolding in slow motion for some time. Hopelessness and despair eventually led to dysfunction and abuse. The problems in Davis Inlet, at that time, were profound. Alcoholism was rampant.

Just a year before, six young children between the ages of six months and nine years had burned to death. The parents were drinking at a Valentine's Day party; they'd left their kids at home alone. Investigators speculated that the kids had been using a hot plate to try and keep warm. Something caught fire and the house had burned with them inside it.

A quarter of all adults in the community had attempted suicide in the previous year. In barely twenty years, over 50 lives in a community with a current population of just 465 had been lost in alcohol-related deaths.

As we started down the road to the band council office, from a distance I could see a dozen or more huge frozen mounds, some at least three metres high, outside windows. Drawing closer, I now saw the legs of caribou sticking out of the mounds, then a caribou head, frozen human waste, food scraps—whatever was thrown out of the window was now heaped up in an icy pile just outside. It was surreal. I had never seen anything like it in my life.

Inside the band council office we found chief Katie Rich and band constable Simeon Tshakapesh, bundled up in their parkas and stamping their feet to keep warm. Simeon had made the video and sent it to the media as a cry for help. Many adults struggled with alcohol, and their kids, he said, were out of control, lost with no direction. They both seemed lost as well, overwhelmed by the situation they found their people in.

Inside one small house we finally found some heat. We video-taped a family of close to twenty, different generations, cooking, sleeping and living in a room not much bigger than five square metres, all using the same "honey" pail before the slop went out the window. They could at least keep warm by the wood stove. A half rack of caribou ribs and meat lay on the kitchen table on a piece of cardboard. Most avoided eye contact with us, but one elderly woman spoke. "What can we do?" she said. "This is it for us."

I was shaken to my core that this was happening just a few hundred kilometres from where, as a child, I had grown up in relative luxury. It was as if I had stepped back a hundred years into another world.

We got back on the freezing plane and headed for the airport in Deer Lake. From there it would be a forty-kilometre drive to CBC Corner Brook. It was the closest place with a satellite uplink; from there I could do a live interview into the supper-hour newscast. We landed and scrambled. It was almost five thirty, and my interview was supposed to be at the top of the clock, leading the newscast at six. I jumped in a rental car and drove with the heat on full blast. Halfway there I was thawing out, but then I began to shake. I was shaking so badly that I had to pull over. Eventually I regained control and made it to the station, sitting in the chair in front of the camera and putting on my microphone not thirty seconds before airtime.

The world heard about Davis Inlet that day, but its attention soon faded away. The problems for the Mushuau Innu did not. Five of those young, addicted children were sent for treatment. There would be many more. A move to a new townsite in 2002 did not change much. The social problems followed them there and continue to this day.

BOOZE, POLITICS AND FISH—A SLIPPERY COMBINATION

Down on Newfoundland's Burin Peninsula, the Mounties decided to try to do something about the French island of St. Pierre's booze business. They confiscated huge amounts of illegal booze and cigarettes—several warehouses full. I will never forget the shot, standing at the mouth of the huge incinerator (the kind that looked like a giant salt shaker). We rolled tape as a young constable threw case after case of booze into the fire. At one point he turned to the camera, and in an almost wistful voice said, "You know, this is breaking my heart."

Premier Clyde Wells was stirring things up as well. You could almost argue he was driving his fellow Liberals to drink. He had floated the idea of privatizing Newfoundland Hydro, an unpopular notion, but he decided to proceed with public consultation and feedback sessions anyway. One of them was being held at the Holiday Inn, just down the road from the provincial legislature. It was also probably the closest bar to the House of Assembly. The reason I am pointing this out will become clear in a moment.

In one of the conference rooms in the back, the public, numbering about two hundred, was demanding answers on why privatization was necessary. One fellow went up to the microphone to ask why his MHA, a gentleman named Tom Murphy, wasn't here to answer his questions.

From the back of the room someone shouted, "He's here, but he's in the bar!" Could this be possible? I signalled to cameraman Ty Evans, and off we went. Ty had a very bright light, called a sun gun, attached to the top of his camera. We made our way into the darkness of the bar, and there with his back to us was the Liberal MHA for St. John's South, drink in hand, playing at a video lottery terminal.

With the camera rolling I said, "Mr. Murphy, one of your constituents is at the public forum on privatization down the hall asking why he can't question his MHA about what's happening with Hydro. I'm just wondering why you're in here, and *not* in there."

Looking as if he might have a heart attack, Murphy leaped past us, right over a couch, before disappearing through the main doors without saying a word. Tom Murphy never did show his face at that public forum, and Clyde Wells never did carry on with his plans to privatize Newfoundland Hydro.

Time ticked on. In April 1994 came the story that would seal my fate as a network national reporter. Once again, it was thanks to the fishery.

The *Kristina Logos*, a fishing vessel registered in Panama (but actually Canadian owned, with a foreign crew) was seized by Canadian authorities and charged with fishing without a licence. Forced into St. John's, the defiant captain sneered at the cameras. I had a contact inside the federal Department of Fisheries and Oceans, and I got him on the phone.

"Gerry," I said, "I need to get on that vessel." "You can't," he replied. "Its been impounded." "Gerry," I insisted, "I want to show people exactly what these guys were up to, the net liners, the size of the catch, everything."

Canadian moratorium or not, some vessels continued to take as much fish as they could, just outside Canadian jurisdiction, even lining nets with much smaller mesh so nothing could escape. He called back in half an hour. "Meet me down at the dock."

On deck we found the net liners, but what we found in the hold was disgusting. Tiny frozen fish, flounder barely the length of my small finger, boxes and boxes of them. To make sure people understood just how small they were, I used a pencil for comparison. The story aired across the country.

The next day, standing on that very same deck, was Liberal federal fisheries minister Brian Tobin. In one hand he held the liner net, in the other a tiny fish. Tobin, a former television news reporter himself, knew great theatre when he saw it. It would be the beginning of a much more aggressive Canadian defence of fish stocks, known as the Turbot War.

Tobin would become the next premier of Newfoundland and Labrador. I, on the other hand, was getting ready to once again leave my home province.

There was an opening at the network level for a reporter in Manitoba. With the threat of cutbacks looming at the local level, I threw my hat into the ring. After the last experience, I applied with few expectations. To my great surprise, even before the process had started, it was hinted that unless I really screwed up, I would be the new correspondent for *The National* in the West. Of course I would still have to go through an interview process like everyone else, but I was feeling fairly confident.

I would tell a few more stories in Newfoundland and Labrador, including one about the closure of Naval Station Argentia, the last American military base on Canadian soil. It was just off the coast of Argentia that Churchill and Roosevelt met to hammer out the Atlantic Charter, the plan to retake Europe. I found so much history, so many characters, so many stories to tell in the province we had called home for the last eight years. But it was time to set sail again. We were already looking ahead to new opportunities, to a new life for all of us out on the Canadian Prairies.

CHAPTER 8

The Big Leagues

Always undersell what you can deliver, even if you know you can do well. Far better to exceed expectations than to fall short. You are only as good as your last story. These are the critical lessons that I learned early on, and they would become my mantra going forward. If you oversell yourself, or proclaim yourself number one, there is only one direction left ... down.

I certainly wasn't proclaiming anything when the phone call came saying I was being flown to Toronto to be interviewed for the national network correspondent job in Manitoba. I remained conflicted, but any future in St. John's was, at best, uncertain. I got on the plane.

That telephone conversation had left me confident things were in the bag. I was assured the interview was little more than a formality to appease union requirements. Then, at the hotel that evening, I received another call, this one from a colleague. I didn't know it at the time, but she was also after the Winnipeg position. "I hope you know all the Manitoba premiers since Confederation," she said. "You know they're going to ask you that, and other details about Manitoba history."

I felt a pain in the pit of my stomach. Of course, I had done some research about current political and social events, but the political history of the province? Names of all the premiers? Who the hell knows that? Now I was in full panic mode. Don't forget that access to the internet was still relatively remote; it certainly was not available on my phone. Were libraries open? Would not knowing who the first premier of Manitoba was (Alfred Boyd, as I soon learned) sink my chances of playing the journalist on the Prairies?

I went down to the hotel's business centre and went online. However, I soon realized it was hopeless—there was no way to fill my head with that sort of detail less than twelve hours before my interview. It dawned on me that my colleague was not a true colleague at all. She was trying to knock me off my stride to give herself a better chance.

I took a deep breath and returned to my room, but I did not sleep. My interview was at 10:30 the next morning. I walked in and sat down to welcoming, smiling faces. No questions about listing the premiers of Manitoba since Confederation were forthcoming. One person asked how much I knew about Manitoba history in general. My reply was, "I know a little, probably more than the average bear, probably not as much as some. But I'll tell you this. If the time comes when I need to know that information as part of my duties, I'll find it and absorb it quicker than anyone else you can find. That's my job, and I feel confident in my ability to do it."

There were nods of satisfaction all around.

I left the room optimistic that the job was mine, and four days later the network-wide memo from chief news editor David Bazay and Don Knox, executive producer of newsgathering, confirmed it. It had to have been one of the more exuberant hiring announcements in the history of the network. I took more than just a little ribbing over it:

Subject: MANITOBA REPORTER CBC

Date: Oct-06-94

We are delighted to announce the appointment of Reg Sherren as national reporter for CBC-TV News in Manitoba.

His search for the good story has taken him far afield. To places like Spain and Portugal where stomachs ache for our missing Cod, across North America to document the falling market for Labrador's iron ore; and to the Gulf War, where Newfoundlanders made up one third of the Canadian contingent. Yet it's at home where Reg's hard work attracted the attention of his network colleagues.

We know you will join us in wishing Reg and his family success in this move into this important network position out West.

Don Knox	David Bazay
Executive Producer	Chief News Editor
Newsgathering	

"Stomachs ache." Yeesh. That was more than a little over the top. But that was that, we were on our way!

FLAT ... LIKE A POOL TABLE

I had been to Manitoba twice before in my life. Once to visit my buddy Larry, who was working there in radio, and another time on a road trip from Thunder Bay. Both times it was in the dead of winter, and as I remember, it was about three hundred below zero. Cold didn't scare me. I had grown up in Labrador. Show me your cold. They were known for their bugs as well. "Show me your bugs!" I thought. Back in the Big Land, I had lived through swarms of blackflies so thick you couldn't see through them.

In those early days in Winnipeg it was strictly daily news, with the news of the day. You could count on two, maybe three, national files a week. Occasionally you could persuade producers to go with a short human-interest feature. Those stories would become my specialty.

Of course, back then *The National* wasn't *The National* anymore. In 1992, after the death of Canadian journalist superstar Barbara Frum, the powers that be decided the show needed to be overhauled, changing the name to *Prime Time News* and moving its time slot to 9:00 p.m. Eastern.

Initially this new flagship show, now hosted by Peter Mansbridge and former CTV star Pamela Wallin, enjoyed ratings success. But that quickly waned. People missed the old format, with two distinct parts to the hour (*The National* and then *The Journal*) and they could sense friction on the anchor desk. Some tinkering with the format and a return to 10:00 p.m. improved ratings, but by the spring of 1995, Wallin was replaced by the very talented Hana Gartner, and the show's name reverted to *The National*.

Much of that stuff was of little concern to the new national reporter from Manitoba. At that point, I just wanted to get stories on the air and not screw up. I was fortunate enough to eventually land John Bronevitch to work with me. John was older, a small twist of muscle and tendons who could jump over a house with the camera on his shoulder if he needed to. He was fearless. He had been born in the generation of film cameras and was among the best sequential shooters I had ever worked with—a true artist. We would become an unstoppable team.

I set about trying to solidify my place on the flagship news show. I would work six or seven days a week, whatever it took. By now Pam and the kids had settled into our new home. Pam knew the business, and her understanding of the dedication it took was an ongoing source of support and comfort to me.

TROUBLED TIMES

My first story as Manitoba's new national reporter was to cover the signing of an agreement between Ottawa and an organization of Manitoba First Nations chiefs, giving their people more opportunity, at least in theory, to govern themselves. It was said that the agreement would put an end to a hundred years of oppression.

After more than three decades covering the First Nations file, it remains one of my most important, and saddest, assignments. It has taken me deep into the realities afflicting Indigenous peoples.

One of the first people I met and interviewed was Phil Fontaine. He was a quiet, thoughtful man who carried himself with great dignity. At the time he was Grand Chief of the Assembly of Manitoba Chiefs, but he would go on to become the National Chief of the Assembly of First Nations. It was an honour he would carry three times.

Phil was from the Sagkeeng First Nation north of Winnipeg. He was also a residential school survivor, and one of the first to speak publicly about the abuse he and fellow students suffered while attending the Fort Alexander School. Grand Chief Fontaine was also credited with placing that great shame on the national agenda for the first time. His disclosure and what came later evolved into the Truth and Reconciliation Commission on residential schools.

Over the years, Phil was an immense help, always willing to talk and to take the time to make sure I understood his position or that of the people he represented. I would do many more stories looking into the lives of First Nations people, but far too many of them were sad stories.

EYES OPENED

CBC Manitoba was ahead of the curve when it came to Indigenous issues and to giving Indigenous reporters opportunities.

Newfoundland and Labrador had a relatively small Indigenous population, certainly compared to Manitoba's. There are over sixty First Nations in the province, and the capital, Winnipeg, has the largest Indigenous population of any major city in Canada. Over ninety thousand First Nations, Métis and Inuit people call Winnipeg home. Although CBC Manitoba may have seen the benefits of this diversity, it wasn't an opinion shared by everyone, not by a long shot.

It was and remains an uneasy, uncomfortable situation, particularly in the city. From the first day I arrived, I could see evidence of the social conditions far too many Aboriginal people found themselves in, especially as I walked the twenty or so blocks from my hotel at Portage and Main to the CBC. Some people on the street were openly racist, making insulting comments or expressing disgust. In other social situations it seemed quite acceptable to make derogatory jokes about Aboriginal people or to publicly share disdain for having "their kind" in "our" city. Not everybody had this attitude, but even one person was too many.

I had never experienced such open expressions of bigotry before, at least not about Indigenous people. As a Newfoundlander, however, I did experience some bigoted humour. After I left my home province, I found that as soon as some people learned I was from Newfoundland they would say, "Jeez, you don't have that stupid accent," and proceed to tell as many ridiculous, insulting, derogatory "Newfie jokes" as they could think of. Charming. But what I heard too often on the streets in Winnipeg was more than just bad taste—it was hatred.

CBC had made it an important part of its mandate to cover Indigenous stories—the politics, the social conditions and, with any luck, the truth. More than once I heard spoken under someone's breath or through backhanded comments that the people at the CBC were a bunch of "Indian lovers." But we weren't going anywhere, and we had lots of airtime. The First Nations communities weren't going anywhere either. Their population was growing faster than any other demographic, and their voices were growing too.

Protests were an almost weekly occurrence in the city. One of my first, in the fall of 1995, dealt with the fact that Dwayne Archie Johnston had been given day parole. Johnston was a nasty, brutal character. He was the man eventually convicted of stabbing Helen Betty Osborne to death in The Pas, Manitoba.

Helen Betty Osborne was the first case I'd covered of a murdered or missing Indigenous woman. It was particularly disturbing, not just because of the disgusting lack of concern for human life it represented, but because of the fact that it took over a decade and a half to find any semblance of justice for her (if it could be called that) even though practically everyone in town knew who was involved.

Her tragic end took place in November 1971, long before my time in Manitoba. Helen Betty was a young woman of just nineteen when her life was taken from her. She was the eldest child of Justine and Joe Osborne of Norway House First Nation, and she dreamed of going to college and finding a career as a teacher. But to make that dream a reality she needed more training than was available in her First Nations community, so she attended a residential school near The Pas, and later a local high school.

Four local men were implicated in her brutal murder: Dwayne Archie Johnston, James Robert Paul Houghton, Lee Scott Colgan and Norman Bernard Manger. I could describe what happened to her that night, but it seems more appropriate to offer an excerpt from the report of the Aboriginal Justice Implementation Commission, which was set up after her death:

> Betty Osborne was accosted by four men in a car. Houghton, who was driving, stopped the car and Johnston got out, attempting to convince Osborne to go with them to "party." She told them that she did not wish to accompany them. …

In spite of her screams and attempts to escape, Osborne was taken to a cabin belonging to Houghton's parents at Clearwater Lake.

At the cabin she was pulled from the car and beaten by Johnston while the others stood watching and drinking wine they had stolen earlier. Osborne continued to struggle and scream and, because her assailants were afraid they might be heard, she was forced back into the car and driven further from town to a pump house next to the lake ... Wearing only her winter boots, she was viciously beaten, and stabbed, apparently with a screwdriver, more than fifty times. Her face was smashed beyond recognition. The evidence suggests that two people then dragged her body into the bush. Her clothes were hidden. The four men then left, returned to The Pas and went their separate ways.

Now, twenty-four years later, in 1995, Johnston was on day parole. The other three men received no punishment at all.

Helen Betty Osborne's mother Justine was seventy when I flew to Norway House First Nation to meet her. She was quiet and soft-spoken but still possessed a tremendous resolve, particularly when it came to justice for her daughter.

Johnston had been granted day parole after serving just seven years. Justine cried as she talked about her girl and her attempts to be granted intervener status at Johnston's parole hearing. The parole board had felt Johnston was no longer a danger to reoffend.

Members of Helen Betty's community, including her mom, marched all the way to Winnipeg, over eight hundred kilometres, to protest the justice system. On November 17, 1995, the week of the anniversary of her death, they rallied outside the provincial legislature.

Johnston got his full parole in 1999. He eventually told the Osborne family he was there that night but did not kill Helen Betty.

However his new statement did not match with a re-examination of evidence gathered at the scene, and it was rejected. The inquiry that was called after Helen Betty Osborne's death concluded that racism and a certain sense of community indifference played a role in her murder and in the fact that it took far too long to bring anyone to justice.

Helen Betty Osborne's name is now known across the country. Books have been written and a movie was made chronicling her tragic death. Scholarships have been established in her memory and schools have been named after her. Sadly, there are still well over a thousand missing or murdered Aboriginal women in RCMP files. Other estimates say the real number is probably many thousands more. In the next twenty years there would be too many more stories involving the Indigenous community, most of them part of the great shame of this country.

OUR REAL SHAME

I remember picking up the newspaper one day and reading about a homeless woman named Darlene from Northern Ontario who had been charged by the provincial government after building a cabin on the land she had grown up on near Savant Lake. I thought, "There's more to this than meets the eye," and I set about trying to find her. Her lawyer, who had been quoted in the paper, said she wasn't easy to contact. She had no cellphone, no home and she moved around a fair bit. He suggested Facebook. Sure enough, I found her on Facebook and sent her a message. (Facebook was becoming the new Canada 411.) She was on her way back up North and would meet me at her cabin near Savant Lake in two days.

We left and drove to Dryden, Ontario. It was typical December weather for these parts—absolutely freezing. The next day we would head north to find Darlene. Now, I know how fortunate I've been in life—life has been good to me—but once in a while I need a little nudge, a reminder of that fact. Sometimes something, or someone, brings it sharply into focus. That person turned out to be Darlene.

We got ready to leave Dryden at around eight in the morning. It was easily −30°C. We were heading up past Sioux Lookout on snow-covered roads deep in the bush. On the way out of town I pulled into a sandwich shop. It was going to be a long drive, and there was nothing along the way and there would be nothing when we arrived. I wanted to get half a dozen sandwiches, just in case. You never knew what might happen.

We passed long stretches of silver birch and frozen bog. Some fast-running streams were still unfrozen, the condensed vapour crystallizing as it met the arctic air above the water. Four hours later we rolled into Savant Lake, a place where railroad tracks crossed the road. In the summer and fall it was paradise for anglers and hunters, but now it was just cold—damn cold, for early December.

There was no cellphone coverage, not that it made any difference. Darlene didn't have a phone anyway. We began exploring side roads, looking for someone we could ask to learn where Darlene might be. A young woman must have spotted us and came out of what can only be described as a little shack on the side of the road. "Darlene is in that house over there," she offered, pointing, with a big friendly smile. Darlene was staying with friends. She was a small woman in her fifties, with greying hair. Darlene looked tired, but, even so, managed a big grin and insisted we go to see her "home," which was under construction across the way. It was on land where her parents' home used to stand. Back from the road, behind some birch, there was now the shell of a tiny, square cabin with a sheet of plywood nailed across the door.

It was freezing. She had no mitts or gloves. She and her sister had come back on the train in the middle of the night. Darlene had been given a train ticket to get back and forth to Toronto, where some kind folks were raising money for her defence. She had been charged with breaches of the Public Lands Act and ordered to stop building her little home. As far as she was concerned, this was her family's traditional land. She and her sister had dragged their belongings to her friend's house all the way from where the train dropped them off, about a kilometre away. "Hard on my hands," was all she said.

After taping outside, we went back to her friend's house to do a longer interview. As soon as the camera lens hit the heat in the kitchen, it fogged up, as lenses tend to do. We sat there in the pleasant, if sparse, surroundings, waiting for the lens to clear. That was when I remembered the food. I said, "I have some sandwiches out in the van. I'd be happy to share them with you while we wait." I had just enough for everyone.

I noticed that Darlene took only a couple of bites from hers before she carefully wrapped up the sandwich again. I had devoured mine. "You're not hungry?" I asked. "I eat slow," she said, and she did not eat any more.

We started the interview. She talked about how difficult it had been since her son, just twenty, had taken his life. It had sent her on a downward spiral that eventually resulted in her being homeless. She said she was in a better place now, and spent her time trying to help others and trying to help herself. But she was clearly despondent and frustrated at her predicament.

"I still try to remain helpful, no matter what situation I am in. I will always look at other people's situations before mine, and help them first," she said. "I help myself too, but now I am more focused on other people, helping them and making it comfortable for them to live."

Then she said, "I don't eat every day. I sometimes eat just every second day. That's just because I don't want to go to other people's houses and eat, because I know they struggle to feed their families too. So having me as an extra mouth to feed, no, no, I won't do that—I will try to stay away."

The rest of her carefully wrapped sandwich sat on the kitchen table between us. I felt like an idiot. I realized that sandwich might be all there was for her today, and maybe tomorrow. I could feel mine in the pit of my stomach. I felt sick. I felt ashamed.

We finished our shoot and she wished us well, thanked us even for coming, and stood waving goodbye as we left. It was a long drive home. I couldn't get the image of that carefully wrapped sandwich on the table out of my head.

When the story aired, it caused a bit of an outcry. A petition was sent to then-premier Kathleen Wynne. And three months later, mere days before she was headed to court to face the possibility of tens of thousands of dollars in fines, the Crown dropped all charges. Her lawyer told me, "They didn't feel it was in the public interest to proceed with the charges."

Five years later Darlene still lived in her "castle in the woods," as she called it. The last time we spoke she told me she still didn't have running water or electricity, but she was very happy just to have her own roof over her head. We still usually exchange greetings around Christmas time. It's a great feeling when you can change something for the good.

SNAKE SEX

The snakes of Narcisse were up to something. And not just a few of them either—this was one of largest gatherings of these slitherers in the world. Snakes, in general, were somewhat foreign to me, at least the ones without legs. They don't exist on the island of Newfoundland, and I had never seen even one in the wild. But at Narcisse, an hour's drive north of Winnipeg, these cold-blooded creatures gather by the tens of thousands to winter deep in the limestone caves below ground. And now things were heating up.

When these red-sided garter snakes emerged in the spring it was like the ground itself was moving. They were, quite literally, everywhere. In nearby barns they could be found hanging from the rafters. People could not mow their lawns for fear of slicing through snakes in the grass. The highway became so greasy from snakes squashed by fast-moving vehicles that little tunnels were dug to encourage the snakes to go under rather than over the pavement.

But what was really happening during a few warm spring days was one great big, *big* forked-tongued love-in. It was explained to me by an American professor who had travelled all the way from the Deep South to observe this amorous ritual. Basically, the snakes emerge from the limestone caves below with just one thing on their minds: How can I convince her that I am The One? Hundreds of males compete, slithering up the females' backs, flicking their tongues and hoping to impress one enough for her to say, "Okay, *that's* what I see in him." There are several hundred males for every female.

Not that winning her attention is any prize. Once coupling is achieved, she then proceeds to drag him around by his hemipenis (yes, that's what they call it) for about twenty minutes. Sometimes she pulls it right off! That's why nature gave him two. One shudders to think. It all made for a fascinating discussion and even better pictures. At one point, John even persuaded me to pick up one of the writhing orgasmic masses of evil as they attempted to go about their business. It played on CNN for three days. I guess these days you might call it clickbait—it would certainly have had the potential to go viral.

STICKHANDLING

Later that spring, local businessman Barry Shenkarow delivered a stab wound deep into the heart of Winnipeg's pride. He decided to sell the one sporting enterprise that made the city "not Regina": its beloved hockey team, the Winnipeg Jets. It appeared the team was bound for the United States. A low Canadian dollar, an old arena and having to pay salaries in American dollars all meant the team seemed destined to fail.

But that spring there arose such a collective groan from the public and the business community alike that some level of reprieve was achieved. There were stories about rallies, fundraisers and massive demonstrations at the (in)famous corner of Portage and Main. The team survived, for the moment. But that reprieve would be short-lived.

DOWNTOWN BEARS

After stickhandling through snakes and Jets, I found even more clickbait. Yes, I was up to my old tricks. Black bears had invaded the community of Kenora in nearby Northwestern Ontario. They had followed their noses to the overripened fruit in people's yards, and they were not shy about going after it. Bears were strolling through car dealerships. They were meandering through traffic. They were wandering near schools. They were, quite simply, everywhere. The town was overrun. Sometimes they stopped eating fruit long enough to go after the real tasty stuff. We taped a momma and her three cubs in the garbage containers behind Casey's Grill Bar right downtown. People sat in their cars and watched. It was better than a drive-in movie.

And in one backyard, there he was. A four-hundred-pound male, up in a crabapple tree, apparently drunk from feeding on the fermenting fruit. We stood below with the wildlife officer, but Mr. Bear could not care less. He looked at us as if to say, "I'm thinking about a nap. I'll get back to you after that." Then he fell out of the tree, landing right on his bum not ten metres away from us. He staggered to his feet and stumbled sideways like a drunk after being pitched out at closing time, then proceeded to crawl under the homeowner's deck. A tranquilizer dart in the butt didn't seem to faze him one bit. Under he went, and under he stayed. It would take six guys (including me) and an ATV to pull him out of there and place him in a cage for his undignified trip out of town.

It all seemed funny enough, but black bears in proximity to people are no joke. Black bears kill more people than any other species of bear in Canada. They become conditioned to our sloppy ways of dealing with garbage, or too used to us trying to take a picture of that "cute" bear. The entire time we were there in Kenora, schools had to be closed because of bears around the playground. It was dangerous business, and far too often the bears wound up losing.

FLIP THE COIN

But in the fall of 1995 another bear, this time a polar bear, wound up being the winner. I got the scoop to deliver the story on *The National*, but it really wasn't mine at all. The man with the inside information was our anchor. The phone call came from Peter Mansbridge.

For weeks there had been speculation about the Royal Canadian Mint's new $2 coin. Would it be called the doubloon? The toonie? What would be on it? The day before the big announcement, Peter had been slipped the details. Now he was on the phone, less than three hours before deadline. It would be a polar bear, one of Manitoba's iconic symbols (though the province's official mammal is the plains bison).

I beat it over to the Assiniboine Park Zoo and talked my way in. Fortunately, Sailor, the polar bear, was willing to play along and emerged from his concrete cave just as I revealed the much-anticipated news on camera.

The new bimetallic coin, which would be produced at the mint right in Winnipeg, would be called the toonie. For the next few years there would be stories about them wreaking havoc with vending machines, about them coming apart, about people trying to bust them apart. But the toonie was here to stay.

And so were we.

WINNIPEG THE WONDERFUL

As a family we had settled in nicely. Winnipeg was and is a highly underrated city. The cost of housing is low, and so is the crime rate (okay, certain areas are trouble) compared to other major centres. A beautiful urban environment, it is much more European than Western Canadian (the geographic centre of Canada is just outside the city limits) and a fabulous place to raise a family.

At work, people were warming to the guy from the East as well. They were a great bunch with tons of talent, and like me, they were ambitious. Who could blame them for being a little put out and suspicious at first when an outsider got the gig? But really, they should not have been surprised. The national news service back then often hired from outside the local reporter pool. The thinking was that a new person would have fresh eyes, could see stories differently, and not be influenced by familiarity or a feeling that the story had already been told. It was solid thinking that eventually fell by the wayside, the result of budget cuts and shrinking financial resources.

CHAPTER 9

It's Freezing! And Flooding!

The winter of 1995–96 turned out to be extremely cold, even for hardy Winnipeggers. The Winnipeg national bureau had always been handed more than its fair share of cold-weather stories. Ironically, in the business we called them "melts." You would begin the story in a place where it was unseasonably cold, then combine those pictures and interviews with material from across the country, and "melt" it all together into one story.

You could easily get sick of them. It was Canada, and it was winter. Big deal. But if the national desk wanted a cold-weather story, you delivered a cold-weather story. In January of 1996, it was bloody cold for a month straight. Winnipeg had broken its own record: for something like twenty-seven days it never got warmer than −25°C during the day and dropped below −30° every night. Without the wind chill factor.

I went to cold-storage facilities where workers were going inside the freezers to warm up—while still below zero, it was much warmer inside them than outside. I showed how long it took to freeze an egg on the sidewalk (under thirty seconds). I did stories about bulls freezing their vital bits off, about deer starving as they tried in vain to find food, and about the insulating properties of

Jill Oakes from the University of Manitoba and I building igloos at forty below, just outside Churchill, Manitoba. The shotgun, like the polar bears, was never far away!

natural materials, like caribou hair, over synthetics. That last story came from Professor Rick Riewe of the University of Manitoba. I had first met Rick shooting a story near its northern research facility outside Churchill, Manitoba.

Rick, who was originally from Detroit, Michigan, had spent over twenty years living in the high, High Arctic. He had become an expert on traditional Inuit survival skills and was teaching a course on building igloos to a group of Inuit and Dene students. With the arrival of snow machines in the North, many of the young people had lost touch with such traditions as igloo construction. We had travelled with Rick to shoot a feature, one of my first features as national correspondent, and it was bloody cold. It was so cold the camera kept freezing up. We would shoot for ten minutes, then we'd have to place the camera in a truck we kept running so it could warm up enough to start working again. Great story. Cold work.

So when the same kind of cold hit Winnipeg, I gave Rick a call. Sure enough, he and his research partner Jill Oakes had a story.

Extensive research showed that the hair of the caribou had insulation properties far superior to that of anything mere humans could produce. It became another one for CNN.

I have to get back to the bulls for a moment. Those poor creatures. You know the old expression, "It's cold enough to freeze the balls off a brass monkey"? Maybe not. But these were no monkeys. They were breeding bulls, some of them champions worth a *lot* of money. Freezing their whatnots could mean sterility, and that meant instead of a valuable animal, what you had there was now hamburger.

I had gotten wind that a test was about to be conducted on one such animal, a Black Angus bull. This monster weighed over two thousand pounds, or close to a thousand kilograms. When we arrived, he had been contained in a large metal holding cage. We soon learned why.

The veterinarian, no small woman herself, was quite stoic, saying not a word as she donned a plastic glove of sorts that went right up to her shoulder. She lifted the bull's tail and proceeded to probe deep inside the poor fellow's back end. She then turned and picked up something that looked for all the world like a WWII artillery shell and, using both hands, inserted it into the bull's behind. If you could have seen the look in that bull's eyes ... it was terror. Sheer terror. I had spent a little time down on the farm, but this—this was making us all more than a little uncomfortable.

The vet picked up two heavy cables that looked a little like the booster cables you would use on a vehicle's battery and attached them to the posts at the back of the artillery shell. The other ends were attached to a large electrical generating machine with two big dials on the front. She turned to the camera and explained that the only way to determine whether the bull had been permanently injured by the cold was to electrically stimulate him into giving a sample of his cow-making serum. She said this very earnestly, with a straight, serious face. And then she turned those dials.

The noise that came out of that bull was something I had never heard before, or since. He shuddered. The entire building shook along with him. Using a cup on the end of a stick, the vet quickly gathered the liquid that emerged. Then she disappeared, leaving us with one very sorry-looking Black Angus bull. Twenty minutes later, she returned. The verdict was in.

Hamburger.

That poor bull was just the first in a long line of victims that winter. It was not a happy spring for dozens of ranchers. Eventually a fellow in Saskatchewan came up with something that reminded me of those purple Crown Royal bags we used to carry marbles in as kids. It was made from neoprene and could be attached with Velcro to a bull's tangy bits to ward off the cold. I imagine it was worth it to any bull hoping to ward off the vet with the artillery shell!

DOING THE ROYAL TWO-STEP

In the spring royalty came to town. Prince Charles arrived in the colony with the Liberals' deputy prime minister, Sheila Copps, on his arm. The prince had come to unveil a plaque and to travel north to the fort named after him, Prince of Wales Fort, situated at the mouth of the Churchill River. The prince was just doing his royal duties.

Sheila Copps needed to get out of Ottawa. The opposition Reform Party had been having a field day during Question Period in the House of Commons. In the 1993 election, Chrétien and his team had vowed, if elected, to do away with the goods and services tax (GST). Once they had routed Kim Campbell and her Conservative cohorts in the election, however, the new government decided to keep the GST after all. It had turned out to be far too lucrative as a revenue stream.

The problem was that during a CBC town hall meeting for that 1993 election, Sheila had vowed she would resign her Hamilton seat if the Liberals reneged on their promise. Now that it was clear they were indeed going to keep the GST, the howls of opposition outrage echoed through the chambers of Parliament. They demanded Sheila keep her promise and resign. But they were much harder to hear from Manitoba.

The desk called from Toronto. They didn't much care about old Prince Charlie, but they needed me to get an interview with Ms. Copps to put her on the record about her pledge. It would not be easy. Sheila was sticking to the prince like glue, safe behind the comfort of the Crown. Security around the prince was tight, with three or four RCMP escorts always close at hand, and the lowly media had to keep its distance. There was quite a crowd of us, more during his city visit, but things became more casual as the visit went on and we headed up North to see the fort.

Minutes were mounting. Deadlines loomed. I kept making small talk with the RCMP folks, and they were an easygoing bunch, but they made it clear that unless the deputy prime minister was willing to leave the prince's side, I was out of luck. I joked, "Listen guys, at some point I'm going to have to grab her. Please don't shoot me."

The fort had a story of its own. It had taken almost seventy years to complete and was supposed to have guarded English interests in the fur trade. But by the time they had finished building the darn thing, the fur trade had seen its day and was no longer of any significant strategical importance. The one time the fort was attacked by the French, the freezing garrison inside surrendered without firing a shot. The French, it is said, walked in, took one look around that barren configuration of stone in the middle of nowhere and said, "Nah, you can keep it." And with that, they left.

Now Sheila Copps was attempting to do the very same thing, heading for the helicopter under the guard of the RCMP. We had spent all day doing this crazy dance, but just as the whole entourage was leaving Prince of Wales Fort, opportunity knocked.

Out of the corner of my eye I could see that the CTV national cameraman was changing tape and the battery on his camera. I knew this was my one chance. I stepped past the RCMP officers, whispering, "Please don't arrest me," excused myself to His Highness—"Pardon me, Prince Charles," I said, "but I need Ms. Copps for just a moment"—and guided Sheila by the arm.

In her very brief exchange with me she mentioned something about sometimes "shooting from the lip" (as opposed to the hip) in reference to her pledge to resign, just before the RCMP spirited her away again. The RCMP thought it was great fun. Sheila was smiling too, even if the CTV crew was not. They had missed the moment.

On the charter flight back, I began writing my piece on the tour for *The National*, but I also had to let Toronto know I'd gotten Sheila Copps for the Ottawa story. Cell service had been non-existent in Churchill, but as we got closer to Winnipeg, I locked myself in the washroom and flicked on the phone. A signal! I made the call.

Just as the CTV crew was missing at the key moment that day, some weeks later Sheila was missing too, but from the House of Commons. She finally made good on her promise to resign over the whole GST debacle. But not long after that a by-election was called in Hamilton East and soon enough, Sheila Copps was once again a member of Parliament.

That spring was pretty much all politics, as I was asked to work in Ottawa at the parliamentary bureau. It was interesting enough, but the atmosphere was stuffy and boring. As we say in the business, B-roll, clip, B-roll, clip, stand-up. The reporters had almost no say over production or editing. We even had specific rules about how to stand and what movements were allowed during our stand-up presentation on camera. Note to Reg: *Working Parliament Hill is low on the list of priorities.*

I returned to Manitoba and found more great stories with real people and fabulous pictures. There was the woman who had spent years trying to drum up the courage to walk across the Souris

Swinging Bridge, the longest swinging pedestrian bridge in Canada. Turned out the day we were with her wasn't going to be that day. I don't know if she ever made it across.

There was the gentleman out near Brandon, Manitoba, who offered public World War II aerial dogfights in his vintage Harvard trainers. You could shoot at the other plane using machine guns equipped with sensors that sounded just like the real thing.

Then there was Rocket the tortoise. At the age of one hundred years young he was being dispatched from the Assiniboine Park Zoo to New York City to "comfort" three lonely females at the Bronx Zoo. You couldn't make this stuff up. The old boy was destined to become a love rocket!

"THE FLOOD OF THE CENTURY"

Over the fall and into the winter of 1996–97, an ominous sense of foreboding developed in the city of Winnipeg. A lot of rain had fallen before the snow came in early November, and the ground was saturated. Then the snow came, tons of it. The experts were saying the snow also had a very high moisture content. The flood forecast was ramping up from bad to worse.

What many people don't realize is that in this part of Canada, given the Laurentian continental divide, rivers flow north. The Red River, whose headwaters are way down on the border between North Dakota and Minnesota near a place called Wahpeton, flows north to Lake Winnipeg. From there the water keeps right on flowing through Northern Manitoba, until it reaches Hudson Bay.

So when the river overflows its banks, several smaller American cities and eventually Winnipeg are directly in its path. The older folks around were still talking about the 1950 flood. Close to eight hundred square kilometres of the Red River Valley were left underwater for weeks. Much of Winnipeg's downtown was submerged. Four of eleven bridges in the city were destroyed. Over a hundred thousand people had to be evacuated, which at the time was the largest evacuation in Canadian history. Damage estimates approached $1 billion—a lot of money back in 1950.

In the early 1960s, Premier Dufferin Roblin vowed "never again" and pushed to get the Red River Floodway built. Those opposed to the idea called it "Duff's Ditch." It would cost $63 million and become the second-largest earth moving project in the world, second only to the Panama Canal. The idea was to divert some of that flood water around Winnipeg, using this forty-seven-kilometre "ditch," to where it would rejoin the Red River and continue flowing north—at least that was the theory. It would be sorely tested in the spring of 1997.

As early as February I began doing stories. Flood forecasters were worried, particularly for communities south of Winnipeg in the Red River Valley that were not protected by the floodway. Down there they called it God's pool table. Flat as a board. If the water busted its banks, it would spread like soup on a plate with nothing to stop it. Emergency planning got underway. Some town councils began making plans to surround their entire town with a wall of dirt.

By early March, it was starting. The melt was barely underway and already in Wahpeton, North Dakota, they were evacuating the zoo because of flood waters from the river. Now, Wahpeton is almost five hundred kilometres south of Winnipeg but it's all downhill from the US town, and as the river flowed along more spring meltwater would join the flow. It was already a monster and it was growing.

Then, insult was added to injury. In early April some of the worst blizzards on record hit North Dakota and Southern Manitoba's Red River Valley. Over fifty centimetres of moisture-laden snow dropped out of the sky in just twenty-four hours. If the situation was dire before, it had just become downright disastrous.

Flood control workers began drilling holes in the ice on the Red River around Winnipeg—forty thousand of them. The hope was that this effort would help the ice break up quicker, making it easier to get the water to flow the heck away. They were dreaming, of course.

The water first hit in North Dakota's largest city, Fargo. There was flooding but it was somewhat contained by the improvised dykes piled along either side of its banks. From there on, water began flowing very quickly. Grand Forks, North Dakota, was watching what was happening in Fargo and began building its dykes higher. Workers and volunteers didn't have much time—that wall of water was rapidly swallowing everything in its path. Thousands of people were mobilized, including military personnel from the local Air Force base, to pile the earth higher. The flood hit Grand Forks on April 18, 1997, and promptly busted through the dykes. With that, nothing short of disaster unfolded.

On that day's morning assignment call, Toronto could not decide what it wanted us to do—stay and report from Winnipeg or head south to where the story was. They wanted to save money. Right now, the flood was still happening "somewhere else." I, on the other hand, thought we needed to go where the action was *now*, to give people a sense of what was coming. Just before noon they agreed, but by then half the day was gone. You learn in this business that only one time is meaningful, and that is the amount of time you have left before your deadline. You also learn to plan. I had already put a charter plane and a vehicle—a big bloody SUV—on standby, just in case.

In the time it took for Toronto to make up its mind, the Grand Forks Airport had closed. We could still, however, land at a small community field north of the city. From the air we could see what looked like a giant lake slowly swallowing the city. It was unreal. The vehicle rental folks kindly agreed to meet us at the airfield with our truck, a big Dodge Durango, and by one o'clock we were speeding toward Grand Forks.

It was chaos. The mayor had ordered fifty thousand people to evacuate and the main roads were clogged with cars, trucks, RVs and military and emergency vehicles. John Bronevitch, who usually drove like a rally car driver anyway, nimbly darted down side streets, working his way closer to downtown and the river.

We turned one corner, and suddenly a wall of water was hurtling down the street toward us. It was a warm, sunny day and we had the windows down. At the last second, we managed to get them up as John slammed the vehicle in reverse and the water flowed just beneath the side mirrors. To this day I have no idea how we weren't swamped, but somehow the vehicle kept running. We drove full speed in reverse until we could get ahead of the water and turn around.

In this sort of situation you assess and manage several things. It was now abundantly clear we were on our own and potentially in danger. Becoming casualties ourselves, possibly requiring rescue, would be stupid and irresponsible. Emergency personnel already had more than they could handle, and things were still quickly developing.

I needed to do a stand-up to show we were there, on the ground, and to show the situation around us. We got to a spot where you could see water pouring over the dykes behind us and got our shots quickly. It was time to get the heck out of there and beat it back to our charter plane. I knew the American networks would be sticking around on the ground, and we could also use their footage from the syndicated news service. We arrived at the airfield just as they too were about to evacuate. "Another ten minutes and we would have left you behind," said the pilot.

From the air we could see how the Red River—make that the Red Sea—had just about swallowed Grand Forks in the short time we were on the ground. We got back to the edit suite in the relative safety of the Winnipeg station with an hour to spare before deadline. But now we knew exactly what was headed our way—and Winnipeg was directly in its path.

In Grand Forks, the situation became even worse. It looked like a scene right out of a bad B movie disaster plot. The downtown was partially submerged—and on fire. Many people used heating in their homes and businesses. As hot-water tanks popped loose in the flood, the fuel escaped, spreading along the surface of the water, until a spark, probably from a downed hydro line, sent the whole works up in flames.

Note to Reg: *Do not fly blind into an unfolding disaster in another country with no backup!*

THE MONTH OF THE RUBBER BOOTS

Within days, in that late April of 1997, the liquid invasion reached the border. Manitoba premier Gary Filmon called a state of emergency and issued a public warning that twenty thousand people from the Red River Valley might have to be evacuated.

I was now doing live hits on *The National* every night at the top of the newscast. One day we followed Premier Filmon to St. Jean Baptiste, an hour south of Winnipeg, where he held a brief news conference by the bridge. Work crews were placing large concrete blocks on the bridge to weigh it down. They were trying to prevent it from being washed away. The water was moving fast, very fast, less than a metre under the deck. When we returned just a few hours later to rendezvous with the satellite truck, the bridge was already under water.

Just north, in Ste. Agathe, the water stole into town like a thief in the night, from the opposite direction residents had been expecting. I remember being in one poor fellow's house as he showed me the water just centimetres from the ceiling in his rec room. "I worked on this room all winter for my daughter," he said. "Now it's all gone." A small red plastic Minnie Mouse chair floated in the water near the top of the doorway. He tried to reach it but couldn't. He started to cry. I had a lump in my throat. There were now hundreds of families in situations just like his, and even more would be.

The province decided to open the floodgates, driving water into that big floodway even earlier than planned. Huge steel gates were driven up from the bottom of the river by hydraulics, forcing some of the water's flow east and into Duff's Ditch so it could flow around Winnipeg.

But there was just too much water. It began to back up south of the floodway. People in the bedroom communities there lost their homes, one by one. Some had spent weeks building elaborate sand-bag dykes around their bungalows. I went out to one in a small motorboat. As we stepped over the dyke and onto the roof, I realized there was a good three or four metres of flood water swirling around the house. Paul, the owner, was completely exhausted. He was running pumps to control seepage while his wife brought fuel and supplies by boat. I climbed down the ladder to the bottom of the sandbag dyke and looked up to the top, knowing the volume of water swirling on the other side. The pumps' engines droned on so loud you could barely speak. "How do you sleep?" I screamed to him. "I don't," he replied. "Sometimes I pass out from sheer exhaustion." Eventually their house went under.

It wasn't hard to understand the frustration and disappointment of those just south of the floodway gates. The few were being sacrificed to protect the many. There was no right or wrong in it, it was simply a matter of the officials trying to limit the inevitable damage.

The next day started at 5:30 a.m. I drove to meet John at the airport. We had been offered a ride on a government chopper to get pictures of what was quickly becoming "The Red Sea," just to the south, and there was a chance we could jump on a boat ride. As I was driving up Portage Avenue, it was a beautiful morning and the Beach Boys played on the radio. Sun and surf. We had more than enough but in the wrong place.

The pictures showing the extent of the flood were impressive. Water as far as the eye could see. When the chopper landed near

Rosenort, which had now become a small "island" community in the middle of all that water, we were quickly shuttled to a Coast Guard boat that had been brought south from Lake Winnipeg. Soon we were racing across the water, over what used to be farmers' fields, looking for stranded people and hoping the propeller didn't get tangled in an uprooted barbed-wire fence. Several kilometres from town we came across a modern-looking farmhouse. A dyke was built, but it had been breached. The water was mere centimetres from the main floor. A piece of plywood was sticking out with one word spray-painted on it in neon orange: HELP!

As the Coast Guard fellow manoeuvred closer, I yelled out, "Ahoy!" Eventually I heard someone yell "Ahoy!" back, and a scruffy fellow with a weary look in his eyes emerged from a door just above the waterline. "I've run out of fuel and the pumps have failed," he said. "I think it's time to abandon ship." Then he drew himself up straight, and with his chest out inquired, "Permission to come aboard?" Now we were rescuers. I said, "Of course." His wife was with him. She spoke not a word but clutched a cherished potted plant. The Red Sea had now become Manitoba's ocean, stretching over twenty-five hundred square kilometres, more than three times the size of the 1950 flood.

File a report. Sleep. File. Sleep. I was barely home long enough to change my clothes. The days were all blending together. There was talk of a federal election but nobody cared. Not here. Not anywhere. We led *The National* with "the flood of the century" every night. Extra crews were brought in from Toronto. I had to use sharp elbows to make sure everyone knew I did the lead story each night. I wasn't about to have anyone big-footing on my territory or "sinking" my lead!

People from every province and territory came to help. Some used their vacation time so they could fly to Winnipeg, sleep on a school gymnasium floor, and fill sandbags for twelve hours a day. By the end of the flood, the estimate was that over *eight million* sandbags had been filled, which, if they were laid end to end, would be much longer than a drive from Winnipeg to Vancouver and back!

YOUNG MAN LOST

His name was Adam Young. He was just fourteen years old. As young people will, he and some buddies were goofing around in the flooded ditches, when a younger lad fell in. Adam tried to help him. Unknown to them, the cover had been taken off the culvert beneath the surface to improve flow. It would prove deadly. The younger fellow was saved but Adam was swept away into the sewer system. For five days they searched for his body until it turned up in one of the large catchment basins underground.

Every day that they searched, and for many days after, I thought of that young fellow. I couldn't get him out of my mind. So many people on the move, all over the province, and so much danger. Yet there had been only one drowning. But it was one drowning too many, and it would have a much greater impact on me than I realized at the time.

We were going flat out now. Four days later, in the middle of the madness, Jean Chrétien decided to call a snap federal election, even against the advice of senior MPs like Reg Alcock. Alcock turned his campaign headquarters in Winnipeg South into a flood relief centre and ignored the political call to arms. Chrétien showed up and threw a ceremonial sandbag, and he took a lot of flack from the public for doing it.

Eventually the water crested in the city, and ever so slowly the waters of the Red Sea receded. The flood had lasted nearly a month. A big parade was held for the tens of thousands of military personnel and volunteers who had helped to keep damage to a minimum. In Manitoba the cost was estimated around $800 million. Farther south, where cities like Fargo and Grand Forks did not have the protection of a Duff's Ditch, the damage was estimated at US$3.5 *billion*.

Jean Chrétien was lucky to escape the 1997 election with a majority government, something he just barely accomplished. A swing of eight hundred votes in a couple of key ridings and it would have been another story.

And then there was Adam Young. He was on my mind, consciously or not, all through that summer, perhaps because I had a young son of my own. But it wasn't a daily thing. Time marches on and all that. In early December the CBC was getting ready to tape some stuff for the year in review, the top stories of 1997, that sort of a look back. Of course, the flood was at the top. I was in the studio, giving an interview about everything that had happened during the coverage. Our work had led to a Gemini nomination for best reportage, and we were all feeling pretty good about that.

Then I began telling the story about the one drowning fatality during the flood of the century. About Adam. From nowhere I felt this wave of emotion wash over me, not a small wave but a tsunami. Tears welled in my eyes and I began weeping. Gasping and choking back sobs, I said I would have to stop, I could not continue. It took a good ten minutes for me to be able to get myself together. I never saw it coming, and I had never really understood the impact all those days and weeks had on me, what toll Adam's death had taken on me, until that moment. I can still get emotional now, just writing about it, and I've felt my voice crack over the years when speaking about it during lectures.

Perhaps it's some mild version of post-traumatic stress. It was certainly a reminder that the things we reporters sometimes get close to in our efforts to describe them to you can come back and hit hard. Some years later, I remember watching a young journalist in the Winnipeg newsroom, a damn good one, get caught up in the crime beat. Every day it was another big story about an overdose or a shooting or a missing person. I took her aside and said to her, "This may all seem like exciting stuff right now, but believe me, whether you realize it or not, it's taking a toll on you. Be careful—it can come back and bite you." At the time she said she was okay; she really liked the work. Three months later she came to me and said it was starting to get to her. Not long after that, she asked to get off the beat, eventually leaving it. She no longer works in the business.

A certain level of detachment is necessary, healthy even, for a journalist to maintain objectivity and perspective on any story. But to really "get" the story, you also have to let some of it in. Either that, or some of it will push its way in. We are, after all, human. You don't stop caring just because you are a journalist. Finding the balance is the key to longevity in this gig. Too much sadness is never a good thing, in work or in life.

Our coverage of the flood of the century won numerous awards on both sides of the border, but the Gemini for best reportage was not among them. Like many who don't win, I got my share of sympathy from colleagues, with some even telling me I was robbed. I heard myself saying it was an honour just to be nominated, but truthfully it was also a huge disappointment, and a lesson in the "business" of awards. Don't take awards too seriously.

In the end, 1997 was one of those years. The flood had led to another high-water mark—that of my career. Numerous hero-grams came in from Toronto and, even more gratifying, from colleagues I had admired for years, some joking, "Hey, you air hog, give it up so we can get back on the show!" I guess a lot of folks were watching the coverage on *The National* because everywhere I went, people approached me to say how much they appreciated the work. It all felt pretty damn good.

CHAPTER 10

Moving On?

Rumblings were coming out of Toronto that perhaps I was now "too big" for the Manitoba market, and it was time to think about moving me to a larger bureau. Was my weight gain that obvious? Hehe. Seriously though, I felt I had just barely settled in Winnipeg and, although I didn't say it, I didn't know what the rush was about. Then they asked me to go and backfill (fill in for other reporters) in Washington, DC, for the month of July. I had never been to Washington before in my life. This was heady stuff. The Washington sign-off is something every journalist dreams about—at least I had. But it was also more than a little frightening. I was going from rubber boots to Oxfords. For starters, I didn't have enough suits to see me through. I rushed out and bought a few.

Of course, Washington in the summer is normally a relatively sleepy place (at least that's what they told me). And hot, damn hot, and humid. I would see young professionals walking up Pennsylvania Avenue in the morning, dressed in white cotton undershirts, with their dress shirt on a hanger, saving it so it wasn't soaking wet by the time they got to work. I got some cotton undershirts of my own. Some of the best value ever for money I've invested.

The CBC's Washington bureau is in the National Press Building on 14th Street NW, about two blocks from the White House and right across the street from the famous Willard Hotel. During my time there, we shared some space with ABC—the Australian Broadcasting Corporation. David Halton was the CBC's senior Washington correspondent, and reporter Keith Boag also filed from there. David was a lovely man and a talented old-school journalist. If his door was closed and the blinds drawn, it was probably because he was defying the rules and sneaking a smoke. Both were very friendly, but they were soon off for a summer break.

The travel people put me up in a posh hotel on Pennsylvania Avenue, just up from the White House. It was expensive, almost US$300 a night, and didn't have so much as a coffeemaker in the room. I found a Doubletree Hotel a block away and switched. For $99 a night I got a suite with a bedroom and a kitchen, much more suited to a two-week stay, and I could walk to the Safeway, downstairs in the Watergate Apartments, to buy groceries. I smiled and thought of Richard Nixon every time I walked into the place. Don't get me started on some of the penny-wise and pound-foolish decisions made by CBC travel contractors.

MEDIA SPACE CADET

The big deal in July of 1997 was the *Mars Pathfinder*. The United States' little unmanned probe had taken just seven months to reach the red planet and was all set to pitch on the surface of Mars on the fourth of July. It doesn't get much more American than that. People had begun gathering early in the morning for the Independence Day celebrations just down the hill on the National Mall around the Washington Monument and stretching all the way up to the Lincoln Memorial.

I was busy inside most of that day but occasionally had to dart out to do a stand-up. A great spot for stand-ups was at the bottom of the hill, where the Capitol Building could be nicely dropped into the frame just over my shoulder. As I did with many bureau files, I spent much of my time looking at feeds from the American networks CBC had an arrangement with (so I could use their videos, interviews, etc.), reading the wires and figuring out whether an original interview was to be had nearby. If it was too far away, you could get stuck in Washington traffic and never get anything on the air! Washington was also the capital of professional "experts," available to blather on about anything at the drop of a microphone.

Trying to make the piece look like my own was always a challenge. I wound up doing an on-camera presentation, as I recall, in one of the video-editing suites with computer-generated NASA graphics behind me on a monitor. Between updates and the final version for *The National*, I filed three times that fourth of July.

It had been a long day, but as I was heading down the elevator, close to 9:00 p.m., I thought I might wander down by the Washington Monument to check out the celebrations. As I walked out the front door onto 14th Street, I had no idea of what to expect. Literally hundreds of thousands of people were on the street, a much bigger crowd than I had ever seen in my life. I was pulled into the flow. Suddenly something struck me on the shoulder, almost knocking me down. It was a large rock that someone must have hurled from up the street.

What could you do? The chances of discovering who did it or being able to do anything about it were nil. I was now being pushed into the intersection at the bottom of the hill, not far from where I'd done my stand-up earlier in the day. Suddenly at least twenty police officers on large horses were herding us, pushing us back. Apparently there'd been a bomb threat. I made my way across the street and around the Willard Hotel just as the fireworks started going off. "Bombs" bursting over Washington on the fourth of July. Indeed.

There were more stories about the *Mars Pathfinder* and its rover, a robotic six-wheeled vehicle named *Sojourner*. It was the first vehicle to operate on a surface beyond earth and the moon. It was all quite fascinating and made for great television—and not just the fact that they could control this little vehicle from over two hundred million kilometres away, but that it could send back pictures and show the world. More importantly to me, I could tell that story from the relative safety of the National Press Building.

DUKES UP AND PLAYING WITH THE CHAMP

In truth, I can't say I was ever comfortable working or staying in Washington. It seemed a little as though you were working inside a big film production studio called Washington, the one you had been watching on TV all your life. It was tremendously exciting, but the place scared the hell out of me. Murder was hardly even news-worthy. While I was there, in Georgetown, usually considered one the safer parts of the city, three young people were shot to death in a Starbucks at seven o'clock on a Sunday evening.

Then there was the Tyson incident. In June, boxing thug Mike Tyson had decided to bite off part of Evander Holyfield's ear, not once but twice, during a display of dubious pugilistic talent. A hearing (a funny term under the circumstances) decided to ban Tyson from boxing in the United States for a year and fined him $3 million.

The desk in Toronto wanted me to do a story about it from Washington. "Okay," I thought. "How am I going to make this work?" I was determined that the piece would not be just a series of video clips borrowed from the Amnets (American news service) but would comprise material I could gather myself. I did a little research and found a boxing gym in Washington, up in behind the Capitol Building, where Tyson had even sparred a few times as a kid. I called a cab. We took cabs everywhere in Washington, or we walked, even with all the gear. A cab seemed safe. But finding park-ing was impossible and, as I mentioned, often so was the traffic. Impossible.

My first clue about what I was getting us into should have come when the taxi driver said, "This is as far as I go. You have to walk down there about two blocks." Okay, no big deal. We loaded up the gear on our handy trolley and wheeled on down the sidewalk. The gym was located above a big garage set back from the road. Upstairs, it was easily 40 °C, and about fifty young black men were working out, shadowboxing or sparring.

The fellow I had spoken with on the phone, Louie, turned out to be this massive man, over six feet tall. An easygoing guy, he said, "Y'all talk to whoever you like." I set about interviewing a few of the boxers. Some of the young men expressed disappointment that their idol would behave so badly in the ring. One guy symbolically tore a poster of Tyson off the wall. I did a little on-camera presentation in their makeshift ring, the sweat pouring off me, and it was time to go.

As I was shaking Louie's hand, a thought occurred to him. "Hey," he said, "how the heck did y'all git down here anyhow?" I explained what happened. He looked at me as if I was nuts and said, "Okay then, I'll give you a few of my boys to help get you back outta here."

There we were, me and my camera guy, walking up the road with a dozen young boxers surrounding us, when a fellow came hobbling out from between two row houses. He was stripped to the waist. His t-shirt, soaked in blood, was wrapped around his foot. He stumbled by, seemingly oblivious to us, saying, "I can't believe he shot me in the foot, the fool shot me in the goddamn foot!" It was still only about 11:30 in the morning. We got the hell out of there and never looked back. So much for trying to do original storytelling in Washington, DC. It could be life-threatening.

Before I headed back to Manitoba, I had the great pleasure of meeting and working with a real legend in Washington. His name was Henry Champ. Henry is lost to us now, but he was a giant of a man in more ways than one. The only thing bigger than his stature was his heart. By the time I met Henry, he was already a seasoned veteran, a former NBC and CTV News foreign correspondent, one of the last journalists to leave Vietnam as Saigon fell, and one of the first Canadian journalists allowed into the People's Republic of China. Harry was experienced and wise, and above all just a lovely, funny guy.

He had a soft spot for Manitoba, being a Brandon boy himself, and maybe that was why we hit it off. That, and the fact that we both loved to play snooker. We used to play for an hour or so almost every day up in the National Press Club. He was by then Newsworld's correspondent in Washington, but really, he was the go-to guy for the entire CBC system, with information, inside tips, connections. Just about anything any journalist needed to know, Henry either knew it or knew where to find it.

Over a pop, we would duel it out with our snooker cues (he was a competitive guy) and hash over the state of the broadcasting universe. With a twinkle in his eye, he was fond of telling me how the business in general took itself much too seriously, and in many ways was just such bullshit. He was my kind of guy. His straightforward, down-to-earth approach and sage advice helped me realize that chasing politicians and being part of a rat race like Washington, or Ottawa or Toronto for that matter, was not what I was looking for as a journalist. He helped me decide to push back against those who thought they, not me, would manage my career. It was some of the best advice—a gift, really—I have ever received. That, and tickets to his front-row seats on the first base line of his beloved Baltimore Orioles (he had season's tickets). Thanks, Henry.

I returned to Manitoba with a lot to think about. The feedback on my stint in Washington seemed great. People were pleased with the work, but I couldn't be certain of what it all meant. No new gigs were on offer, at least not yet. But although I wasn't entirely sure of what I did want next, I was now coming to some clear conclusions about what I *didn't* want.

154 · CHAPTER 10

THE COMPETITION

Don't ever let anyone tell you the news business is not a competitive environment. It is.

Every good journalist wants to beat the competition to the story. First was always better, although getting the story right also used to take top priority. Not so much anymore. Unfortunately, in today's hyper-charged social media environment, "first" seems to trump everything, even if the story is not entirely accurate or it's not certain what the truth is. I like to joke that we don't make mistakes anymore (at least ones we own up to), we just have updates.

Sometimes the chase can get downright nasty. Such was the case one cold December evening. A few weeks before Christmas an Embraer turboprop aircraft owned by Sowind Air Ltd., with seventeen people on board, crashed near the Indigenous community of Little Grand Rapids in Northern Manitoba. Four people were dead and thirteen others injured. The next morning it was a mad scramble to get up there, made even worse by the weather. Ice, fog and freezing rain made for dangerous flying weather at best.

My competition from CTV was yelling at the charter owners to get his plane in the air. He had a deadline, and he wanted to be first on the ground. I made a point of going to the counter and saying I was okay to wait until my pilot was more comfortable with the flying conditions. Eventually the weather cleared enough to take off. Here I was again, jumping in a small plane to fly into a remote area, this time to a plane crash. Just great.

At least we were in a twin-engine Navajo, a comfortable, reliable machine in my experience. CTV had chartered their own plane. Sometimes broadcast competitors share resources in situations like this to save money, but not today. My competition had sharp elbows and seemed more like he was playing a rough game of hockey than covering a tragic crash.

The weather was still not great, with sheets of freezing rain and some fog. The pilot had to activate his de-icing system as we approached the airport in Little Grand Rapids. The runway itself appeared potentially lethal, especially in these less than ideal conditions. A sizable hill rose on one end of the runway, ran flat for a bit, then sloped downward toward some fast-moving rapids. Rocks awaited if you missed on one end, turbulent ice water on the other.

The Sowind plane hadn't made it to the airport. It somehow lost its horizon trying to find the tracking beacon and crashed in the bush about a kilometre or so away. We got on the ground and taxied into a sad scene. The entire band community seemed to be there. They had responded quickly the evening before, travelling to the crash site by snowmobile, in bad weather, to carry out the dead and care for the injured. But almost a day later, they were still waiting for the military's Hercules rescue plane to land. Some choppers had gotten in earlier to medevac the more seriously injured, but the Hercules was having trouble, given its size, weight and the weather (not to mention that darn runway), getting on the ground.

The CTV crew immediately jumped on the one snowmobile for the media and took off, leaving us behind. A fellow watching nearby came over. I told him how sorry I was that his community was going through this pain and offered my condolences. He thanked me and said he had a snow machine and sled and would take us to the crash site. It turned out he had also helped with the rescue, and he gave us a compelling interview.

As we arrived at the crash scene, CTV was already preparing to head back to the airport. Their reporter made some crack about beating us out there and now he was going to beat us back to Winnipeg as well. But he seemed reluctant to leave. "If you get something I don't have," he said, "my boss will want to know why." I didn't have the heart to tell him I had already done an interview. "I'm sure you'll have the same stuff," I said. "It's a small place." They left.

Two men from the local band council were sitting by a vigil fire. It had snowed heavily, and the deadly site was blanketed in it. You could clearly see how the pilot had lost his horizon, cutting a swath through the tops of the trees for at least a hundred metres before plowing into the ground. Several seats from the plane lay outside the fuselage, looking almost serene with their fresh blanket of snow. Other debris was scattered around, and a big hole gaped farther back near the tail. The front of the plane was almost unrecognizable. I wondered how anybody could have survived at all.

An RCMP officer was also on the scene, guarding the wreckage until the crash investigators arrived. He did not look well. In fact, he looked grey. I greeted him, remarking that he had a sad job to do today. He agreed. Then I said, "I don't mean to pry, but are you feeling okay? You don't look well." He said his wife was in Winnipeg Christmas shopping. She had been on standby all day yesterday trying to get a seat on this very plane. She missed by one seat. My cameraman John had been rolling tape on the entire conversation, and I asked the officer if it would be okay to use his interview. He said yes. Now I had two compelling pieces of tape I knew the competition didn't have.

We jumped back on the snow machine, took to the bumpy trail and headed back to the airport. When we got there everything was on hold again. CTV had not gotten the jump on us after all. The Hercules rescue plane had dumped some of its fuel to make it light enough for a safe landing. It had just landed to drop off investigators and to bring the dead to Winnipeg for autopsies. Nothing else was moving until it took off.

It was a sombre scene as people from the band stood and watched it rumble into the air. As we headed back to our plane, the CTV fellow was yelling at his pilot as he threw his gear on board. He wanted to rush his airplane ahead of ours for the takeoff. I was setting up to screen tape and do some writing on the way back anyway.

"My competition seems a bit too uptight," I said to my pilot. He replied that all the pilots were annoyed with CTV's reporter, and when his pilot got in the air, he planned to slow down their airspeed so we would arrive a good half-hour ahead of him. It was a great laugh, and a good lesson in the adage "What goes around comes around." Treat people with respect and they will generally respond in kind. Act like an ass and you deserve what you get.

The piece attracted my second Gemini nomination. Once again, however, I was destined to be the bridesmaid, not the bride. *C'est la vie.*

TEAR GAS SURPRISE

Later that winter, John and I would find ourselves in another tight spot, this time at the Manitoba legislature. It was opening day, and a big procession into the house was to be held with the lieutenant-governor. Trouble was, there were also about eight hundred angry, protesting Indigenous people out on the front steps, and things were quickly dissolving into chaos.

Newsworld asked us to get over there and possibly do some live hits from my phone in to the network. John was outside on the front steps getting some video. Security had blocked access to the front entrance of the building, so I had to sneak in through a back door and make my way around to the front, near the indoor rotunda, to see what was going on. By now riot police, dozens of them, had also been called in. They were working to keep the protesters outside, but it was tough going. Only a set of big rotating doors kept them there.

I did one hit on air, a debrief with the anchor explaining the situation, and was waiting for instruction from the control room in Toronto when I heard one officer say to the other, "I think they're going to use the tear gas." "That's not a good idea," came the reply. No kidding. Those rotating front doors were now jammed open, creating a wind tunnel that blew directly at us.

The protesters made a big push and burst into the area near the rotunda. I looked up to see John riding along on top of them as if he was in some huge mosh pit, videotaping away. The police were pulling people from the mob and dragging them away. Suddenly John put on hand on a protester's shoulder and launched himself and his twenty-three-kilo camera right over the police line. He immediately began recording the scene from behind the officers. Unbelievable.

To my right I could see the procession coming—the speaker, the sergeant-at-arms carrying the ceremonial mace, the honour guard and the lieutenant-governor—all very solemn, marching in line. And that was when the police outside decided to let go with the tear gas. You can guess what happened next. In it came, wafting right through the doors and filling the whole area inside the legislature. My eyes started burning. I could see the poor sergeant-at-arms, tears streaming from his eyes, stuff coming out his nose, clinging to the mace. The ceremonial mace had once been considered a weapon to be used by bodyguards of the monarch. The irony of the fellow carrying it, now himself being "maced," was not lost on me. People were moving in all directions, trying to get clear of the gas.

Then my phone rang. It was Toronto. Could I do another telephone interview? I was having trouble breathing. I gasped that we had just been gassed and they would have to call back. Goop kept pouring from my nose. I made it down a side hall and to the big public washroom, flushing my eyes until the burning stopped. They were red and swollen.

The protest certainly stopped. People scattered. I called Toronto back and explained the situation. They decided to turn their attention to another crisis elsewhere, and that was that. John and his camera had somehow managed to escape a direct hit. That was John, always quick on his feet. He got the van and we headed back to the station. Just another day in the life of a network correspondent.

BACK TO WASHINGTON

Someone in Toronto was convinced I had to move. And although nobody ever said who decided it, by December I was on my way back to Washington. So off I went, from a tragic plane crash in Northern Manitoba to the mean streets of America's capital. It was a quick trip. In a week it would be Christmas.

But the story they wanted wasn't in Washington, it was overseas. For nearly four years, Bosnia had been the battleground for the bloodiest war in Europe since World War II. After the breakup of Yugoslavia, two factions emerged in what was subsequently known as Bosnia and Herzegovina. The Bosnian Serbs, led by Radovan Karadžić, were determined to carve out their own "ethnically pure" state. The Croatian defence council was determined to stop it. It became a bloodbath, marked by indiscriminate bombing of civilians, ethnic cleansing, mass graves and systematic campaigns of rape and torture.

By the time a level of peace was achieved, thanks in large part to NATO intervention, one in ten Bosnians had been killed or wounded and over 90 per cent were left without work. Depending on whose numbers you believed, over two hundred thousand were killed.

And now, a week before Christmas, the president of the most powerful country in the world had arrived in Bosnia to reassure people that this fragile peace would indeed hold and would continue to receive the support of the United States of America. Bill Clinton also assured them that a hunt for those guilty of crimes against humanity would continue.

Here I was, thousands of kilometres away, expected to cobble together a story about his visit. It was one of those awkward moments in a journalist's career when you have to present yourself as knowing more about something than you actually do and, in this case, do it using whatever video was being shot by other networks and whatever information you could verify from news wires or other trusted sources. Of course, the internet had now become a valuable tool, offering background research and details on the conflict that would have been nearly impossible to gather quickly even five years earlier. What fun.

So you find yourself retreating into standard phrases such as "It's been reported that ..." or "While unconfirmed, it's believed that ..." I found myself drifting back to a song I had written with my good buddy Larry some years before: "How's it feel to be a media man, as the cameras start to pan? Talking to people you've never seen, coming from places you've never been."

I filed the story, reporting the basic facts and leaving the analysis to the experts. The next day President Clinton was hamming it up with those troops still on the ground. A little holiday cheer in what was an ugly place where humans had been doing the worst that humans could do to one another.

And then it was Christmas Eve. Along with producer Tim Richards, I made the mad dash home to Winnipeg with, it seemed, millions of others in the great Washington escape.

Ronald Reagan Washington National Airport was a disaster zone. Besides the already dysfunctional state of holiday traffic, it was snowing. Lots of snow and lots of delays. We sat on our bar stools, chugging back pints of airport craft brew with visions of sleeping on the airport floor on Christmas Eve dancing in our heads. Five hours late, our Toronto flight was finally called, and I made the last Winnipeg flight out of Toronto Pearson home, landing just after midnight.

Merry Christmas.

BILL CLINTON'S PROBLEM

Two weeks after the Christmas break, I was on my way back to Washington. Bill Clinton was in trouble. Nothing as heady as failed foreign policy or a domestic economic crisis. Nope. It was the oldest political problem in the book: a woman. A much younger woman who was not his wife. Come to think of it, it was probably a bit of a domestic crisis after all.

Her name was Monica Lewinsky, and she was a twenty-something White House intern from San Francisco. The word was that she and the president were having one-on-one consultations of a carnal nature. This news exploded with much more ferocity than any bombs in Bosnia. The whole world was immediately transfixed on Bill Clinton's zipper, and journalists from every corner of the planet converged on the capital.

I remember going with a camera operator to a potential sighting of Ken Starr, the independent counsel investigating the mounting scandal. Starr had initially been tasked with investigating Whitewater real estate holdings and the Clintons when this much juicier accusation emerged.

While we waited, it became pandemonium. In fact, it damn near became a riot. Hundreds of cameras, reporters and spectators were all crowded together waiting for Mr. Starr to emerge from a justice building. When he did, a kind of journalistic feeding frenzy ensued—yelling, pushing and shoving, even a few punches thrown.

It was every journalist for themself. This journalist quickly realized the situation was useless, and my cameraman and I retreated to the bureau where we could get pictures on the news feed. There you could see the person they were chasing on the ground without running the risk of being trampled or having the side of your head caved in by a media gorilla wielding a twenty-three-kilo camera on his shoulder.

It was clearly out of control. A sitting president, an intern with fire-engine-red lipstick, talk of things like fellatio and stains on dresses. And now, perhaps, President Clinton caught in a lie. "Yikes," thought the leaders back in the Toronto mother ship, "better put more boots on the ground."

By mid-week, well over a dozen extra CBC types had been flown in. When it came to a good sex scandal, money apparently was no object. Over a beer one night I told them I had found a block of available rooms at my new favourite hotel, the Doubletree, and suggested they all move out of the expensive hotel the travel folks had put them in. Many of them did. This could be a long haul. Video emerged showing Ms. Lewinsky with the president as he moved through a crowd. They clearly knew each other. Every day a little more of the story was revealed.

I was doing my stand-ups now right on the lawn of the west wing of the White House. At least I started on the lawn. Within days they had to build scaffolding four storeys high to accommodate us. It was like something from TV's *Hollywood Squares*, that game show where each celebrity had their own little cubicle. In this case, it was each correspondent, all looking for that same backdrop of the White House lit up at night. To my left, up there on my third-floor perch, was a reporter from Japan. Another from Germany was on my right.

And Bill Clinton, right in the crosshairs, was in the middle. Oh, the debates. What actually constituted sex? If there was no intercourse, does that mean there was no sexual relationship? "I did not have sexual relations with that woman." That was Bill Clinton's explanation, given in a televised nationwide address.

> But I want to say one thing to the American people. I want you to listen to me. I am going to say this again: I did not have sexual relations with that woman, Miss Lewinsky. I never told anybody to lie. Not a single time. Never. These allegations are false. And I need to go back to work for the American people.
> —President Bill Clinton, 1998

It became known as the Clinton–Lewinsky scandal. We called it Zippergate, and Monica Lewinsky had her own version to tell. In testimony she swore there was indeed an affair, one that had gone on at least a year and a half and included no fewer than nine sexual trysts, right in the Oval Office. Monica has also saved a certain blue dress, acquired by Mr. Starr, with the stain "evidence" down the front. Just plain weird.

It was ruled that sexual relations, by whatever definition, had indeed occurred, and the president was caught in a lie. It would lead to his impeachment, only the second of a sitting US president in American history. Andrew Jackson was the first in 1868; both were later acquitted by the US Senate. It was scandal at its finest, and I got to enjoy it from a front-row seat. But eventually it was time to head home.

THE COST OF DOING BUSINESS

It must have cost a fortune. By my conservative calculations, moving some of my fellow scribes down the block to the Doubletree had saved the corporation thousands of dollars, if not tens of thousands. I say this to illustrate a point—or to present the CBC version of penny-wise, pound foolish.

Not long after returning, we were all called to Toronto for a meeting of national reporters. We arrived from the many corners of Canada. A week or two before the meeting, an email had been dispatched telling everyone the meeting would be on a Saturday, and that all reporters, producers and others should fly in that morning and fly out that evening to save on hotel costs. Right. Good plan. I then dispatched an email of my own.

I respectfully pointed out that if they were trying to save money, why were they holding the meeting on a weekend when everyone was on overtime? Also, back then Air Canada had a rule designed, I suspect, to gouge business traffic. If you did not stay overnight on a Saturday, the flight cost went up significantly. As I pointed out, if I did what they asked, the cost of my ticket would be about $1,800. If I stayed overnight on Saturday, the ticket cost would drop to about $340. I ended by saying I would expect them to pick up my hotel costs and expenses, still saving well over $1,000. Within hours another email was dispatched from Toronto instructing all participants to stay over the Saturday night.

Close to thirty people were flying in for that meeting. You do the math. But that wasn't the best of it. When I returned, I put in a $12 claim for my lunch, which I had to buy at a local sandwich shop. It was denied because they had apparently served some carrot sticks and other snacks (that didn't get past the head table) during the meeting. Penny-wise (debatable), pound foolish (without a doubt).

I won't go on about this too much, but Toronto decisions were becoming increasingly frustrating. For example, in the spring of 1998, I saw the potential for a funny story down near Minot, North Dakota. The village of Granville, population under three hundred, had won a contest to change its name to McGillicuddy City for a couple of years. It was being paid $100,000 to do so as a promotional stunt for the Dr. McGillicuddy's brand of schnapps. The problem was, the town had been established by teetotallers and had always been run by members of the temperance movement. Descendants were talking about forefathers (and mothers) rolling in their graves.

It had the potential to be a cute story, and it was just a few hours' drive southwest of Winnipeg. The desk said great, off you go. But there was a condition. They needed the story for *The National*, so I would have to fly back and file that night. The only way to do that was to hire a small charter plane to come get me, a cost of about $2,500. They said fine, and off I went.

It really was a great story. The characters were funny. The owners of the Branding Iron Saloon had agreed to change the name to the Shady Eye Saloon (the reputed name of the fictional Dr. McGillicuddy's favourite hangout). Even though they had never heard of the schnapps, they started serving it. A brass band awaited us with all the bunting and colour to make the story shine.

After getting the story, we raced to the small airstrip and flew back to Winnipeg, and I sent the script to Toronto. The senior producer of *The National* called. "Why would I want to put this story on *The National?*" she demanded. "It's not even Canadian." I pointed out that the schnapps (at that time) was owned by Seagram's, a.k.a. the Bronfmans, one of Canada's wealthiest families. That information was in the script but she had apparently missed it. "Besides," I replied, "you guys assigned me to this story and even paid for a plane to come pick me up so I could get the story in time for the show." That decision had apparently been made before she came to work.

I told her I would file it anyway and release it to the syndicated news service. She asked why I would do that. I said we'd already spent the money to shoot it, so why wouldn't we release it? It ran on every regional news show in the country, and for two days on CNN. That didn't matter. She had painted herself into a corner and was determined to stay there, so the story never ran on *The National*. Frustrating? You bet.

By the way, in the end the village of Granville decided, in one way, to keep the name McGillicuddy City. The little town received so much national and international attention, attention that Granville had never received, that they decided to keep the McGillicudy City sign up. A clan of McGillicuddys even showed up for a big reunion!

Situations like this that came up in the process of daily newsgathering convinced me that I needed to do more work for the "back half" of the show. Longer features were my thing—always had been, really, since CBC had first hired me. I was also starting to realize that for me, public broadcasting was about Canada. Canada's people, its history. Its story.

CHAPTER 11

Treading Dark Water

DOCTOR DEATH

In 1999, I got my chance. Across the Prairies, dozens of South African doctors were quietly emigrating and starting up practices. This was a good thing, especially in rural Saskatchewan where it was hard to attract and keep physicians. But some of these doctors had a past, a dark past attached to the apartheid regime. Back in South Africa the Truth and Reconciliation hearings were ongoing, exposing some of the former regime's more sinister plots. One was code-named Project Coast. It was the stuff of genocide: sterility experiments in the black community, even torture and murder, all in the name of protecting the apartheid regime.

It came to our attention that one such individual, Dr. Jack Bothma, was practising orthopaedics in North Battleford, Saskatchewan. He had once worked for a man named Dr. Wouter Basson, also known as Dr. Death. Basson, as testimony revealed, was a nasty character known for the development of various chemical and biological agents, many designed to help maintain control over the black population in South Africa. The techniques he employed drew comparisons to those used by Josef Mengele during the Nazi regime in World War II. For five years, Dr. Bothma had been under the radar in the small city in Northern Saskatchewan, but if I had anything to do with it, that would soon be coming to an end.

I worked on the story with Carmen Merrifield, a fabulous producer, but it soon became apparent we wouldn't be getting any help from the community. Nobody wanted to speak with us, on or off the record. Door after door was closed in our faces, and at that point we had not yet revealed the details of what we knew about the doctor's connection to "Dr. Death" or the South African military program. North Battleford appreciated having the doctor there and no doubt he was badly needed, but he also had a past. Even so, we could not even confirm a) whether Dr. Bothma was still working at the city's hospital, or b) where he lived.

As we circled around the parking lot of the hospital, I noticed an area for physicians' parking. Five vehicles were parked there. Licence plate numbers! I had a way, one that I won't get into here, of attaching names to those plate numbers, complete with addresses. We focused on a dark red Chevy Blazer. We waited in that parking lot until eventually the doctor emerged. Still having our element of surprise, with the camera rolling, we pounced. He said nothing, jumped in his vehicle and left. So much for the element of surprise. But unknown to him, we knew where he was heading.

We waited a bit and then pulled up in front of his house. No answer came when I knocked on the door, but I could hear someone inside. Through the door I explained who I was and why I was there. Unfortunately, I added, I was not able to go away, and I would be waiting at the end of his driveway for as long as it took. We would set up lights if necessary. If the neighbours became curious, that would be unfortunate. I also said I knew there were two sides to every story, and this was his opportunity to tell his.

Ten minutes later, he emerged. He shook my hand and was extremely friendly. At first. As the questions became more pointed, however, questions about people being tied to trees, injections, about bodies being dumped from planes into the ocean, his tone changed. He admitted he knew Dr. Basson and had worked with him in the South African Army's Seventh Medical Battalion. He denied knowing anything about torture, or human experiments, or death.

We left, but that was not the end of it. Far from it.

He had already been implicated several times in testimony before South Africa's Truth and Reconciliation Commission. Witnesses testified about his involvement in a program designed to assassinate opponents of the regime. An attempt was made to develop a vaccine to render black women sterile. Furthermore, Bothma was directly implicated in the murders of three black detainees. According to witnesses, under Basson's instructions they were handcuffed to trees by Bothma and others and injected with a substance that suffocated them. Their bodies were flown out over the ocean and dumped.

When we went to the College of Physicians and Surgeons of Saskatchewan, they were decidedly indifferent about hearing this information. The head of the college simply said allegations were allegations, and without knowing their veracity the college could do nothing. But then he added that Dr. Bothma would not be practising much longer in Saskatchewan anyway as he had failed three times to pass the necessary exams.

After the piece aired, Dr. Bothma disappeared, seemingly without a trace, as did another South African doctor with military ties we had been trying to track down. Our investigation was widely reported across North America. Dr. Bothma re-emerged some time later as a state witness for the prosecution in South Africa, hoping to avoid being charged himself. With tears in his eyes, he admitted it was all true.

After years of trial and testimony, Dr. Basson walked free. The judge in the case concluded there was not enough evidence directly linking him to even one of the many crimes he was charged with, even though he was clearly involved in the development of chemical and biological weapons. Bothma had already freely admitted what he had done as a medical doctor. But because he had turned state witness, he avoided prosecution and has never faced any formal sanction. His whereabouts are unknown.

Other daily assignments came along, but once I developed a renewed taste for longer-form journalism, it was hard to go back to a minute and a half. It just seemed so limiting.

I did another stint in Washington and covered a Manitoba election scandal, but Toronto was now placing constant pressure on me, telling me I had to move. Apparently I was needed more in Toronto or Ottawa or Calgary. Toronto leadership argued that the idea was to get me on the air even more, which, from their perspective, would be a good thing for me.

I pointed out that I was filing more stories for *The National* than my counterpart filed from Alberta, and it was a much bigger place. I had also taken on the responsibility of covering Saskatchewan, so I was already a busy guy. I was more than willing to travel wherever the story took me, but I could not see how uprooting my family, especially my children, and dragging them somewhere else in the country was going to benefit anyone but the good folks in Toronto.

I simply said no, I was not leaving. I spoke with my colleagues. Some thought I was nuts, defying Toronto like that. "Career limiting" was a common refrain. The thinking was that at this level they owned you and could do with you as they pleased. But I held my ground—I was not moving. They countered with, "You'll have to leave *The National*." I said, "Okay, I'll leave *The National*." They said, "You don't have to be like that." I said, "You don't have to be like that either." It was a standoff that continued all summer and into the fall. Meanwhile, another story was always waiting.

THOSE KILLER EYES

Larry Fisher was a cold-blooded murderer, no two ways about it. For years he had kept his mouth shut, knowing that another man,

David Milgaard, was serving time for a crime Fisher had committed: the brutal slaying of nursing assistant Gail Miller. She had been raped and murdered and left in a Saskatoon snowbank back in 1969. Fisher had lived in her neighbourhood. Milgaard, just sixteen at the time, was travelling across the country with some buddies and had the misfortune of being in the wrong place at the wrong time. They had stopped in Saskatoon to pick up a friend. The friend's family just happened to be renting out their basement apartment to Larry Fisher.

After Gail Miller's body was discovered, suspicion fell on the young lads from out of town. Milgaard was found guilty and on January 31, 1970, he was sentenced to life in prison. He would serve twenty-three years behind bars before being released and then exonerated by DNA evidence. The hard and relentless work of David's mother, Joyce, who stood beside her son every day of his incarceration, finally cleared his name.

Fisher, meanwhile, had spent twenty-three years in prison himself, convicted of numerous rapes committed in Manitoba and Saskatchewan. He was finally charged with Gail Miller's murder in Calgary in 1997, and now I was at the provincial courthouse in Yorkton, Saskatchewan, for his rape and murder trial.

It was the first time in my life I had come face to face with pure evil. Fisher was not a big man, but he was cold and nasty. It was clear the police escorting him to the courthouse each morning did not like him either. We stood with cameras rolling by the back door where he was brought in. They made sure we had a long, clear shot.

I got to throw him the usual questions the accused never answer. "Did you do it?" "Are you being treated fairly?" He turned and looked me right in the eye. Those eyes were black and murderous. My blood went cold and I felt the hair go up on the back of my neck. It was pure evil—pure hatred. He did not reply. With his hands and feet shackled, the police shuffled him inside.

Fisher sat unemotional, almost detached, throughout the trial. When he was found guilty he showed no emotion either, and he was taken away without speaking a word. The right man had finally been convicted, but on top of committing a murderous act, he had allowed another young man's life to be destroyed. David Milgaard was eventually compensated $10 million for his wrongful conviction, but the best part of his life had already been taken from him. Money could hardly compensate for that.

Fisher tried to launch numerous appeals, but they were all denied. Eventually he was eligible to apply for parole, but he never did. He died in prison in Abbotsford, British Columbia, on June 10, 2015.

HOW ABOUT MOVING ... WHERE?

My battle with Toronto was ongoing. The latest suggestion was that we should think about moving to Calgary again. In a moment of weakness, I agreed to give it serious consideration. Pam and I talked it over and even decided we would visit Calgary to get a better handle on housing costs, schools, amenities and other things we would need. I had lived there before, of course, but the city of Calgary had exploded in the almost fifteen years since.

Then one morning while I was in the office preparing for a new assignment, the phone rang. It was the CBC's real estate division. They said they needed some details on our Winnipeg house to do a market comparison between it and a similar house in Toronto. I said they must be mistaken—that comparison was supposed to be for Calgary. They said no, the email from the individual in the news department who handled these matters clearly stated Toronto.

I knew exactly who that individual was and I got him on the phone. I told him, "I think you made a mistake. You have the real estate folks looking at Toronto." There was a brief pause before he said, "Yes, we've been thinking about it, and we've decided Toronto would be a better fit for you than Calgary." *They* had decided, and they hadn't even told me directly! I was so mad I could barely speak, but I managed to tell him to tell the real estate division not to waste their time. I was going nowhere.

Of course, I now knew I was trapped. They were not going to stop, and the situation had come to a head. I briefly considered other news organizations. Several overtures had come my way in recent years, but none that I had taken seriously. I had always remained at the CBC because I believed in the importance of a public broadcaster and its value to Canadians. But these people were driving me nuts. It was becoming a bit of a nightmare.

MEDICAL DARKNESS

Journalists are often asked, "Where do your story ideas come from?" The answer is that they come from all over. Everywhere. Some are driven by community events that are deemed newsworthy, sometimes you see a thread of something happening and develop it into a story, and some come from good, solid investigative research. The South African doctor in Saskatchewan would fall into that last category. So did my next story.

A team of researchers at CBC Toronto was working to develop a number of threads into stories. One of them was Bonnie Brown. She was whip smart and thorough. She had developed a lead about the Anishininew (often known as the Oji-Cree) in the Northern Manitoba communities around Island Lake, an area that was nothing short of a national disgrace.

Island Lake comprises four Aboriginal communities—Red Sucker Lake, Garden Hill, Wasagamack and St. Theresa Point—spread across several islands, just over six hundred kilometres northeast of Winnipeg. It is remote and accessible only by air most of the year, the exception being during the few short winter months when an ice road is built through the bush.

Close to ten thousand people lived in those communities, many with no running water. Can you imagine any non-Native community of that size anywhere in Canada—places like Winkler, Manitoba, or Swift Current, Saskatchewan, or Smiths Falls, Ontario—where a situation like that would be allowed to exist? Every day they hauled water in buckets and pails, summer and winter, from a central tap that could be a kilometre or more away. Sometimes in winter the community water taps froze.

Poverty was the norm. Living conditions were deplorable. But that wasn't the worst of it. Island Lake was in the middle of a medical crisis: an epidemic of type 2 diabetes. It could be argued that the onset of type 2 diabetes is generally the result of poor diet and exercise. It was certainly true that maintaining a healthy diet in those communities, with little money and astronomical prices in the single food store, was wishful thinking at best. A jug of milk could be $12, but a sugary can of pop was still just a buck. However, that was only part of the problem.

The Oji-Cree, as a people, used to be much more active, almost nomadic. They hunted, fished and ate primarily wholesome, natural food—food gathered from the land. Back in the 1950s, type 2 diabetes in the Ojibwa-Cree population was almost unheard of. But slowly, as the influence of the Department of Indian and Northern Affairs increased, the health of the people living in Island Lake, and indeed in many Indigenous communities, began to decline.

People used to spend a lot of time in the bush, cutting their own wood for housing and for fuel. The department said that was no longer needed—the government would bring in oil heat for them to keep warm. Many hunted and fished. At one time there had been a thriving fish-canning operation in Island Lake. But eventually people turned away from traditional foods, and instead to the one local store, with its sugary drinks and fatty foods, and a slow-motion medical disaster unfolded.

There was also the controversial suggestion that the Anishininew were genetically predisposed to developing type 2 diabetes—that their illness was a direct result of what was called the "hunter-gatherer" gene. Whether true or not, what *was* true was that these four Indigenous communities were now immersed in a full-blown medical crisis. Diabetes was rampant. This was the first place in the world where type 2 diabetes had developed in children. Many now required dialysis.

But here's the thing. You had a community of close to ten thousand people, and most had *no* running water. They had a water-treatment system, but it was hooked up only to the school and some teachers' residences. But Bonnie Brown had discovered that instead of providing clean running water and the medical care these folks clearly needed in their community, the federal government was spending over $5 million a year flying those needing dialysis to Winnipeg for treatment.

Invariably these patients, already sick and weary of the constant travel, would be forced to relocate to the city with their families. A community team in Winnipeg did its best to help them settle, but it was an impossible situation. Limited resources meant living in poverty. Unfamiliarity with the big city meant their children often got caught up in gangs or drugs or, if their parents succumbed to diabetes, were left to fend for themselves.

I travelled to St. Theresa Point with producer Lynn Burgess and a crew from Toronto in the dead of winter. It was bitterly cold. Driving up the gentle slope from where the ice road came off the lake, we couldn't help but notice the many small white crosses, all the way up the hill, in the community graveyard.

As we drove by the town's garage, I saw what appeared to be a brand-new fire truck sitting in a snowbank. All the windows were smashed, and every compartment door on the truck was hanging open. Fire hoses snaked across the snow. I asked the local fellow helping us out with transportation what had happened.

He said a man had taken the fire truck out of the garage to do some work on his own vehicle and hadn't bothered to put it back inside. The water in the truck's tank had frozen and the tank split. He said because it was no longer of any use, the kids had messed around with it, and this was the result. It was my first indication of the profound problems in this community.

We then spent the better part of a day before the chief and council, trying to persuade them to allow us to videotape so we could shine a light on their tragic situation. Until they agreed, no recording. Finally, they said yes. I thought surely they understood we were there to try to help, but at that point, who could blame them if they were skeptical?

We travelled down to a house by the lake to meet Harry Wood. Harry was a dignified man, tall and straight, with a shock of jet-black hair. Harry's brother was J.J. Harper, an Indigenous man shot by a police officer on the street in Winnipeg some ten years before. Harry's official complaint against the police officer had led to an inquiry into the treatment of Indigenous people in the city.

For two hours, as we sat in folding chairs in the snow down by the lake, Harry gave me a lecture about what the "white man" had done to his people. I took it willingly. The more I learned, the more I realized how much we had to answer for. Harry was angry, and we were his opportunity to tell the entire country what had been done to his people. He spoke of pushing people away from traditional ways, of the hopelessness of young people, of having no chance at a future, of watching this other world via the grainy images on TV, knowing it was a world you could have no part in.

Not that Harry watched it himself. Harry was blind. He too suffered from the ravages of diabetes. His tiny wife Maggie helped him get around by leading him by the elbow. She barely came up to his elbow herself, but at sixty she was still more than capable—and she still played hockey.

Once the interview was over, hospitality followed, and we returned to their small bungalow with its scrubbed plywood floors for a cup of tea. Harry even played the old upright piano in the corner of the room for us.

Other homes were not as cozy. In some, as many as twenty people lived in just a few rooms. Others had cracks where daylight shone through the walls, kids sick with runny noses and, at one home, a slash right through the metal front door that had clearly been made with an axe. The social and economic challenges seemed almost insurmountable.

Jack Harper, another man from Wasagamack we interviewed, was also struggling with type 2 diabetes. His wife still worked at the local school, but he could no longer work full-time—travelling to Winnipeg for dialysis made it impossible. Even so, he was one of the few left who still cut his own firewood. We recorded him as he sawed and carried logs on his shoulder, sometimes almost up to his waist in snow. He was worried. Worried about what he had seen happen to other families forced into the city. Worried about his kids. Worried about the future. But he was determined not to leave.

Not that the government had given him much choice. And while Ottawa and the province of Manitoba fought over jurisdiction, the people of Island Lake were slowly dying. Communities like Island Lake were a federal responsibility, but health-care delivery clearly came under provincial jurisdiction. In the meantime, Ottawa was spending over $5 million a year to ensure the cycle continued. It was nothing short of a disgrace.

We got back on the small commuter plane headed south, surrounded by folks heading the same way for treatment.

In a few weeks the piece was ready. We knew it would hit hard. It was powerful and profoundly sad. The plan was to air it on Monday night; it would be a full edition of the back half of *The National*, close to twenty-five minutes in length. I made sure the communities all knew. But in the middle of the afternoon, the senior producers of the show changed their minds. They called to say they needed to air something on the NDP leadership race that night, and there wasn't room for both in the show. The story of the people of Island Lake would have to wait until Tuesday.

On Monday night Harry Wood died. He had been in Winnipeg for treatment and had died of a heart attack in his sleep. He went to bed disappointed, I am sure, and died never knowing what impact his story would have.

The next night, Tuesday, Harry's wake was held in a funeral home in the middle of the Indigenous community in the north end of Winnipeg. The weight of what had happened, of how we had let him down, was heavy on me. As I reached the steps, a van pulled up and his wife Maggie got out of the back seat. She grabbed hold of me and hugged me as if I were life itself. I told her how very sorry I was for her loss, and how sorry I was that Harry never got to see himself telling the country what had been done to his people. I will never forget what she whispered in my ear: "Don't worry about that, my son," she said. "Harry knew you did your best." Even in her grief, she was comforting me.

We walked up the steps and into a crowded funeral home, with Harry in a coffin at the end of the room, lying there in a powder-blue tuxedo. Later that night, while we waked Harry, the documentary aired.

The next day the story was raised in the House of Commons. It was a travesty, a nation's shame. Something had to be done. Something. The health minister of Manitoba called a news conference to say negotiations would begin immediately with federal counterparts to get proper water treatment and a proper medical facility installed in Island Lake, one where residents could get dialysis.

Then for five years nothing happened. Well, nothing much. There seemed to be, finally, goodwill between the two levels of government, but the four band councils involved could not agree on where the new facility should be built.

Ten years after my initial story, I returned to Island Lake. All of the people interviewed for the original story were now dead. Diabetes had killed them. Jack Harper's widow still worked at the school. A big plastic tank to hold water had been delivered to her house so she wouldn't have to haul it in buckets anymore, but it came with contaminated sludge inside and you couldn't drink any water that came out of it. Only a handful of homes had finally been hooked up to the water system.

Almost twenty years later, Island Lake now has a renal treatment centre in one of its communities, Garden Hill, that can treat eighteen people a week. But there is still a waiting list, and the ongoing water and sewer issues in the community cause frequent problems. Medical care remains an issue. The community's plight was raised again in the House of Commons as recently as 2019.

My frustration with this story, as a journalist and as a Canadian, would not go away. In my naïveté, I thought it was simple: expose the problem and someone would realize that not only would it be much more cost-effective to help these good people where they lived, it would also tremendously improve their quality of life. It seemed as though no leaders on either side, in the federal government or the Indigenous communities, were really interested in a solution. They seemed more interested in power and protecting their turf.

You can't help but feel that the undercurrent of racism that seems to run through far too many things affecting Canada's First Nations people also played a role. I remember quite some time ago running into a fellow who was on his way north to work on water and sewer problems in a number of Indigenous communities. He said he knew of four where the intake for the new water system had been installed downstream from the sewer outflow. He mused that only one thing could allow that to happen in so many places—not incompetence, but racism, pure and simple.

911 UNANSWERED

My next story was part of another great shame of our country—that of murdered and missing Indigenous women.

The events of my story happened in February 2000. Two Métis sisters, fifty-two-year-old Corrine McKeown and Doreen Leclair, fifty-one, called 911 from Leclair's north-end home.

The call was disconnected. When the operator called back, a woman said someone had been shot. A car was dispatched but a man answered the door—and gave a false name. He was William Dunlop, McKeown's former boyfriend. A restraining order had been filed against him, supposedly backed up by a police zero-tolerance policy. But nothing happened. The officers simply left.

Over the next eight hours, four more 911 calls would be made. All the taped recordings of the calls, after a fight between police and the media, were released so the public could hear what happened for themselves.

On the second call, the women were told to call police directly.

On the third call, a woman said McKeown had been stabbed by a man who was violating a restraining order. But rather than sending another car, the operator told the woman to deal with it herself, even suggesting the two women were partly to blame.

On the fourth call, the women were very difficult to understand, but one could be clearly heard saying, "Please help me." The operator promised to send a car, but no car was dispatched.

On the fifth and final call, only muted sounds could be heard, perhaps from the sisters, but they were drowned out by barking dogs. When the operator called back, William Dunlop answered but seemed evasive as he tried to convince the operator that everything was okay. Finally, a car was sent, but it was too late. Both sisters were dead.

A police inquest was called, but not much information was forthcoming. Eventually an independent inquest concluded that a mix-up in communications between different 911 operators was primarily to blame. Right. Aboriginal groups responded that if those same calls had come from non-Indigenous people, or from a better part of town, perhaps those women would still be alive. So much for a restraining order. So much for protection. William Dunlop pleaded guilty to second-degree murder and was sentenced to life in prison with no parole eligibility for seventeen years.

It was all taking its toll on me—not only the deaths of those two sisters, but so much sadness and too many terrible stories about other murdered or missing Aboriginal women. It kept me up at night. It bothered me that so many people simply shrugged it off. "That's just the way it is," people said. Yes. But why?

Then there was the pressure of quick turnarounds and looming deadlines. That pressure was becoming relentless. For me, change was in the wind. I struggled to find a way forward. I knew how lucky I was to be a correspondent for *The National*, but I also knew, more than ever, that I did not want to force my family to uproot and start all over somewhere else. As the spring of 2000 moved into summer, my mind was made up. For the first time in my career, I started developing a plan—a strategy, really. Perhaps I could stay in that world *and* embark on an exciting new adventure without having to move anywhere.

I decided to try and pull it off.

CHAPTER 12

Country Canada

I saw it up on the CBC job board: a producer was needed for the network program *Country Canada*. The show was based in the Winnipeg plant, but its staff usually kept to themselves. They had stepped up in a big way, helping with coverage during the 1997 flood of the century, but they were busy enough filling over twenty shows for their network seasonal run.

I had grown up with *Country Canada*. It was a rural affairs show, one that had survived almost since the inception of television in Canada. It had signed on as *Country Calendar* back in 1954. Over the years it'd had several hosts, one of the longest serving being Sandy Cushion, who had been there twenty-five years.

I thought it over and decided to apply. I had almost always self-produced and felt confident that I was up for the job. I knew it could mean not being on camera anymore, but it would also mean we could stay in Winnipeg.

At the time, Jane Chalmers was the head of CBC Winnipeg, and she would have a critical role in the decision-making process. I was a huge fan of Jane and had respected her work for many years. When I'd first gone to Calgary almost twenty years earlier, she had just been named as a new national reporter. Her compassion for the people in her stories always shone through. It was a style built around empathy, and one that I had always tried to emulate.

In the interview I was asked, quite rightly, why I was intent on blowing up my career with the national news service. I explained that consideration for my family and what was best for them had to come first, and that I did not see this move as in any way blowing up my career.

Then they asked me what I thought of the show. I didn't really expect to hear what came out of my mouth. Or maybe I did, but just hadn't known how I would say it. They seemed genuinely interested in what I had to say, so away I went.

I said I'd been a fan of *Country Canada* since I was a kid in Labrador, and the program was a beautiful showcase for all things rural in Canada. But it seemed a little too agricultural. I had learned a long time ago that it was the people, the characters, who made any piece shine, and said I thought the show was already very good at that. The people should be the primary focus, whether they were farmers, or those who fished, or those who raced horses.

The show already had a lot of talented staff, and I said I'd be happy to be one of them, but if I had a choice, I'd prefer to remain on the air. At the time there were two other producers, Marie Thompson in Halifax and Jim MacQuarrie in Edmonton, who fronted their own pieces, so I thought I could be a third. I would self-produce, but I had another little card up my sleeve.

I said I thought the show also needed to be more responsive to events in the news. There was a method to my madness in this reasoning. Through ongoing discussions with folks like Jonathan Whitten and Mark Harrison at *The National*, I had been given assurances that if I got the job, some of the pieces I produced for *Country Canada* would also find a home in the current affairs segment of the flagship show. This way I could maintain my close relationship with the news organization, embark on an exciting new phase of my career and keep the family right where we wanted to be, in Winnipeg.

I also knew there was increasing scrutiny on current affairs programs to get more value from them for the money they cost. I thought, "What the hell, nothing ventured, nothing gained," put it all on the table and thanked them for their time. To be honest, I didn't know what I was going to do if the job didn't work out.

Country Canada

A new direction. A new logo. A new host. Reg Sherren, host of *Country Canada*. I couldn't believe it!

In less than a week they came back to me with a shocker of their own. Was I was interested in becoming the new host of *Country Canada*? They had spoken with Sandy Cushion and he had agreed to retire. I would still self-produce half a dozen or so pieces a season, but I would also help write and "front" the pieces created by other producers.

Over the summer we hammered out the details, and by September of the new millennium I was announced as the new network host of *Country Canada*. It was without a doubt one of the most exciting moments of my entire career. Not only would I host the show, I would have significant editorial input and still get to be in the field producing stuff of my own. It was like a dream come true. You could not wipe the grin from my face.

An exciting new season was about to begin!

Who are all these people? Every host on CBC Television, back in the day. How many can you name? I'm in the front at the extreme left, next to Luba Goy from *Royal Canadian Air Farce*.

SEASON ONE

Things were coming at me from all directions. The season premiere was just weeks away. The show's talented producers needed me, as the host, to do interviews, travel on their shoots and write and voice material. We also had links to shoot: on-camera intros, extros and promos to welcome folks to the show, guide them between stories and say, "See you next time." I decided the sign-off should be, "Thanks for spending some time with us. Until next time, take good care of yourself. We'll see you again soon."

I was also determined to get out of the gate quickly with a piece or two of my own. They needed to be researched and organized to shoot, write and edit. I wanted to find material that *The National* would be interested in, to establish my new relationship with them as quickly as possible. Busy was an understatement—the pace was insane! More than a few times, I wondered whether I could pull it off, but I plowed forward.

THE DAY THE TOWN DROWNED

Vanguard, Saskatchewan, was the location of the first story I would produce myself for *Country Canada*. I had seen the news video from earlier in the summer. The town's residents had almost, quite literally, floated away. On July 3, 2000, they were hit by a perfect storm. One hundred and eighty-seven souls still lived in the town that had stood since 1912. When the skies opened up that afternoon, an ocean of water fell right on their heads, 345 millimetres of rain in just over eight hours. That's fourteen inches, or two-thirds of a billion cubic metres of H_2O—all dumped on little Vanguard. Homes were lost. Crops. Farm equipment. One fellow's combine harvester was tangled in a length of barbed wire from a picket fence that had washed into his field. The railway lines looked like picket fences themselves, pushed up by the force of the water and standing on their sides with their ties still attached.

When I arrived, weeks later, they were still cleaning up. Busloads of Hutterites from nearby colonies showed up, rolled up their sleeves and began to rebuild. They even brought their own lunch, only stopping long enough to gobble it down before getting right back to work. They cleaned the local butcher shop of mud and debris, built new barns and did whatever else needed to be done. They were very shy. The most I could get out of one young woman was a lovely smile for the camera and the words, "For me, it is just a pleasure to help."

It was exactly the sort of story I would have sought out for *The National*, had I stayed, and it was a perfect story to start the new season of *Country Canada*. Drama, strong emotion and that wonderful sense of community, of all hands pulling together.

The National couldn't have been happier. Free material from a fellow their audience was already familiar with. Except I decided it wasn't going to be free. With a little negotiation, I convinced *The National* to pay us $3,000 or $4,000 an item. It was still a bargain for them, and it was money I could then use to shoot longer documentaries, one-hour specials to complement the program's presence on the network. Sitting in the edit suite with the extremely talented editor Christine Ladan Gurniak, watching that first show come together, I knew I had made the right decision.

Reg Sherren, network host of *Country Canada*. Never in my wildest dreams.

That first season was mostly about catching my breath, about learning as much as I possibly could from great producers like Andy Blicq and shooters like Bert Savard. The show already had a reputation for beautiful pictures and wonderful storytelling, and I did not want to screw that up. Besides the full complement of stories for our season, I managed to file over half a dozen documentaries with *The National* and elsewhere on the network, everything from deer mice carrying the deadly hantavirus to a ghost story from New Brunswick to ongoing cod troubles in Newfoundland and, of course, the little town that damn near drowned, Vanguard, Saskatchewan.

SHOWCASING THE COUNTRY

I was determined to make sure *Country Canada* kept living up to its name, covering the entire country. Besides all the great work the other producers were doing, I sought out stories of survival and heroism.

There was the young diver from Digby Neck, Nova Scotia, who was on the bottom of the ocean one morning, harvesting sea urchins, when he looked up to see a porbeagle shark "the size of a station wagon," as he described it, bearing down on him. Again and again it attacked while he burned through precious oxygen. He survived by hitting it repeatedly on the snout with the metal rim of his mesh basket while keeping his back on the bottom and slowly making his way to shore.

There was the elderly fisherman from the Burin Peninsula of Newfoundland, George Buffett. George had bad asthma, one lung and a plate in his leg. But when his crew mate was dragged into the water while they were fishing for scallops, he didn't hesitate, diving over the side into the freezing North Atlantic and saving his young buddy's life.

In British Columbia I found a black market worth millions of dollars, created by stealing four-hundred-year-old cedar trees and using them to make, of all things, wooden shingles for people's houses.

All these stories had great visuals. The show had a history of being primarily agricultural, and my goal was to get people to begin thinking of it as simply rural. That went a long way toward giving it more universal appeal.

We had two weekly time slots. One was in what they called early prime (7:30 Eastern) on Thursdays, and we aired again on Sundays at noon. But *Country Canada* was at the bottom of the pecking order when it came to network promotion. The people in Toronto instead focused on three main programs they wanted to push each week, and we were never one of them. That lack of promotion meant getting *Country Canada* items on *The National* and elsewhere (supper-hour news shows back then were called *Canada Now*) was critical, and the kind of advertising money couldn't buy. And it didn't cost us a cent. In fact, that first season it generated about $25,000 in additional production money. Production money was tight, but as a team we punched way above our weight. An incredible ride was moving into high gear.

WE WILL REMEMBER THEM

One part of the CBC mandate I always took seriously was the responsibility to tell the stories of our history, of how we came to be who we are. A big part of that was our military history, from Canada's involvement in two world wars and numerous other conflicts.

My great-uncle Nelson, my father's namesake, was gravely wounded in the battle of Monchy-le-Preux during World War I and died as a prisoner of war. Pam's mother Phyllis had a narrow escape when an air raid in May 1943 flattened the hotel right next to where she was on duty at the Bournemouth telephone exchange. Phyllis's father, Henry John Burden, received the Military Medal for his bravery during World War I but suffered from the effects of mustard gas for the rest of his life.

My father-in-law, Minor Tennant, was a young radio operator from Saskatchewan when he landed on D-Day. He survived shrapnel wounds from a mortar attack that killed his best friend and worked his way through the liberation of Europe, on the radio every day and always a target, without ever firing a shot. Jack and Phyllis met in Bournemouth, which was a huge staging ground for Canadian soldiers on their way to Europe. The rest, as they say, is history.

I took every chance I got to tell a military story. I had always been greatly impressed with the fine work of Dan Bjarnason, who produced many historical pieces for *The National*, and I was determined to carry on in that fine tradition. It would become a big part of *Country Canada*'s programming, especially around Remembrance Day.

The money I was able to squirrel away by "selling" pieces to *The National* was soon put to good use. My first one-hour special to find its place on the network came about when my father told me of a fellow living in St. John's who I really had to meet.

RETURN TO NAGASAKI: THE JOHN FORD STORY

When John ("Jack") Ford was a young boy of fourteen or fifteen years old, living in Port aux Basques, Newfoundland, he had a dream. "I had a dream that the Japanese were landing on the shores of Port aux Basques. We met them on the beach and tried to stop them. That has lived with me all my days because that premonition, at that age, that was a true story. Some years later I witnessed exactly what I had dreamed. Uncanny, but true."

I first met John Ford in the small bungalow he shared with his wife Margaret in the west end of St. John's. John was in his early eighties when Dad took me down to meet him. He had a big smile and a firm grip, and had been a career man with the Newfoundland Railway.

Indeed, John's dream had come to pass. He did fight in a great war against the Japanese, in World War II. He was captured and managed to survive being a Japanese prisoner of war. More than that, he had lived through the second atomic bomb ever dropped in wartime—in Nagasaki. He had the conviction of a man who knew his own mind, who spoke it freely and who had every reason to carry through his life a great resentment for what had been done to him. And yet, in the end, he didn't.

John still had his wooden identification badge from his internment in a Japanese prisoner-of-war camp. He still had the small metal can from which he'd eaten his allotment of rice when he could get it. And he still possessed an unbelievable memory for the smallest details.

As a member of the British Commonwealth, he signed on to serve with the Royal Air Force in 1940. He was barely twenty-one, a young man working with the railroad, just as keen as any other young man from Port aux Basques to get in on the action. He left his girl Margaret behind, thinking he would be back in a year, not much more. Instead, he was gone for six years, into a war that would change him forever.

After a period in England, he soon found himself travelling farther and farther from home, eventually sailing around the Cape of Good Hope in Africa to the far-off British base in Singapore. The

John's handmade prisoner ID badge from the prisoner-of-war camp in Nagasaki. It, like John, survived a nuclear explosion.

British thought Singapore was a fortress, but John Ford wasn't so sure. It turned out to be anything but. In just seven days, the Japanese brought Singapore to its knees. It surrendered on February 15, 1942. Eighty thousand Allied troops would be taken prisoner, among them John Ford. British prime minister Winston Churchill called it the worst disaster in British military history.

John was marched in the stinking heat, exhausted and starving, to Changi Prison on the far end of the peninsula. I remember the matter-of-fact way he described his predicament: "In my personal opinion, they didn't want prisoners anyway. There were many people who were murdered in small groups. There were people dropping all the time. As they dropped, they didn't move after. There was no ... anybody who dropped, you didn't pick anybody up. If you can't make it, you stay there. The guards would put a bullet in them as we passed on."

After several months, John and his fellow prisoners were all placed in a huge line. As their Japanese captors walked along, deciding who would be sent where, they broke the line right between John and a good friend. His friend would die in a torpedo attack while being shipped to another prison camp.

John's fate was to be thrown into the darkness of a ship's hull for days on end, which eventually landed him in Nagasaki, Japan. "I arrived in Nagasaki at five o'clock in the afternoon, on December 17, 1942." He was interned in Fukuoka Prison Camp #2. For three years, he was systematically beaten, starved and forced to work as a slave labourer in the nearby Mitsubishi naval dockyards. The conditions were brutal and the workdays long and hard. Guards, in general, showed little mercy. Some were just plain cruel. Many prisoners simply couldn't survive the abuse.

One by one John watched his comrades fall, the result of starvation, abuse or disease. "Every man that was sick, your ration was cut because they couldn't go to work and produce anything. Their philosophy was so different from ours." John described volunteering for cremation detail. It was a chance to get outside the camp, to maybe scrounge some morsel of food from a civilian as they passed by. Sometimes his guards would force him to remove the searing hot bones of his dead comrades from the oven with his bare hands. He recalled how they thought it was quite funny.

John was certain he too would die there. But on August 9, 1945, at 11:02 in the morning, everything changed. The most powerful plutonium bomb ever produced, nicknamed "Fat Man," was unleashed over downtown Nagasaki, not seven kilometres from where John Ford was working.

"The day the bomb dropped it was a beautiful day. Beautiful clear sky. Then I heard it. *Boom.* I looked toward Nagasaki and the mushroom was just forming, and there were pieces of shrapnel, pieces of glass, pieces of rock, and people running and screaming in all directions.

"The blast and the intense heat struck me, and I struck the ground. There was rocks and glass and bolts, everything that was movable was flying with the blast and the intense heat. We didn't know what had happened to us. The only thing one could think, under the circumstances ... you thought the world was coming to an end. It was that bad."

John was protected somewhat by large sheets of metal they had been working with in the shipyard. Tens of thousands more were not as lucky. An estimated seventy thousand people were killed. Just as many more were left horribly burned or wounded. Tens of thousands more would die later of radiation sickness.

Now here we were, over sixty years later, sitting on his couch while I held his prisoner ID tag in my hands. His wife Margaret made us tea. It all seemed surreal.

We met several times over the course of the next year and found more connections between us. I got to know a man of great civility and, much to my surprise, learned that Margaret had gone to school in Grade 5 with my grandmother on the tiny island of Ramea. We became good friends, and eventually I discussed with him the possibility of returning to Nagasaki. I wasn't sure how he would react. John Ford owned no Japanese electronics, had never owned a Japanese car. His house contained nothing made in Japan. He said to me, "I have no abiding love for the Japanese people, but I have no particular hate for them either."

When I finally did ask him, he did not hesitate. He agreed to travel with me back to Japan. Remember, he was in his eighties, and he had not set foot in Japan since being liberated. His one caveat was that he needed his family's blessing to return. They gave it, and in the summer of 2002 the trip happened.

John flew from Newfoundland to Vancouver with my cameraman, Keith Whelan, on this historic journey. Keith was another old-school shooter who had cut his photographic teeth in film, a real professional with an amazing eye. He was the perfect person for the job and, being a fellow Newfoundlander, he had a great appreciation for the project and for John. I met them on the West Coast and we headed out over the Pacific.

I had booked John into business class for this part of the flight. I was worried about his long journey and wanted him as comfortable as possible. Keith and I were in economy. As soon as John was settled in, I went up front to make sure he was okay. On the way back I said to the flight attendant, "I hope you don't mind, but I'll be coming up from time to time to check on this gentleman. He is the last Canadian alive to witness the atomic bombing of Nagasaki, and we're filming a documentary with him. He's returning for the first time since being liberated from a prisoner-of-war camp there in 1945."

"That's incredible," came her reply. "As soon as we're in the air, we'll move you up so you can be with him." It was a lovely gesture, and it sure made the ten-hour flight more comfortable—for all of us.

Now, I know many people don't believe in such stuff, but John had this unnerving ability to see things. My first indication was when he told me of his premonition as a young boy. His war with the Japanese had come to pass. But many other unusual things happened on this overseas journey—some might even call them supernatural.

When John first agreed to return to Japan, I realized we would need an interpreter. I sent an email to various media relations offices at post-secondary institutions in Nagasaki. The man who replied was from Winnipeg! Not only that, but his father had worked at the very same CBC station as I did. Brian Burke-Gaffney, who readily agreed to interpret, was a wealth of knowledge and an immense help.

Nagasaki is a small, modern city of fewer than half a million people, located on the island of Kyushu. The houses rise among steep hills that surround its naturally protected harbour. The day we arrived, after settling John in our hotel for a rest, I went for a walk to clear the cobwebs. As I turned the corner just outside the Holiday Inn, I ran smack into a Japanese man walking two large Newfoundland dogs that were bigger than he was.

The next day we were out in the harbour on a small cruise boat that toured us around (it was much cheaper than privately renting a boat and our production was on a tight budget). The idea was to get some video of the harbour itself, the surrounding hills and the still-operating Mitsubishi Dockyard, where John had been forced to work as a slave labourer. The cruise boat company was entertaining some Korean businessmen—who were there, as it turned out, doing business with that very same company. As we floated past the dockyard, John saw a cruise ship under construction. "Has that ship been on fire?" he asked me. I said I didn't think so. It was still being built, and on its side was some black primer paint that could easily be mistaken for smoke damage. I thought no more of it.

That very evening, the head of the Mitsubishi Dockyard came aboard our little vessel to take care of those Korean businessmen. Uncanny. Of all the tour boats for hire in that harbour, what were the chances we would choose the one holding the Mitsubishi Dockyard event? Keith struck up a conversation with the company's head man. When he learned who John was, he insisted on sending a car to pick us up the next day, inviting us to lunch and a tour of the dockyard facilities.

The next morning, at eight o'clock sharp, a Mercedes limousine arrived for us at the hotel. Given that we were in Japan, I found it curious that the car sent to pick us up was made in Germany, another of the Axis powers in World War II.

At the dockyard, we toured their small museum, which was fascinating. Mitsubishi had played a long-standing role in the development of various weapons and warships, especially during World War II, for the Imperial Japanese Navy. In other areas, huge liquefied natural-gas carriers were being assembled. Eventually we happened upon the cruise ship we had seen in the harbour the evening before. It was now tied up alongside the dock. Hundreds of workers were toiling away on every level of the massive structure.

Again, John asked the question, "Has this ship been on fire?" The manager assured John it had not, adding that it was going to be one of the biggest cruise ships ever built. John said nothing. But that would not be the end of it.

Brian, our interpreter, had arranged for us to meet with another survivor from the bombing, who was Japanese. Koichi Wada had been a young streetcar operator on the morning of August 9, 1945. We met in a town square and John immediately stepped back in time, using a traditional Japanese greeting instilled in him sixty years before. Koichi kindly invited us back to his home up in the hills for tea.

We sat, legs folded, around a beautiful low table while his wife poured us each a cup. Then Koichi made what I thought was a startling admission. Because he did not believe in the war and did not want to serve, he had lied to the Japanese military authorities about his vision, saying he was colour blind. As a result, he was assigned as a streetcar operator. That fateful morning he had been upset about a car derailment that forced him to switch lines. As he entered the train depot, he was still grumbling about having to work later. But it turned out that derailment would save his life.

He was in the building, not three kilometres from the hypocentre, when the bomb exploded. He said the building seemed to float for a moment before everything went black. After a time, the air cleared somewhat and he could feel a weight on his back. Eventually some friends pulled him from the rubble and, while grateful for having all his arms and legs, he was horrified to see the destruction around him. "The first thing I said to myself," said Koichi, "was 'Where did the city of Nagasaki go?'"

As he continued with his story, I could see John becoming more emotional. We all were. Koichi said as the days passed, they tried to help the injured but it was very difficult. There were no medical supplies—little more than axle grease to soothe burns.

Koichi then told a story I will never forget. "One thing that really stays in my memory was one of my colleagues. He had been in Nagasaki at the time of the atomic bomb explosion but managed to return to his house. I went to visit him. His mother was there with a candle—there was no electricity at the time. In the light I thought he seemed to have something stuck to his face, and I went to brush it off and then realized it was his eyeball that had come out and was stuck to his cheek. He was on the verge of death, quivering, and when I came close to him, he tried to say something.

And what he said was, 'I didn't do anything wrong.' After that his quivering stopped."

With tears in his eyes Koichi recounted how he helped ignite the funeral pyre to burn his friend's body. We all wept together. The handshake between Koichi and John lasted a long time. I think something changed in that moment, for everyone.

The next day we were to travel to the site of the former prison camp. It used to be on a small island near the main island. Now much more land had been reclaimed and it was hard to find. We got lost. Eventually we found our way to the place, which was now a junior high school. Then we experienced one more uncanny coincidence. A large clock hung outside on the wall. As we pulled up, John noted that the time read 11:02, the exact time the atomic bomb had exploded over Nagasaki.

There was no sign or plaque, no indication of what this place had been, but John could recognize the outline of his former prison immediately. As he wandered around the schoolyard he almost seemed to be in a trance. Flashbacks flooded over him, he told me later. The comrades he had lost overwhelmed his thoughts. Their ghosts still haunted this ground. Nobody spoke in the cab back to the hotel. Not a word.

The next afternoon we were scheduled to meet with the mayor of Nagasaki. It had turned into a media event with gifts and drinks and dozens of cameras. John had brought a gift of his own, a Newfoundland flag. "I would like you to receive this as a token of Newfoundland friendship," he told Mayor Iccho Itoh. The mayor apologized on behalf of the Japanese government for what had been done to John and offered him free medical attention should he ever require it. John replied, "The Canadian government takes care of me and they do it very well, thank you very much."

With tears in his eyes, John continued. "I talk to the schools in my community in St. John's, Newfoundland, and I tell the kids what happened. And I always end up with the phrase, "Let there

The room was full of emotion when John Ford met the mayor of Nagasaki, Iccho Itoh. By the time the meeting was over, there wasn't a dry eye in the place. Brian Burke-Gaffney, front left, served as our interpreter.

be no more Hiroshimas or Nagasakis." You could have heard a pin drop in that room.

It was a very long journey back home to Newfoundland, almost two full days, but in some ways it had taken John almost sixty years to truly get there—to finally be able to leave all that sadness behind.

Some time after we returned to Canada, Margaret told me John had changed again. He slept through the night for the first time she could remember. The next car John bought was a Honda Accord. John's story became a bit of a sensation in Japan and began to be taught in Japanese universities. There is also now a memorial acknowledging the POWs of Nagasaki.

John had been told, given the radiation exposure, he would be lucky to reach the age of forty. As he was proud to say over the years, he had doubled that and then some. With Margaret by his side, he raised a fine family, full of children, grandchildren and great-grandchildren. He lived to be ninety-four. After the funeral Margaret told me she still talked to him every day and would see him soon. She joined him not a month later.

One last thing. The *Sapphire Princess*, that luxury liner under construction at the Mitsubishi Dockyard? Not long after we returned home, it caught fire and burned. A thousand workers on board were lucky to escape with their lives. The ocean liner, worth an estimated forty billion yen, or US$326 million, was all but destroyed.

Someone should have listened to John.

CHAPTER 13

Getting UP to Speed

Country Canada was getting attention. Our ratings were climbing. Even without network promotional support, people were finding us. The strategy of offering material to air on other shows, always with the tag line "You can see more on that story this Sunday (or later tonight) on *Country Canada*," was paying off.

At that time, CBC.CA was still in its relative infancy. I remember being called to Toronto around 2002 for a meeting with top executives from this newest platform for the CBC. They told us things were moving quickly and described how we could use the internet to help get word out about the show. Don't forget, this was still in the days before YouTube, Twitter, Instagram, Facebook and other social media had taken hold.

It was all very exciting. When I returned to Winnipeg, I thought, "Why don't we put the whole show on the internet? Then folks can watch it whenever they want!" I had been in contact with a new company in Calgary that was willing to provide a third-party streaming service for us free of charge. It seemed a great way to build an audience and give taxpayers a more user-friendly experience. Keep in mind, this was over fifteen years ago, long before Netflix or Crave TV or Gem (CBC's streaming service).

I contacted Toronto and suggested a plan. The response was somewhat less than enthusiastic. They replied (I'm paraphrasing here): "It's people like you who don't know what they are talking about, that are ruining CBC.CA. People do *not* want to watch TV on the internet. People want alphanumeric [few pictures or video]. Please stop messing around with things you don't know anything about."

Well. Nice.

So I replied: "Thanks for that. You know, back in the sixties when they invented colour television, they didn't keep broadcasting in black and white because nobody had a colour TV. They started broadcasting in colour as quickly as they could because they knew in five minutes *everybody* would have a colour TV. You can lead or you can follow, it's up to you."

The next idea in Reg's grand design to get *Country Canada* to viewers came to me on an Air Canada flight. The airline had just begun introducing personal viewing screens on the back of every seat. I thought, "*Country Canada* on Air Canada. What a perfect fit. It's a captive audience, and what a great way to get new eyeballs to watch the show!" I contacted the company that bought programming for Air Canada and, after some negotiation, had all but signed a deal.

They were willing to pay US$5,000 an episode for the show. At the time our production budget per show, excluding salaries, was only about $4,800 Canadian. This was looking like a great deal. Then I was told I had to get in contact with international sales in Toronto as we were "not authorized" to do the deal ourselves.

I received another note tearing a strip off me and asking who the hell did I think I was, going off and negotiating such a thing by myself. I apologized for my ignorance and explained that I hadn't meant to step on anyone's toes. I gave them all the contact information and details on what that company was willing to do. I handed the whole file over to them. It disappeared. Not a word for months. Emails I sent were not answered.

Undeterred, I moved to Plan B. Even I could realize that in a universe with viewer choice expanding every day, anything that got us attention could only be good. I went to my bosses in Toronto and said, "Okay, international sales won't sell the program to Air Canada, so let's give it to them. The taxpayers have already paid for it, so why shouldn't they be able to watch while flying from Calgary to Winnipeg—or wherever. It's the kind of free advertising money can't buy!"

Well, although nobody could ever exactly explain why, they couldn't do that either. Not one episode of *Country Canada* ever appeared on an Air Canada flight, but it wasn't because I hadn't tried. Lord knows I had.

GRAIN AND POT

The show carried on. In the summer I travelled to England to meet a charming young family named the Walkers who had a mixed cattle operation northwest of London near Bridgenorth. After the huge mad cow disease scare in Britain, farming, and especially raising cattle, had become a bureaucratic nightmare. The Walkers had decided that a better future for them and their young boys lay on this side of the pond, in Manitoba.

We followed their move to Canada as they set up shop on a huge grain farm just northeast of Brandon. Their land in Britain was so valuable that they were able to pay cash for almost everything they needed for their new made-in-Canada farming operation.

The first season flew by and already we were deep in planning for the next one. I had an idea about doing something on Canada's real cash crop, marijuana.

As a national reporter I had covered one of the largest pot busts in Canadian history, just outside of Winnipeg. These guys were sophisticated. They had set up in a massive barn out in the country. They ran hydro wires out to the power line and spliced them right into the main line, cutting a wedge out of the hydro pole so nobody would notice their cable running up it. In this way they also bypassed the power meter, leaving no evidence of spiked power consumption to alert authorities.

They had closed-circuit TV. White lab coats hung neatly just inside the door. Huge mixing bins full of hydroponic chemicals and plants, three floors of them, were all in various stages of production. There were huge bins of buds—the potent tips of the plants—going through various drying stages. Massive fans exhausted pungent air out the side of the building. Now that I think about it, today these fellows would be considered just another legitimate business oper-ation. Back then, they very much were not.

A neighbour had reported suspicious activity. I rode along with the RCMP. A dozen cruisers busted into the farmyard. As we drove in with lights flashing, I yelled, "There's a guy coming across the field to your right." The RCMP spokesperson said, "Well spotted!"

The guy I'd spotted was the only fellow caught in the entire multi-million-dollar operation. The RCMP didn't even get close to the real operators, who were long gone. Just one fellow looking after the place for the weekend, and a sign on the fridge reminding him to WATER THE PLANTS.

Not long after that, I was contacted by a fellow living in Northern Ontario, just outside of Thunder Bay, who was an organic pot farmer of the most unusual variety. Doug MacKay did not mind being identified. He was what you might call a mari-juana advocate. He strongly believed in the medicinal value of pot, especially for those battling various illnesses, and he felt the criminalization of those folks who liked to partake of a little bud was nothing short of ridiculous. You might say Doug was a man ahead of his time.

He agreed to let me follow him through his entire crop year, just as *Country Canada* did with many other farmers, and he allowed me to identify him. I knew the story would be television gold. It would be quite the summer. Doug was living off the grid in a large teepee he had constructed with a friend of his. He always grew his crop on Crown land, deep in the bush.

His area of choice was a bog. He lugged in garbage bags of soil and fertilizer, humping them through the bush and polka-dotting the landscape with them. He had easy access to the water from the bog, and the garbage bags kept his plants from getting too wet. He tended to them faithfully, like any good farmer—with one possible exception. Doug liked to do all of this work naked. It was his thing, being a back-to-nature sort of guy.

And, of course, the beauty of growing his crop on Crown land was that if anybody in authority came across it, or him, he could simply claim he was enjoying a day picking berries in the nude and knew nothing about the cash crop in the bog.

Much of his crop went to people suffering from various ailments. He took us to a small cabin in the woods where we met some of them, folks battling cancer or multiple sclerosis. Everyone was smoking *a lot*—well, except us. But by the time we were finished, we realized we needed a little break ourselves. We weren't just high from the shoot.

We decided to serialize the stories as his season progressed. The series also aired on *The National*, eventually attracting the attention of the Thunder Bay Police Department. One day, two officers appeared at our offices in Winnipeg, demanding all of our videotape. That wasn't going to happen. We informed them we would fight them every step of the way before handing anything over and they could expect a protracted and expensive legal battle. They went away.

Meanwhile, Doug was enjoying a bit of celebrity. His story had attracted the attention of like-minded individuals, including folks on the internet who ran a website called Pot TV. *Country Canada* now had the dubious distinction of producing the most popular video on their website. We hadn't given it to them; they'd simply taped it off TV and put it up on their website. We couldn't do a thing about it—not without an expensive legal challenge anyway.

Besides like-minded individuals, Doug was also getting attention from the authorities, who probably thought he was thumbing his nose at them. He was charged with various drug offences—not related to his appearance on *Country Canada*—and faced many legal battles. Not that it slowed him down much. He also ran for mayor of Thunder Bay—twice. He wasn't successful but his story was number one on Pot TV for many, many years—and you can still find it on their website!

THE TIMES, THEY ARE … WELL, YOU KNOW

The show was hitting its stride. Besides fabulous producers like Andy Blicq and Gary Hunter, and satellite contributors Jim MacQuarrie in Edmonton and Marie Thompson in Halifax, executive producer Nigel Simms was testing out new people. Some worked out. Some didn't.

The show's ratings were more than respectable given the time slots and lack of network promotion. For a time we managed to get a few commercial slots to promote the program, but they soon disappeared. The network decided to revert to promoting just a few shows (at least that was their explanation). I never understood why, when we had two English television stations and two English radio stations, we couldn't get thirty seconds to promote one of CBC's own shows. It didn't make any sense to me.

On the upside, Winnipeg executive producer Cecil Rosner had persuaded Toronto to embark on an ambitious and exciting new network program based in Winnipeg. Called *Disclosure*, it was intended to offer CBC viewers an alternative approach to investigative current affairs. More irreverent than *The Fifth Estate*, faster paced and interspersed with some sharply focused humour, it came out of the gate in 2001. Cecil was one of the sharpest investigative minds inside the CBC, and hopes were high. At the last minute, though, the network decided to pull some of the control over the program back to Toronto. Almost before *Disclosure* started, storm clouds appeared on the horizon. With the addition of *Disclosure*, three network programs now originated in Winnipeg.

For *Country Canada*, I continued to resort to getting shorter versions of our stories placed on local supper-hour shows or, when possible, on *The National*. But both of our time slots were problematic. The early prime slot on Thursdays at 7:30 was set up so that not all stations that were part of the network were obligated to run the network's programming in that time slot. Affiliate stations could run their own programming, which took potential viewers away from us.

Sundays at Noon was a repeat of the show from Thursday. It aired right across the network, but often, just as the show was picking up momentum in a new season, it was pre-empted, usually in the West, because of live events like football, hockey or curling.

Even so, for a show that got kicked around a bit, it managed on a good week to get close to six hundred thousand combined viewers. Not bad considering it was probably one of the CBC's most cost-effective programs to produce. But that too was starting to change.

The National's budget was getting tighter. The show was still happy to take items from us, but the amount of discretionary money available to pay for them was shrinking. The CBC had also decided to change the way it accounted for costs. It used to be that while our camera crew was with another producer somewhere in the country, I could fly off to Vancouver or Halifax and shoot a piece there using a camera from the local news pool. In exchange we would give them the finished piece shot in their region, which they could air on their supper-hour show. This arrangement was good value for them (free) and it was cost-effective for us. It also gave other talented shooters, and there were many of them, the opportunity to work with a network show.

But the bean counters in Toronto put an end to that. They decreed that if you used a local camera person you had to pay the same rate as if you had hired a freelancer, regardless of the location. Immediately two things happened. First, our production costs took a big jump. Second, local camera people looking for network opportunities didn't get them—not from *Country Canada* anyway. It was a sad and, to me, somewhat senseless development. Our season got cut. Fewer shows. I should have realized then that the CBC had a much bigger plan—to get out of producing current affairs in-house—but, as they say, hindsight is 20/20.

MURDER ON THE PRAIRIES

If you told most people that tens of thousands of German prisoners were held across Canada during World War II, they would tell you, "You're nuts!" I knew nothing about it myself until I saw a brief story from back in the '80s about a group of Germans who had returned to their old camp in Alberta to reminisce. In my drive to produce more historical work I started a file, and the research led me to a fascinating tale—and to murder.

It all happened in Medicine Hat, Alberta, on what is today that community's rodeo grounds. Over twelve thousand captured German troops were held there for years. The camp was bigger than the town itself. They were guarded by what was known as the Veteran Guard, a group composed of World War I vets too old to serve overseas. The guards had no machine guns, just rifles, and the joke was that guards often ate with prisoners because the latter had better food. German prisoners could play in the orchestra, act in a theatre group or play on sports teams. They had training courses, even university programs, offering the opportunity to get a degree. They had the best of medical care. They even had access to beer to help celebrate various occasions. You would have thought their lives were fairly content thousands of kilometres and an ocean away from the fighting.

But the Nazi regime was never far away. Unknown to the guards, senior SS officers were mixed in with the regular German army prisoner population, and they had control of the inner workings of the camp. As time marched on and Germany's grip on Europe loosened, those Nazi officers inside the Medicine Hat camp became increasingly determined to suppress any talk against the fatherland. At first those accused of being unfaithful were beaten by the Nazis in the camp, and later they were murdered. It would end with the second-largest mass hanging in Canadian history.

I was able to get some money from CBC Newsworld on the promise of delivering a one-hour documentary. With a little more from *The National*, and the money we would have spent producing two programs for *Country Canada*, I was in business. As I recall, it was a budget of less than $15,000 to make an hour of network television. Today, that same hour would cost between $500,000 and over $1 million. But more on that later.

During my research I came across a book by David J. Carter entitled *POW, Behind Canadian Barbed Wire*. David turned out to be a wealth of information and played a critical role in my efforts to tell the story of what happened inside that camp.

I can't rightly remember how I found Max Weidauer. It may have been through David. A tall, handsome fellow, Max was living in Southern Ontario—and he had one hell of a story to tell.

Max had fought with German general Erwin Rommel in Africa on the "other side" of the war. He considered himself a faithful and good soldier, and received the Iron Cross and other decorations for bravery. Even so, he was relieved when he was captured in the African desert and happy to be sent to Canada, a place he had read about before. He didn't expect, however, that his life would be threatened by his own kind. It took a little persuasion, but he agreed to participate in my documentary. I would call it "Murder Behind the Wire."

In Calgary, I found the RCMP officer who was sent in among the thousands in that camp to investigate. Bill Westgate, a big, jovial fellow, had kept his own secret RCMP files about the case. Bill told me he would never forget walking into that camp and down the rows of bunkhouses with German soldiers all lined up in front, clicking their heels and giving the Nazi salute as he passed. He had even kept the photos of the fellow he found with a rope around his neck, the one he'd had to cut down that day.

Max Weidauer remembered how the Nazi officers had murdered two of his friends and threatened to kill him. Fearing for his life, he escaped and hid on a farm. Eventually, through spies inside the camps, Canadian authorities were able to gather enough information for a trial. In all, seven men were charged with the two murders, but none of them were the Nazi leaders who had ordered the killings. Those Nazis wound up giving evidence against their own men. In the end they were all hanged. It was the second-largest mass hanging in Canadian history (the largest took place in 1885 after the North-West Rebellion in Battleford, Saskatchewan). Max was eventually recaptured and sent to another camp.

Eventually the remains of all those who died were moved to the German prisoner-of-war cemetery in Kitchener, Ontario. Those convicted and hanged were placed side by side with those they had murdered. I took Max there so he could pay his respects.

Some months after the story aired, Max passed away. His son called to tell me and to say thank you. His whole life, he said, his family had harboured a deep shame around their German heritage, a great weight they all carried, especially his father. But he said giving Max the opportunity to tell his story, as a man, a German soldier serving his country, helped him to resolve feelings that had haunted him for decades. That gave them all some comfort in Max's last days. I was happy to hear it, and grateful his son had taken the time to call.

I knew some would think, "Why should we give a damn about what happened to German prisoners?" In fact, I received several letters saying exactly that, and criticizing me for telling any German soldier's story on Canadian television. We would have to agree to disagree. The story of the POWs was a fascinating and important piece of Canadian history and I felt duty bound to tell it. Thousands of those former German soldiers went on to become Canadian citizens, just like Max, and made huge contributions to this country. Their story is our story.

IT'S NOT A LIVING ANYMORE

That same fall of 2003, another in-house network production at CBC Winnipeg got the axe. *It's a Living*, hosted by Peter Jordan, was no more. The show had been ahead of its time in the world of reality television. Peter was a funny, talented guy, and he and the show had won a pile of well-deserved awards. But it wasn't enough. The thinking in Toronto was changing, certainly about the willingness to produce shows "inside" the CBC—no doubt about it.

The next season, it was *Disclosure*'s turn. As good as it was, and it was very good, it never seemed to catch its stride or find its audience. I remain convinced that splitting leadership between Winnipeg and Toronto played a big part in that, but the CBC's increasing unwillingness to produce its own products also probably played a role.

Country Canada was the last network show left standing in Winnipeg. It left local CBC management scrambling to absorb the damage. There were lots of hard feelings. And *Country Canada* was not immune. By moving our two satellite positions in Edmonton and Halifax back to Winnipeg, the show's leadership was able to save two positions in Winnipeg. Unfortunately, that didn't help some others.

Country Canada itself also got a change in leadership. Executive producer Nigel Simms and producers Marie Thompson and Jim MacQuarrie, all talented people who had been with the show since before I arrived, were moved into other positions in Edmonton, Regina and Halifax. The program had survived, but they took away our Thursday-evening time slot and cut the number of shows we would produce. That meant just one airing of the show on Sundays at noon. It also meant the writing was on the wall.

Toronto now had a new head of English television. He made it clear that he didn't give a damn about mandate—all he really cared about was ratings. If the ratings didn't live up to his expectations, the show did not survive. To him it was as simple as that. It meant the start of a new era at the CBC, one that was driven almost entirely by the search for eyeballs. In some ways, I think it was the beginning of the CBC losing its way.

In fairness, the reality was that television ratings had already begun to erode, and there were reasons for that. Some of it was driven by an increasingly wider selection of programming available to viewers through their cable systems. That new kid on the block called the internet was also getting attention from increasing numbers of people. Streaming video technology was improving rapidly. The CBC's new leader would have to quickly learn to adjust his belief that any program that couldn't attract a million viewers (a big number by Canadian standards) wasn't worth keeping. Almost no shows on CBC were achieving ratings like that. In some ways, the fact that *Country Canada* wasn't really on the radar for programmers probably helped it survive a little longer. But make no mistake about it. We were now fighting for our television lives.

CHAPTER 14

Upping Our Game

It was 2004 and the game was changing—and fast. *Country Canada* decided to change too. Instead of doing two or three shorter stories in the half-hour, we would dedicate the entire show to just one subject, one that usually involved an adventure or a journey. It meant searching even harder to find material that could sustain a full half-hour.

FLYING HIGH

One of the good things, if I can put it that way, around the misery of the other shows in Winnipeg being cancelled was that it left two talented producers available to work with *Country Canada*. One of them was Terry Stapleton, a consummate, detail-oriented professional who had a sharp eye when it came to making pictures work.

But our first time out of the gate with one of the new guys was with Ryszard Hunka. Ryszard always went about his craft in a quiet, almost gentle way. But make no mistake about it, he was always thinking in pictures and developing his keen ability to sew them together.

I had been looking, as I always was, for another great Remembrance Day story to tell, and I found it with the Guinea Pigs. The Guinea Pig Club was a group of airmen from World War II who had been badly burned in air crashes, many of them during the Battle of Britain. Beginning in 1941, they were all treated together at the Queen Victoria Hospital in East Grinstead, Sussex, England. These individuals were the guinea pigs in experimental plastic surgery techniques as medical experts attempted to rebuild them, body and soul.

What did this have to do with Canada? Well, Canada had its own chapter of the Guinea Pigs, a support group that had survived over sixty years. Some were fighter pilots, a few were from the Army or Navy, but most belonged to the Allied Forces Bomber Command. One of them was a gentleman named Hank Ernst. I found Hank living in Calgary, Alberta. Affable, funny, kind and humble, he had carried the weight of his war experiences quietly, almost privately, over the years.

He told me about his bombing run as part of the crew in a Vickers Wellington bomber, assigned to attack a German U-boat basin on the French coast in January of 1943. He was just twenty-two. They headed out over the English Channel with a massive eighteen-hundred-kilogram bomb designed to bust through thick concrete hanging beneath their aircraft. Unknown to them, it had become frozen in place. When they tried to release it, it didn't budge. Fuel was becoming an issue. It was also getting dark, so they decided to fly in over the English countryside, set the plane on a course back over the channel, and jump.

As they approached Plymouth on England's southwest coast, they came under attack by British anti-aircraft gunners who did not recognize who they were. Just as they managed to escape that gun-fire and were preparing to jump from the plane, the bomb released, dropping harmlessly in the English countryside.

With little fuel left, the pilot had one last chance to head for the airfield at Exeter. They didn't make it. Hank has no real memory of the crash itself. He was told he was found underneath the starboard engine, on fire and screaming for help. He woke up days later in the hospital in East Grinstead, badly burned and injured, only to eventually learn his crew mates were dead.

Hank was a leading member of the Canadian arm of the Guinea Pig Club. But the Canadian arm was now coming to an end. The club was having its final gathering in mere weeks in Victoria, British Columbia. We would be there.

After many hours on the telephone, it was the first time Hank and I met face to face. Many of the old gang had come

Hank Ernst standing proudly in uniform before leaving Nova Scotia to head overseas.

to say their goodbyes and to reminisce together one last time. One gentleman in his eighties told me that in recent months he had developed a severe fear of flying, to the point where he'd driven to the reunion rather than get on another airplane. This, after getting past his terrible fiery crash in the war and flying on vacations and for work all his adult life. Another man told me he'd had a flashback the previous evening about his crash. His plane was on fire, and in his dream he went through the emotional turmoil of trying to get his parachute harness off so he could get out. He had woken up still trying to wrestle with it.

We took a tour of the local war museum. Hank and I came across the Air Force's *Book of Remembrance*, which held eighteen thousand names of those who never came home. Hank's buddies were in that book, along with the details about the crash of DF 626. Hank could barely speak. His entire life he had wanted to visit the site where they crashed, but no known records existed of the precise location.

Only in that moment did the realization hit me. I asked Hank, "If I can find your crash site, would you go there with me?" I had never discussed this with Hank before, and I really didn't have a clue how I would go about finding it, but I thought I had to try. With tears in his eyes, he said, "I would be honoured to go back and pay my respects." I knew we now had a sixty-year-old mystery to solve and an incredible journey was about to begin.

After the crash, it took many months for Hank to recover physically. Decades later, he still struggled with the emotional impact of losing his buddies and of never getting to say goodbye. He told me that at times he was racked with guilt, asking, "Why me? Why did I survive when they did not?" It was a weight he could share with his fellow Canadian Guinea Pigs when they met on occasion to share old war stories and to remember. It was not, however, something he had shared with his family, even over sixty years later.

I knew I would need some serious help. I tapped my usual sources for funding—one problem solved. The bigger issue was expertise. I contacted Dr. Emily Mayhew, a military medical historian overseas who had written a book about the British Guinea Pigs, and solicited her assistance. Her knowledge of the British war archives would prove invaluable. I also placed a request for information in the local daily newspaper in Exeter, the community near the crash site. Perhaps someone in the area would remember.

When I contacted the hospital in East Grinstead, we were invited to come and tour the facility. By coincidence, the British Guinea Pigs were also having a reunion, and Hank would see some fellow patients he hadn't laid eyes on in decades.

The one big problem left was finding the crash site. War records were sketchy. Most wrecks were removed and recycled during the war effort, leaving almost no trace of them in the countryside. One other smaller issue was Hank's family. They were understandably concerned. After fifty-four years of marriage, Hank's dear wife Mary Rose had passed some years earlier, and the kids were worried that Hank, now in his eighties, was also in decline.

We went to a big family dinner—kids, grandchildren and great-grandchildren all jumbled together—to sort through it all. They wanted to get a closer look at this journalist who planned to drag their father off to England. I shouldn't have been surprised, but his children knew very little about what happened to their father during the war. It was something Hank never spoke about. After their mother passed away, concern grew as they noticed that he seemed depressed and a little lost.

Now suddenly at the age of eighty-three he was heading off to England with this television fellow they didn't know from a hole in the ground. They were very gracious, but Hank's daughter Rosemary summed it up well: "The whole family is a little bit worried because he's going over to somewhere where he went through this horrific thing, and he never talked about it with us, so it opens a door, and Mom's not there anymore to kind of buffer that."

When I interviewed Hank's son Bruce about what his father had been through and what he had achieved, his emotion bubbled to the surface. Bruce would accompany us overseas to offer support for his dad. We were happy to have him along.

After a long flight from Calgary to London, we met Emily Mayhew at the British War Museum. The museum kindly allowed us to tape there. Its records revealed precious little solid information about the crash site, but Dr. Mayhew was able to lay one of Hank's abiding concerns to rest—the official cause of the crash. It had always been deemed a pilot error, and she confirmed that was just a standard phrase the Air Force used in the absence of a definitive cause. The vague designation had always bothered Hank. Dr. Mayhew now said that, in her opinion, the pilot was nothing short of the hero in getting them as far as he did, given the situation they had found themselves in.

Later, during a visit to the Brooklands Museum, we were allowed to crawl around inside a real Wellington bomber and gain an appreciation for how little protection you had sitting inside that glorified tin can. But so far, we had nothing solid to go on regarding the crash site. Even so, I refused to believe things would not work out.

And, as fate would have it, mere hours later I received some good news. Two gentlemen had come forward as a result of our newspaper inquiries. They were amateur historians and weekend World War II addicts. They spent practically every free moment in the British countryside around Exeter, searching for old crash sites. Convinced they could locate the site, they wanted to make us their project, and I can't tell you how relieved I was to have them on board. Call it good karma. Up to that point I had been going on faith and precious little else. Now I dared to let myself think we might actually pull this off.

East Grinstead was a sturdy little British hamlet of predominantly brick construction, with its tangle of downtown shops dominated by the hospital on the hill. It became known as the town that never stared. It would have been understandable if they had. These fly men, heroes every one, had survived with some of the most horrific of burn injuries. Many of them had lost lips, eyelashes, noses and ears to the fury of fuel-fed fires.

But led by plastic surgeon Sir Archibald McIndoe, a New Zealander, the team at Grinstead had been determined to put these young men back together, body and soul. One of the plastic surgeons was a Canadian, Dr. Ross Tilley. Together the surgeons developed new reconstructive surgery techniques, some of which are still in use today.

The men were understandably quite a sight, but Dr. McIndoe and his team would not allow any dwelling on that. The beer flowed freely, on the wards and in the local pub, where they mixed right in with the townsfolk, singing songs and trying to rebuild their spirits. The group became known as the Guinea Pigs, and they were soon, sadly, over six hundred strong.

Hank was one of them. His fire injuries were painful but not extensive, certainly not as severe as some others—he had second-degree burns to his hands and face. But his other injuries were much worse—a broken nose, lacerations to his face and scalp, a dislocated hip, a broken heel and a broken neck.

Hank and his son, Bruce, visiting the Canadian wing of the burn unit at Queen Victoria Hospital in East Grinstead, England.

At the reunion, the spirit and camaraderie were something to behold, with jokes that had been shared for decades and friendships seared in common injury and recovery. These were truly remarkable men. In Exeter we toured the airfield they never reached. The air traffic controller dug out an old photo of the layout of the runways.

He also knew about some lights the military used to put up in a place called Woodbury Common. They were fake landing lights used to fool the Germans. This was important information. Hank remembered seeing some lights that looked like the approach to a runway just before his plane crashed.

Days passed. We were scheduled to return in seventy-two hours but still had not found the crash site. Hank grew increasingly emotional. He was despondent but tried not to let it show. To pass time, we drove into the community of Exeter. Hank had never walked through its streets. In a small side lane, we ran into a group of rambunctious school kids. Hank was entertaining them and giving them all little Canadian flag pins when my phone rang.

It was Graham Lewis, one of the amateur historians and crash site searchers. He was pretty much certain he had found Hank's crash site. He and his buddy had figured out the confusion in the crash co-ordinates. I could have kissed him. When we met that evening, Hank was like a kid on Christmas morning. His emotions were all at the surface—elation one minute, tears the next. Graham had turned up discrepancies in the mapping and sorted them out. When he hiked in, he found some scrap using his metal detector that could only have come from a Wellington bomber.

The next day we were all nervous, anxious to get there. We learned that the crash site was close to the fake lights put up in Woodbury Common. It was just a short drive down a country road, but it had taken Hank over sixty years to get back. As we walked through the woods to the spot, you could almost feel the weight of the history the place held. It was powerful stuff, as Hank walked the ground where his buddies had lost their lives and he damn near had himself.

Graham Lewis pulled out his metal detector and found more pieces of the plane. Hank placed a Canadian flag at the crash site and smaller flags on the graves of his comrades, who were buried in a cemetery not far away. That night we raised a toast of the very finest single-malt Scotch to Hank's comrades, to their heroism and to their memory.

The magic of producer Ryszard Hunka's touch, the beauty of Bert Savard's pictures and the stellar editing skills of Gil Tetreault made for one hell of a story. I flew out to Calgary and arranged a private advance screening of the piece at the Glenbow Museum. It was packed with Hank's relatives and his buddies from the Royal Canadian Legion, Gyro International and the Air Canada Pionairs. That's right. After everything that happened to him, Hank had returned from the war and went to work for Trans Canada Airlines, later Air Canada. There wasn't a dry eye in the house.

A few weeks after we returned, a handwritten letter arrived from his daughter Rosemary:

Dear Reg, Bert and Richard [Ryszard],
I want to extend to you, and all your team, my sincere congratulations on the exceptional piece of work "Final Flight" turned out to be. It is an inspiring and touching tribute not just to Dad, but to the countless others in this world who have endured the ravages of war. The quest portrayed was personal, the theme universal.

More than anything else though, I want to extend to you, and all your team, my and our family's heartfelt gratitude. It is rare for a family to receive such a precious gift in the waning years of their Father's life. We have been allowed a glimpse into the closed world of Dad's private war, and had it brought to light (and screen) for us. Moreover, this process has brought so much into Dad's life ... new connections, re-connections, excitement and focus. It has been a reawakening of sorts for him at a time when he so needed it. There have been so many extraordinary "coincidences" associated with this for Dad, and the family. One of the most powerful for us revolved around your most appreciated and thoughtful dedication to Mom. We were all so touched that you had included this (to us) vital component. And when "Final Flight" aired, Dr. Eric Wasylenko, who was Mom's palliative care physician and so much more to her, and to all of us, happened to walk into his hotel room in Winnipeg, and saw on TV only that very last portion "dedicated to the memory of Mary Ernst." He phoned us immediately as we were, once again, all gathered in the house that held so much of Mom and Dad.

I can't imagine any of the work (or working with the Ernsts!) was easy, but I do want you to know how much this work has touched our lives, and those who've seen it. You are all magicians, and we thank you so much, one and all.

Rosemary

PS: Forgot to mention how grateful we all are for the special care afforded Dad while away. He was in such good, kind hands. Thank you.

My relationship with Hank continued until the day he died in September 2016. Hank was a real gentleman and, I like to think, a true friend. I miss him. I am still in contact with his son Bruce, who's truly his father's son, and you can bet we will raise a toast to remember Hank and his buddies the next time our paths cross.

COWS AND THEME PARKS

We had lots of great pieces that season. One, produced by Timothy Sawa, an up-and-coming producer at the time, was called "Shoot, Shovel and Shut Up." It was the truth about how the American cattle industry and the government were covering up suspected cases of BSE, a.k.a. mad cow disease. Rather than testing a suspected sick animal, they would grab a rifle and a shovel and get rid of it. This was happening at the same time the Americans were costing our

Canadian industry millions of dollars, claiming *we* were the ones with the problem.

Our journey led us to a confrontation with Ann Veneman, at the time the US Secretary of Agriculture, on the ranch of one of her supporters in California. She didn't see us coming. Timothy had somehow managed to secure an invitation to a barbecue, and poor Ann just had the misfortune of being there. There were several awkward moments, all on camera, where Ann had to squirm her way through some pointed questions until her PR guy jumped in and said, "That will be the last question from the Canadian reporter." It all made for great television.

With producer Gary Hunter and cameraman extraordinaire Don Scott, we also followed Bonnie Peigan, a forty-two-year-old single mom and proud member of the Nakota First Nation, to Sweden where she worked in a Wild West theme park. It was surreal. There in the heart of Sweden was a place where people from all over Europe, tens of thousands of them, dressed up in cowboy and Indian outfits, a desire apparently born out of some romantic notion acquired from John Wayne movies and Louis L'Amour paperbacks.

Bonnie worked on a place called Indian Island, in the middle of the theme park, where she performed traditional Native dances while little blond-haired children, dressed as cowboys, shot at her with pop guns. Even so, she insisted her culture received more respect there than she had ever found back in Canada. Go figure.

WE'RE ALIVE!

You had to wonder: with so many dead programs lying all around us, were we next? We must have done something right, or maybe Toronto's attention was elsewhere, but the spring came, and then the summer, with no announcements other than the fall schedule—and we were on it!

For *Country Canada*, 2005 would prove every bit as strong as the previous year. Producer Andy Blicq had been developing an idea for a special series called *Legacy* that would find a home on *Country Canada* and also be used as a stand-alone network presentation. It was our first dabble into "reality TV."

I have always found that to be an interesting term. Usually very little about reality television is actually "real"; it is often highly scripted and staged. But not in this case. We all knew the face of rural Canada was changing dramatically. Towns were struggling to survive. Some were succeeding, some were in the middle of turmoil and many others were disappearing.

Andy had the brilliant idea to catalogue these changes in a unique way. He commissioned three of the finest still photographers in the country and sent each into a specific community to chronicle what they saw. They could each choose their style and format, but they would have only a limited amount of time to get those shots.

Ottawa photographer David Trattles was sent to the fishing community of Fogo Island, Newfoundland, Nance Ackerman went to the logging town of Hazelton, British Columbia, and Benoit Aquin from Quebec was assigned to the farming community of Theodore, Saskatchewan.

It would all culminate in a judging session where the one who best reflected the changing face of rural Canada would win. The pictures were so incredible, and so different, that it was impossible to judge. We did—that's what television does—but as far as I was concerned, they were all fabulous. The project was a huge undertaking for Andy, and a real success. I was just happy to be along for the ride.

I produced a piece of my own for 2005 about the instability in the design of middle-distance fishing boats in Atlantic Canada. There was real concern those designs were killing people. Fishermen were spending millions of dollars to build boats that met federal government regulations, but in certain conditions they could roll bottom-up, and they had. It was my first piece on the topic. Sadly, it would not be my last.

LLOYD AND OLGA: A LOVE STORY

When you are young, you don't think you can die. You certainly don't spend any time thinking about the prospect—at least I know I never did. But it was something I thought about a lot on the long flight to Amsterdam. I had been asked by the network to find a series of stories around the sixtieth anniversary of the end of World War II and around the liberation of the Netherlands.

The Dutch had proclaimed neutrality heading into World War II, but that did not stop Hitler from invading. Life was difficult in the occupied kingdom. During the last occupied winter, for many it meant starvation and death. Then, kilometre by kilometre, Canadians drove the Germans out of the north and west, finally allowing food and water to reach a desperate nation.

So as I sat on that airplane, I thought about how little I had been touched by death in my life, how I had never considered, for even a moment, how some of the crazy things I'd done as a kid could have meant my end. I thought about how little sacrifice I had endured in my life. The same could be said of my entire generation.

Now here I was, on my way to tell stories about the liberation. With me again was producer-director Ryszard Hunka, that gentle soul with the incredible ability to put together moving images, as well as Ray Bourier, a tremendous talent behind the lens. Ray was old school—he had begun his career in film and made every picture a work of art.

If you ever want to feel proud to be Canadian, take a trip to the Netherlands. In the province of Zeeland, built entirely on ground reclaimed from the ocean, I went to meet a fellow who had taken it upon himself to start a museum of all the Canadian war artifacts left behind after the Battle of the Scheldt. It took five weeks to clear the estuary of German defenders and cost the Allies almost thirteen thousand lives, over half of them Canadian. It was brutal combat. The Germans reflooded much of the ground as they retreated, leaving mines and bombs in their wake.

For sixty years, from the time he was a young boy, this gentleman gathered every piece of Canadian war memorabilia he could find as a tribute to his Canadian liberators, his heroes. His museum was laid out with great care and attention in a huge room above his garage. We spent several hours videotaping as he described where each uniform, each bayonet, each gas mask had been found.

When we stepped back into the sunlight, close to two dozen people were waiting for us. Word had spread around the village about a Canadian TV crew. As we emerged, they began to applaud and cheer, to welcome us and say thank you—again, sixty years later. Never had I been prouder to be Canadian.

Later, at a cemetery near the city of Groningen, we happened upon a ceremony by an honorary regiment of the Calgary Highlanders. The local Dutch had formed a regiment to honour the Highlanders killed in the brutal battle for Groningen. Forty Calgary Highlanders had died and were lying in the graves around us.

The day was cold. As the group prepared to march in and lay wreaths on the tombstones, a bitter rain was falling. I watched a young Dutch girl fall into line at the end of the procession, carrying a big bunch of flowers. After the service, I asked her why she was there. She explained that her friend had planned to lay the flowers as part of the service, but her grandfather had died that very morning. Her friend asked if she could take her place. "For me," the girl said, "it is an honour to do this." I thought, "How many young people in Canada even know what honour is, let alone how to act on it?" All the Canadian war graves in the Netherlands are cared for by Dutch schoolchildren. It is part of their school curriculum. I looked down at one grave. I don't remember the name, but the Canadian was just eighteen when he was killed on May 4, 1945, one day before the Germans surrendered. He must have gone through basic training, sailed to the Netherlands, gotten off the ship—and died. Such a waste.

But it wasn't all sadness. I was most anxious to meet Lloyd and Olga Rains. Through research, I had learned a little about Olga and the organization she had founded, but it was the story of how they met that I was really after.

We found them tucked into their small home in the back streets of Haarlem, on the outskirts of Amsterdam. We had spoken several times on the phone and exchanged some emails, and now we were here to tell their story.

You see, Olga had been just a teenager when the Nazis occupied her country. She quickly learned that death was close at hand. She had lived through the Dutch famine (the "hunger winter"), but only barely. She knew what it was like to be near death from starvation. She knew the very definition of salvation as the Allies, and her man, Lloyd, arrived to literally save their lives. And she knew about love.

That was what ultimately attracted me to their story. The horrors of war they had lived through, yes, but much more importantly, that love could still blossom out of such misery—and it truly had. Sixty years on, they were quite clearly still in love. We recorded them as they walked down the street arm in arm.

They brought us to a small café not far from where they had first met. That meeting had been just outside the café, where a celebratory Lloyd and some fellow members of Princess Patricia's Canadian Light Infantry had been goofing around when Olga came by on her bicycle. He asked her for a ride. She asked him for a chocolate bar. That was all it took.

Above the café was a small dance hall. It was the same dance hall they had glided around that crazy summer of 1945, the summer of love. We put on some music and fired up the camera. As they twirled together, sixty years later, it was pure magic. It was as

226 · CHAPTER 14

if they were those giddy young kids again, bumped together by a world war and sneaking that first kiss.

As our days together went on, I could see them conferring intimately about things that darn journalist was poking around in. Close moments, difficult memories, deep emotions. A cross word was never spoken, just the warm familiarity of two people who had lived through something only they could truly understand.

Lloyd was having a tough time. His was a code of conduct born of that era, when young men like him would leave their homes in places like Sault Ste. Marie, Ontario, and head off to war. A band of brothers, they faced death together all across Europe, shared in its darkness up close. But they rarely talked about it.

Lloyd had been a commando, at the spearhead of many front-line operations. He had seen the worst of what war had on offer. In the Battle of Ortona, Italy, he recalled, a young buddy suddenly began telling him all about his family and the special occasions in his life. Lloyd wondered why the hell he was being told all this stuff. As the boy finished talking, he stepped around a corner and was shot dead by a sniper. Lloyd was convinced that young man had known he was about to die.

Much of what he'd witnessed, Lloyd preferred to keep to himself. His code of honour would not allow him talk about the war. Those emotions were deeply personal and had been locked away for decades, and each time I prodded, he deflected. And yet somehow he knew he had to go there in some fashion. In fact, as time went on, we both realized he needed to go there.

Lloyd showed me where he and his comrades had begun their final push, where they crossed the river and then used flame throwers to clear the Germans from the forest. Walking through those woods with him raised the hair on the back of my neck. It was as if those ghosts were walking right along with us.

The village bell tower now stood where the last remaining German machine-gunner had held out, and nearby was the foxhole where Lloyd had been trying to sleep when the commanding officer arrived to say it was all over. Of course, as Lloyd recalled, nobody trusted the information for several days. It was difficult to believe the long war was finally ending.

As Lloyd was fighting his way closer to Olga, she had lain near death. Early in the occupation, she and a girlfriend had been arrested and thrown into the damp brick jailhouse in the basement of city hall to be interrogated by the Nazis. As they were still young, the Germans let them go, but they could not escape the *Hongerwinter*. Through sheer determination, and the scraps of kindness and bits of

Lloyd and Olga married on December 24, 1945, in Haarlem. Army supply slices of Spam and powdered eggs were served at their modest reception.

food from those who were themselves emaciated, Olga managed to survive. And liberation was at hand. Soon, those young Canadians, their heroes, filled the streets, as a grateful nation emerged, finally free, to thank them.

And thus they met, fell deeply in love and were married in the very same city hall in Haarlem where she had been terrorized by the Nazis. Olga wore a wedding gown made from parachute silk. But there was more.

After the war, Lloyd and Olga moved to Canada, but they still travelled back to the Netherlands, particularly for liberation anniversary celebrations. On one such occasion, Olga noticed a group of young men and women holding up signs reading, ARE YOU MY FATHER? She thought it was disrespectful and rude and went over to confront them, only to realize they were indeed looking for their fathers. These children were the results of that "summer of love" as a grateful nation celebrated with their liberators. Most of those soldiers were long gone before their Dutch lovers realized they would have to deal with the consequences.

The estimate was that as many as seven thousand "liberation babies" were fathered by Allied soldiers, most of them Canadian. Project Roots, as she called the organization she formed, became Olga's new mission in life. For decades she searched for those fathers. Lloyd helped and supported her. Together they managed, over the years, to match hundreds of them. Olga was even recognized for her efforts by Queen Beatrix of the Netherlands. It was all part of their wonderful love story.

Spending those days with Olga and Lloyd, watching the loving way she took his arm, his gentle hand on hers, a quiet word of encouragement or a little kiss between them, was indeed an honour—and a lesson in commitment, duty and love. The entire trip was an honour—the young woman in the cemetery, the man keeping the memory alive of the Canadians who came to save the day. He asked only one thing: "Carry this message home. We have not forgotten. We will never forget."

Lloyd has passed now, but I still hear from Olga occasionally, and it is always a pleasure. Olga and Lloyd had an enduring message: love conquers all. It's still enough to put a smile on this cynical journalist's face.

CHAPTER 15

The North

I don't know quite what it is about our North, the Arctic. Maybe it's because I spent so much of my young life in Labrador, but every time I am lucky enough to be in the land of the northern lights, I always feel as if I'm right back home.

It never ceases to amaze me how many Canadians I run into who have never seen the Atlantic provinces, or even Vancouver or Toronto, yet they have been to Mexico half a dozen times. And if you ask them whether they've ever been up North, they tend to look at you as if you have asked whether they've ever been to another planet. Sad.

I have been fortunate to see at least some of it. I spent an amazing day Ski-Dooing and filming with cameraman Wayne Vallevand in the mountains between the Yukon and Alaska. I've found myself slip-sliding to Tuktoyaktuk down the longest ice road in the world, deep inside the Arctic Circle. Driving on the frozen Beaufort Sea—unreal. I've sat in the igloo church in Inuvik and later toasted the midnight sun. I've driven down the Dempster Highway and almost been carried away by flies. I've flown over the Mackenzie River and the mountains to Old Crow in the Yukon, on the trail of the Porcupine caribou herd. I've even motored up the Peel River out of

This Gwich'in elder couldn't speak a word of English, but graciously allowed me to take her picture. Near the Peel River, NWT.

Fort McPherson in a plywood riverboat and had a Gwich'in elder show me the place under a spruce tree where she was born.

There was the time spent with drunken polar bears at the dump in Churchill, Manitoba (they had been eating fermenting grain and were quite snozzled), or walking among the tens of thousands of snow geese in La Pérouse Bay. And, of course, my time in the Hebron Fjord of Labrador where I searched for the only black bears in the world that lived above the treeline.

ON TOP OF THE WORLD

But of all my travels in the Arctic, it was the trip to Grise Fiord that left me literally on top of the world. Located on the southern tip of Ellesmere Island, less than sixteen hundred kilometres from the North Pole, it's the mostly northerly non-military community in Canada. The calving grounds of icebergs, the home of the narwhal, this is where we found a story of perseverance and community that remains unrivalled.

It wasn't even my idea to go. Terry Stapleton, a first-class producer who had worked and lived up North before, had the idea to do a story about the sealift. Once a year, a ship pushes its way through the ice to provide all the supplies many small communities rely on to survive the *entire* year. Grise Fiord was the most remote. From Christmas presents to toilet paper, new vehicles to chocolate bars, everything you needed to survive the next twelve months would arrive on the big freighter from Montreal. With any luck it arrived sometime in early to mid-August—*if* it could make its way through the ice. There, for us, was the gamble. Could we afford to spend what amounted to a small fortune in our budget to travel all the way there, only to find the ship had not made it?

I knew I could sell the story to *The National*. Stories from the Arctic always played well. People might not travel there but they certainly liked to see the stark beauty it had to offer flashing across their television screens. Perhaps, I thought, I could attract money from Newsworld as well. The news network was still sometimes interested in a stand-alone hour of television that they could use to help fill gaps in programming.

But in order to make the risk acceptable, we needed something more to tell than just the story of the sealift. The tension around its arrival would make good television, but if it didn't appear, the piece was in danger of being a bit of a dud. I began researching Grise Fiord and the people who lived there. What I found was a more profound story of survival than I could have ever imagined.

Grise Fiord was not some ancient Inuit village. Its genesis had been founded in fear. Back in the 1950s there was a lot of fear to go around. First there was the Cold War, and fear that Canada wasn't doing enough to assert its sovereignty in the North. Then there was the fear that some Indigenous communities were becoming too dependent on handouts from the white man (their words, not mine). Some bureaucrat in Ottawa came up with an experiment designed, I suppose, to try to kill two birds with one stone.

They persuaded seven families from Inukjuak, then known as Fort Harrison, to move over two thousand kilometres from northern Quebec up to basically the top of the world. They left by boat with the RCMP on July 28, 1953, and headed due north to Ellesmere Island, to a land they had never set eyes on before. They were told that if it wasn't to their liking, they could return home after two years. That turned out to be a lie.

They were landed on a small beach beneath a massive mountain of rock and gravel and told to fend for themselves. They were given some provisions: canvas tents lined with buffalo hides, and the equipment to hunt, to ostensibly live off the land. But the hunters were unfamiliar with the land that far north, and they had never experienced twenty-four hours of darkness before. It was a disaster.

Fifty years later, only one person who arrived during that misguided "experiment" remained in Grise Fiord. His name was Larry Audlaluk. We spoke on the phone and I learned a little more about this story of profound loss and sadness. His father, one of the leaders of the original group, had died not ten months after they arrived. Larry was just three.

Larry was happy to spend some time with us, and to guide us through the arrival of the sealift. He also had a few pictures from those olden days and some documents that told what had happened. But he wanted to make one thing clear. Ultimately his was not a sad story. Larry had come through many things on his journey, and he wanted to make sure I understood that he was a proud Canadian, right to his core.

Now we had a story that would resonate with all Canadians, whether the sealift arrived or not. It was full speed ahead. Well—almost. Getting to Grise Fiord is an exercise in patience, perseverance and blind luck. Speed, not so much.

Early in August 2006, Terry Stapleton, Bert Savard and I flew from Winnipeg to Ottawa. The next morning, we headed to Iqaluit, switched planes and kept going due north to Resolute. We crossed Baffin Island and finally landed on the southern tip of Cornwallis Island. Night two would be spent there in what, at first appearance, looked like the world's largest gravel pit. There was not a tree, a bush or even a blade of grass growing.

But the folks were wonderfully friendly, and after a fabulous supper I enjoyed a long walk by the water's edge. Not far from town you could see the rusted ghosts of military installations long since abandoned. At a pond I watched two young fellows running a Ski-Doo on top of the water. I had never seen that before. They were able to get the machine going fast enough that it would skip across the surface until it reached the other side. I grew up practically living on snow machines, but this was something else.

We learned that the weather in the morning was changeable and the next leg, the crucial leg of our journey, might be delayed. We would fly in a Twin Otter owned by Kenn Borek Air. Based out of Calgary, the company had developed a stellar international reputation for its work in the Canadian Arctic as well as Antarctica. It was a comforting thought.

In the morning things had improved, and we were off! Our last flight would be less than two hours, but it would take us across the stark beauty of Devon Island, then out over Jones Sound to Ellesmere Island. As we drew closer, we saw icebergs scattered everywhere, dropping off the edge of the glacial icefield and dotting the water as far as you could see. The colours and shapes were mesmerizing.

So was the landing. At first, Grise Fiord appeared as a speck on the horizon. All I could see was the mountain behind it, which kept growing bigger. A Twin Otter is not a big plane, and we could see right out through the pilot's windshield. Yep, that was a mountain all right. Soon all we could see was that damn mountain. It filled the view. Just as I was thinking this could be my last view of anything, we banked and immediately touched down on the dirt runway. My heart was pounding.

Welcome to Grise Fiord. The population when we landed was 145. Four babies had just been born. Meeting us at the airport was

Admiring some muskox horns in Grise Fiord on Ellesmere Island. The local hunter who gave them to me assured me the animal had died of natural causes!

Ray Richer, the man who made the town tick. Not only was he the Kenn Borek Air agent, he ran the local Co-op store, the post office and the lodge we would be staying in. A good fellow to know.

After chucking all our gear in the back of a pickup truck, we headed down the gravel road along the water to our accommodations. People seemed to be moving everywhere. Some were in boats just offshore, where the water was as smooth and clear as glass. There was so much to take in, we hardly knew where to start. Someone approached us on an ATV. It was Larry, grinning from ear to ear. He invited us up to his home after we settled in.

The community itself was one of the tidiest I had seen in the North. A school, a hospital station, the big Co-op store with a post office, a sort of community hall, an RCMP detachment, rows and rows of little houses and of course our lodge—all were tucked in under the shadow of this massive mountain rising out of the ocean.

The lodge couldn't have been any more than thirty metres from the shoreline.

When it came to meals, we would have to fend for ourselves. The cook had decided to pack it in just the day before. Not a big problem. I liked to cook, Bert had experience as a short-order guy from his younger years and the freezer was filled with lots of grub. I appointed myself head chef and even agreed to cook for a couple fellows there from Transport Canada.

We were eager to get started and headed over to Larry's. Up on the hill, two dog teams started to howl. Down by the brook three or four people appeared to be hunched over, cleaning something. It turned out to be a narwhal tusk, the first I had ever seen. It was about two metres long, a twisted rod of ivory. They got the beast the day before and if the weather held they would head out by speed-boat again tomorrow to hunt for more.

About a hundred metres offshore the water seemed alive. I looked through the digital zoom on my video camera and realized there had to be close to five hundred seals, all swimming together on the surface.

Outside Larry's, two sealskins were stretched on a frame to dry. He and Annie met us at the door. I had brought some fresh Manitoba corn on the cob and wild blueberry jam for them. Larry said he and Annie hadn't had fresh corn on the cob in years; theirs usually came in a can. All fresh produce had to be flown in and was quite expensive. The wild blueberry jam was a big hit. Larry, it turned out, had a sweet tooth.

On the wall in the living room was a picture of a young Larry with his mom and dad, taken back in 1954 by an RCMP officer just after they arrived. It was the only picture he had of his father. I told Larry he looked like him. He looked out the front window as if a million miles away, past the Canadian flag flying on his front lawn, and focused on the water. The wind was coming up, he said. Perhaps in a few days it would calm down enough to go to the original campsite, about eight kilometres away on the water, and visit his father's grave.

"I think he died of a broken heart," said Larry. "My mom said he got more anxious, hoping to go back to Inukjuak, even though it was just ten months later. Earlier than that, she said he started to faint. He would have spells. He would collapse every now and then. It got to the point where it got so frequent my mom thought, 'Well, here's one of his spells, and in time he'll get up again.' But one day, he just didn't. I think he lost the will to go on. I think he felt abandoned. I think he felt that there was no way out of this." Larry grew up without a father, watching the other kids learn skills from their dads. It would take him years to conquer the demons that arose as a result.

We spent the next few days visiting in the community and getting updates on the approaching ship. Many folks were concerned about the ice lurking just offshore. One day it would disappear and the next it was everywhere. If it pushed in tight against the shoreline, the ship would not be able to get close enough to unload. That, quite frankly, would be a disaster for the community. If practically everything they needed had to be flown in, the cost would be astronomical.

That evening there was quite a commotion along the shore. Everyone was down there, throwing nets and hoops into the water. They were fishing. All these small fish, which to me, a Newfoundlander, looked like capelin, were floating on the surface. Someone said they were Arctic cod that seals had driven up from the bottom. Apparently this huge herd of seals would swim deep under the school of Arctic cod, forcing them upward. As they got closer to the surface, their bladders would expand with air and they couldn't get back down. A feeding frenzy ensued. The seals fed. The gulls fed. And with any luck, anybody who liked Arctic cod in Grise Fiord was going to have a feed as well.

One man had fashioned a big hoop from some metal packing straps and covered it with netting. He would cast it out with a big swinging motion and then haul it back in with a rope he had attached. It worked very well. His family's buckets were almost full. His name was Looty Pijamini, and he was a carver who lived a little farther up the side of the mountain. He invited me for a visit and the very next morning, up I went. I found him in his studio, out behind the house, covered in soapstone dust. Looty was a renowned carver and silversmith, fusing the elements of his northern home—soapstone, antler, bone and wood—into stunning one-of-a-kind pieces. Several of his pieces are in the National Gallery of Canada.

Looty spoke quietly about the challenges of living so far north: the isolation, the continually escalating prices of basic food items, not to mention the price of a plane ticket just to get to Ottawa. One ticket cost more than we would pay to spend a week in Europe.

He wasn't upset, just stating the facts as they were. Over a cup of tea, he told me he was determined to stay right where he was. I'd brought him a Hudson's Bay scarf as a gift. I thought afterward that the Hudson's Bay Company might not be viewed in the best light by some Inuit people, but he graciously accepted it.

In the afternoon we met again with Ray Richer over at the Co-op. He had developed a unique way of looking at his responsibilities, supplying the food for an entire community. In order to make nutritious food more accessible to folks, the Co-op subsidized the cost of fresh fruit or milk by charging high prices for stuff like cigarettes and pop. Right now, as supplies dwindled, a can of pop could cost five bucks. It was a strategy that seemed to work. Food prices were not as exorbitant as I had seen in other northern communities, not by a long shot.

But Ray was anxious. That sea ice was creeping closer. They had heard from the ship as it picked its way through the ice—it hoped to arrive about three in the morning. That wouldn't be a problem. In August, the light hardly leaves the High Arctic. But that ice, *that* was a big problem.

While we waited, we visited with some of the teachers. Many of them had travelled north from Newfoundland. School attendance was at 90 per cent. Unemployment was low. The people here seemed very engaged in their community, and still solidly connected with the land. I was mulling all this over as I strolled along the dirt paths that passed as village streets, heading back to our accommodations.

Someone pulled up beside me in a pickup truck. "Nice evening," I said. "Yep, but don't walk over by the dump," he said. "There's been a polar bear over there the last few days and he's not friendly." I decided to head back to the lodge. As I crossed a crystal-clear stream, I happened to look down, and was startled to see the big eyes of a seal staring back up at me. Then I realized it was just its head—the rest had been harvested for other uses. It was a stark reminder of just how fragile life could be up there. I started walking much faster, looking over my shoulder—often.

Life as the locals knew it was hanging on the arrival of that ship. Finally, at 3:00 a.m., word came: it had made it through. The towns-folk sprang out of bed with the all the excitement of Christmas morning. The ship anchored just offshore while crate after crate was barged to the beach. The place was buzzing.

Over at Larry's, he and Annie were figuring out where to store a year's supply of everything from frozen peas to pizza pops. Later in the day we caught up with him at the Co-op. Larry was walking around with a big grin on his face. "Ask me what I'm doing," he said. So we asked. His reply? "I'm buying a freezer. That's right, they're selling a freezer to an Eskimo!" He laughed and laughed.

After all the crates were unloaded and things had settled down, Larry took me to the small church where he was an elder in the congregation. Life, for him, hadn't always been happy. For years he had struggled with depression and alcohol, two of the demons that arose from losing his dad and from having such an unpleasant start to life. But, he said, he was done with all that now. Then he said, "Tomorrow will be a better day. We'll go to the old homestead."

The next day, it felt good to be on the water. As we drew close to the original community's location, you could see a couple of buildings still standing, not much more. On shore, the rise of the mountain from the beach was even more pronounced. It was downright scary. Fifty metres straight were boulders the size of station wagons that looked like they could let go at any minute. And folks slept here, lived here, in canvas tents. It was a wonder any of them survived. Larry led me along a steady incline to the place in the side of the hill where his father lay beneath a pile of rocks. A simple white cross marked the spot.

Back in Grise Fiord, Larry said he had no anger anymore, not toward the RCMP or Ottawa—in fact, he called himself the town's biggest ambassador. He greeted cruise ships whenever they happened by, sat on the Co-op board and did whatever it took to ensure the survival of his little community on top of the world.

And in came the weather again. Bert and Terry would stay another day or two to finish shooting, but I had to get home. My son Mitchell was turning sixteen and I was taking him to New York City. Nobody was sure the plane would make it, but right on time it dropped out of the clouds. Moments after we took off, the clouds kissed the ground and the guys were stuck there for almost another week. Three days later I was in New York City, on top of the Empire State Building with my son. But my mind was still wandering north, back to Grise Fiord and the quiet beauty of that isolated locale.

The piece caused quite a stir when it aired. Larry's spirit, and that of the entire community, shone through. Although the federal government had acknowledged what had been done to Larry and the others, they'd never received a formal apology, a fact I made sure to include in the documentary. Hundreds of emails came in, from viewers across Canada. Many were like this one from British Columbia:

Sometimes the words hero or heroic can get a little over-
used, however, I think they are apt words to describe the
original seven families, and their descendants, that were
taken to Ellesmere Island to form a new community there.
I was struck by the humanity and courage of people like
Larry who are keeping this country alive and protected in
that very important part of our country.

A doctor from Calgary wrote to ask how she could nominate
Larry for the Order of Canada. She did, and Larry received Canada's
highest civilian honour in October 2008. In 2010 the federal government finally read a formal apology to the people of Inukjuak in the
House of Commons, and later that year a memorial carved by Looty
Pijamini was unveiled on the shoreline of Grise Fiord, honouring
Larry's dad and all the folks who persevered and survived the
government "experiment" in the High Arctic. Larry and I remain
friends on Facebook, which is the best way to communicate across
the frozen North.

CHANGING THINGS

Larry's story is a great example of the power of journalism to
change things. Several times, a story I was involved with managed
to effect change. It's one of the things that helps prevent you from
becoming too jaded (and believe me, that's possible) and keeps you
pushing forward.

The first time I really felt this power was years earlier, back
in Calgary. A non-profit organization was raising money for homeless kids on the street. Christmas was coming, and they had set up
a couple of Christmas tree–selling operations downtown to raise
money and help support the big Christmas dinner held every year
at their drop-in centre. Unfortunately, one of their troubled young

people lashed out one night, burning down both tree operations and the drop-in centre itself.

The next day I was assigned to cover the story and did a straight-up minute-and-a-half story for the supper-hour news program showing the damage, with folks saying how much this was going to hurt so close to Christmas. Within moments of the piece airing, the phones started ringing. By suppertime the next day, tens of thousands of dollars had been donated along with presents for all the kids and, amazingly, a new facility complete with a Christmas dinner for anyone from the street who needed it.

HONOURING A TRUE HERO

Besides Larry Audlaluk, twice more in my career stories led to more permanent recognition for the individuals profiled, both times from shows related to Remembrance Day. The first was the story of Francis Pegahmagabow of the Wasauksing First Nation near Parry Sound, Ontario. Francis is the most highly decorated Aboriginal soldier in Canadian history, yet most people have never heard of him. I hadn't either until he was brought to my attention by Toronto producer Sheila Rider, who knew of my interest in military history.

Corporal Pegahmagabow is also considered the deadliest sniper of World War I, credited with downing some 378 German soldiers and capturing as many as 300 more. For his selfless courage in battles like Passchendaele he was decorated three times with the Military Medal. He was known to be fearless. Francis would do something called "counting coup" in Indigenous warrior circles. It involved crawling into enemy trenches in the middle of the night and cutting off parts of German soldiers' uniforms while they slept. It was said Pegahmagabow felt he couldn't die because of the protection afforded him by a medicine man, which was a small sacred pouch he carried with him in his boot.

Several times, while lying in his sniper's nest, he was buried alive by shellfire. Through it all Francis survived, and he returned home to a hero's welcome. Tens of thousands lined the streets of Toronto, where he was decorated by the Prince of Wales.

But the reality for Indigenous people at that time was that they were not considered citizens of Canada, could not vote and were reduced to counting on the Indian agent to see to their welfare. That was not good enough for Francis. He was elected chief of his own nation several times and became active on the national scene, helping to form some of the first national associations of First Nations and being elected supreme chief.

But the war had taken its toll on him. Thunder and lightning storms could drive him into a sort of madness, taking him back to the battlefields of France and sending him into the bush, alone, for days on end. His lungs had been so badly damaged by German mustard gas attacks that as he neared the end of his life, he had to sleep sitting up in a chair so they didn't fill with fluid. He died at the age of sixty-one and is buried in a small cemetery on his home reserve.

Even though these events had happened long ago, I managed to find his granddaughter, Teresa McInnis Pegahmagabow, and another relative who knew him, Priscilla—Francis was her father-in-law. Teresa was born just after Francis died in 1952. Following in her grandfather's footsteps, Teresa sat on her tribal council. We walked together to his grave, shared a cup of tea while looking at the few old photos of him, and I learned more about this man who persevered in the face of tremendous odds.

After my story aired, I received an email from some provincial government representatives who were so moved by Francis's story that they wanted to erect two plaques on the Wasauksing First Nation to honour him and his accomplishments. Plans were also approved for a statue to be erected in nearby Parry Sound.

I was honoured to be asked to participate in the ceremony held at Wasauksing. Later, the new statue of Francis, standing proudly in his uniform and holding an eagle up for launch, was erected. Look for it the next time you are lucky enough to be in Parry Sound.

MEMORIES OF MONA

The second story that highlights an act of heroism was brought to me by a colleague. One day I received an email from Heather Spiller, at the CBC parliamentary bureau in Ottawa. "Check out this story about Mona Parsons," she suggested. So I did. What a tale! Mona was a young woman from Nova Scotia who, prior to World War II, had sought her fame and fortune in New York City. Through sheer nerve she landed herself a place dancing in the Ziegfeld Follies.

Through her brother, she met a young Dutch millionaire. They travelled back to his home country, married and became part of high society. But all that came crashing down with the German occupation, which began in 1940. Her husband wanted her to flee, but Mona stayed, determined to somehow resist. Together they helped Allied pilots who had been shot down, hiding them in a small secret compartment in their home. But an informer turned them in. Mona became the only Canadian woman to be taken prisoner by the Nazis. She was sentenced to hard labour at a camp in Germany.

After the camp was bombed, she and a fellow prisoner escaped, making their way across Germany and back to the Netherlands just in time for the liberation. At first, they were suspected of being German spies, but the interrogators turned out to be Canadian. In fact, they were from the North Nova Scotia Highlanders. Some of them even knew her!

She was rescued and was reunited with her husband, but he died in 1956 and Mona was left penniless. She returned to Nova Scotia and remarried. When her second husband died, she lived out a quiet life in Wolfville until her own death in 1976.

Mona Parsons had received a citation for bravery from the British as well as from American president Dwight D. Eisenhower for her war efforts. But back home in Canada she was refused a pension, and had never been officially recognized by the Canadian government.

Writer Andria Hill-Lehr was determined to change all that. A biographer, she wrote a book about Mona and made it her mission to ensure she got the recognition she deserved. And she was the perfect person to help me tell Mona's story. As Andria put it, "This is a person who was willing to give her life, to stand up for what she believed in, in justice and in freedom, who very nearly forfeited that life and yet has received no recognition whatsoever."

Andria managed to raise enough money to commission at least the beginning of a statue of Mona, and when my piece aired, folks across the country spoke up, all saying the same thing: "This woman needs to be recognized." Well, today, in front of the post office in downtown Wolfville, Nova Scotia, you can find that statue of Mona, dancing for joy.

Mission accomplished.

CHAPTER 16

Country Canada Cancelled

You could smell it coming. The tone of the chatter from Toronto had changed. All through the fall of 2006 and into 2007, any ideas for stories, new approaches or new sources of funding were all met with a certain bureaucratic banality.

I had been talking with a huge American rural affairs specialty channel. It had launched in 2000 and boasted over forty million available viewers across the United States, plus more in Mexico and Central and South America. I didn't contact them; they had contacted me. They knew about *Country Canada* and wanted to buy the program.

After the backlash I'd received the last time I dared to try to find additional revenue for the program on my own, this time I immediately mentioned it to our leadership. They were less than enthusiastic. I even met with the head of the current affairs arm of news at the time. She was polite but noncommittal. Then she casually asked if I had given any thought to what I would do after *Country Canada*. That was the first nail in the coffin. They were obviously *not* interested in more cost-effective ways to produce the program; instead, they were interested in taking its budget and killing the show. Not that they ever said that outright.

Wildfires raged in Eagle Plains, but it was a beautiful day outside the tourist office in Inuvik. You can hardly tell the bugs were about to carry me away.

Ironically, that last season was one of our strongest. Great characters. We spent some time with Patrick Moore, past president of Greenpeace, an environmentalist who had turned his back on the movement he helped create, choosing instead to work on what he called "realistic" solutions. He had ultimately rejected the notion that another tree should never be cut down, and that all nuclear development was necessarily bad. It made for an interesting piece.

On another show, our team travelled up the Dempster Highway inside the Arctic Circle to Eagle Plains, halfway to Inuvik, and videotaped as wildfires devastated both sides of the highway. That was more than a little unnerving. A fellow had driven us down the highway in his pickup truck, and too late we learned he had several hundred litres of fuel in a tank in the truck box. The flames were ten metres high on either side of the narrow dirt road we were on. I politely suggested we "get the hell outta here." Later, eighteen-wheelers came through with the paint on the sides of their rigs bubbled up from the heat.

In The Pas, Manitoba, we celebrated the Trappers' Festival, ice fishing with Queen Trapper Tricia Dick on the Saskatchewan River at −50°C. I remember because I went through the ice! The fast-flowing water underneath had prevented any safe buildup of ice, but the snow on the surface made everything look normal. Only my big puffy arctic parka kept me from being swept under. I went in up to my waist and remember the feeling of my feet kicking in the stones on the bottom. By the time I got back to our truck, barely a hundred metres away, my ski pants, boots and gloves were frozen. My teeth chattered for several hours after that.

We told stories from Harbour Breton, Newfoundland, and from Ontario with Sally Nielsen and her Newfoundland pony rescue, and in the land of the polar bear, Manitoba. Then, after fifty-four years on television, *Country Canada* told its very last story on Vancouver Island at the Lester B. Pearson United World College of the Pacific. There, kids from around the world were working on the future and learning to harness electricity from the ocean using tidal energy.

But there would be no future for *Country Canada*. In the end, the powers in Toronto didn't even make a formal announcement. Instead, in the spring of 2007, in a news release announcing other programs for the fall launch, they mentioned that *Country Canada* programming would now be seen "on other platforms," whatever that meant. The CBC was jumping into the world of reality television with programs like *Battle of the Blades* and franchise programs they had purchased like *Dragon's Den*. These were entertaining shows that would enjoy success, but they were hardly the kind of mandate programming that *Country Canada* had provided for decades.

To say it was a profoundly sad time would be a gross understatement. At CBC Winnipeg, it felt like a death in the family. The last network current affairs program was gone. By now, most of the network sports produced through CBC Winnipeg had also been lost to other networks. The CBC had eliminated all current affairs in the local newsrooms as well. For the people working there, the journalists and technical folks, the future was looking bleak. Where were the opportunities to work on network programming, to develop new skills? Where was the logical career development? Not at CBC Winnipeg, or anywhere in the regional system, it seemed. Not anymore.

MY OWN "MARKETPLACE"

At first, it seemed as if the Mother Corp. didn't really know what to do with me. I wasn't sure I knew what to do myself. At this point in my career, all I could see was the long, slow slide toward retirement. I wasn't sure I had another decade of just hanging on left in me.

But through the support and guidance of good friends and colleagues, I found a way forward. Jonathan Whitten, a big part of the leadership team in Toronto, was overseeing *The National*, and he assured me a place was still there for what I had to offer. Cecil Rosner, who I have mentioned before, was now the managing editor of the regional news operation and was respected across the network for his knowledge and dedication to the craft of investigative journalism. He wanted me to jump in and oversee a consumer beat, producing stories for the regional system and for *The National*.

To be honest, I did not really want to go back to doing daily news. My heart was still with doing longer-form work, documentaries and features. But in the absence of any other concrete offers, I agreed to give it a go.

It was interesting work—pieces about everything from electric cars and trucks to cold and flu medications. Some of it involved simple little consumer tips, what we call take-away journalism. For example, did you know that in many cases, you can negotiate a lower interest rate on your credit card simply by calling the number on the back and asking them to lower it? It's true. One day we decided to test that theory in a local shopping mall. Nine out of ten people had their interest rates lowered. That story still gets loads of views online.

The internet was also becoming a much bigger part of our lives and social media was starting to explode. Crime followed people online. I had been doing some research on identity theft and contacted a team of cyber-security experts located in Woodlands, California. But where these experts were really operating was on the dark web. They had infiltrated chat rooms where thieves were buying and selling credit card numbers, social security numbers, even bank account numbers of people from around the world.

Now, if you are like me, you are probably too trusting, and more than a little lazy, about regularly changing passwords or upgrading online security. Well, I'm not anymore. As we sat and watched and taped, the financial lives of thousands of people were being bought and sold, right before our eyes. My expert told me that at one time a platinum credit card number was quite valuable. Now, so many of them had been scammed that a package of a dozen would sell for less than twenty bucks.

I found contact information for several Canadians whose personal information was being traded in one of these chat rooms and gave them a call. Some were already aware they had been compromised, but others were stunned to learn their social security number was being bought and sold in some cyber bargain basement for thieves, and potentially used halfway around the world.

In one case, identity theft almost destroyed a fellow's video store business in Vancouver. It took him years to restore his identity and credit rating. The story was a real eye-opener and wound up being a four-part series on *The National*. Ironically, it was also shown on Air Canada's new onboard personal entertainment systems. Jeez, I'd finally managed to get something on there!

I was always looking for information that challenged the accepted norm. I found what I thought was a huge story at Dalhousie University in Halifax. A research team had examined cellphone use while driving. Everyone knew it was dangerous, potentially five times more dangerous than drunk driving. Almost every province and territory in Canada had passed legislation making hand-held cellphone use illegal, while also passing legislation making hands-free use of cellphones perfectly legal.

But here's the thing. Their research, and it was an exhaustive study looking at crash results and surveys from over a dozen countries, showed that hands-free cellphone use in a vehicle was *more* dangerous than hand-held use. Why? They concluded it was the conversation itself that caused the distraction for most people, not the physical use of the phone. People using hands-free technology tended to drive faster, so they had more severe accidents. People who held on to their phones seemed to be more aware they were driving, so they drove slower.

I thought, "This should shake things up." Nope. It passed by with a collective shrug from the public, now well on their way to being addicted to their phones. Over ten years later, legislators are only now upping fines and penalties for those who insist it's their right to text, watch videos or talk on their phone while driving. I see it every day. The carnage continues.

But all too often, my job became a scramble to put together a minute-and-a-half news item on the latest consumer recall. It was tedious stuff that, as in the case of the cellphone study, rarely changed anything and began to make me feel as though I was moving backwards in my career. It seemed like the internet and social media were already desensitizing people to just about everything.

Fortunately, salvation was again at hand. Jonathan Whitten was working on the latest retooling of *The National*. As mentioned, he was also the boss, and a damn good one. I think he could sense my frustration (or maybe it was the emails!), and in the summer of 2008 he asked me whether I would backfill in the London bureau for a month. He didn't have to ask twice. A month in one of the greatest cities in the world? Rough gig.

Turned out to be rougher than I thought, but not because of the stories. After Washington, I already knew the drill of being in a foreign bureau. So, why was the London gig so rough? Two words—sleep deprivation. The CBC had rented a small apartment kitty-corner from the office. It was handy and saved them a lot of money, but the problem was the heat. It was the warmest summer in a decade, and there was no air conditioning. The only way to get a breath of fresh air was to open the massive windows that lined two sides of the flat. Outside, both ways, were pubs. Because of the great weather, people would buy three or four pints at last call and stand in the street talking and joking until two in the morning. Every. Single. Night. Often I would drag pillows into the small bathroom to try to get any sleep at all.

Then, cranky and not at all well rested, I would arrive at the office to the sound of the sidewalks being replaced around the building using stone, which they sawed *all day long*. Once again, you couldn't close the windows or you would melt into a puddle on the floor.

I did my best to remain unperturbed. There were stories about military dust-ups between Russia and former Soviet republic Georgia. I covered former Bosnian Serb leader Radovan Karadžić, also known as the "Butcher of Bosnia," as he finally faced war-crimes charges after thirteen years in hiding. In August of that summer, Barack Obama came to meet the British prime minister as part of a multi-country tour. I finally got to do a stand-up outside 10 Downing Street, the prime minister's official residence. With all the security, that was a feat in itself.

But the most interesting story that summer was delivered compliments of my good friend and colleague Manjula Dufresne. Manjula was a producer from Vancouver who was also backfilling at the London bureau on Little Titchfield Street. She knew that Canadian Lawrence Hill was about to receive the Commonwealth Writers' Prize for his amazing novel *The Book of Negroes*, and that he was to be presented with it by Queen Elizabeth herself. Not only that, but through some research, Manjula was able to get access to the original historical *Book of Negroes* itself at the British National Archives.

That original leather-bound ledger documents the names of over three thousand former slaves, loyal to the British, who escaped with them from New York to Nova Scotia (then part of British North America) at the end of the American Revolutionary War. They were promised their freedom, but instead found more of the same in their new home until finally they set sail for Africa, where they established the community of Freetown in Sierra Leone.

Hill tells the story of that journey through the eyes of Aminata Diallo, a young woman originally captured in West Africa and brought as a slave to the Americas. It was a riveting tale that shone an ugly light on the reality many faced in the New World.

Hill himself agreed to sit down with me to discuss his book and let me walk with him to Buckingham Palace as he was on his way to meet the Queen. It turned out we had something in common. As a younger man, Lawrence had worked for a time at the *Winnipeg Free Press* as a reporter. He was a kind soul and a real gentleman, and it was my great pleasure to spend time with him. The front gates of Buckingham Palace, however, were as far as I got. Unlike Puss in Boots, I was not to meet the Queen.

The last two weeks of heat and lack of sleep had me ready for the nuthouse. Pam came to visit, took one look at me and said, "Let's get on a train." We spent two weeks travelling about while I decompressed and regained my sanity.

Far too soon it was time to cross the pond again. I was not looking forward to the fall season. But as I have often said, it is better to be born lucky than rich. Good old Jonathan had come up with a plan. I would get to set up a dedicated current affairs unit for *The National*, based in Winnipeg. I might be expected to file the occasional news story, but they were leaving the local national reporter in place so I would be free, for the most part, to put together features for the show. There was funding for a dedicated producer and camera operator/editor. I couldn't believe my luck. This would be the only unit of its kind outside of Toronto.

I put together a team and we got to work, determined to show that you didn't need to be in Toronto to deliver network-quality features that would resonate across the country. I could breathe again.

"TELL ME A STORY"

There was new leadership at *The National* as well, and they wanted a close-up look behind what appeared to be happening on the street. There was always another story, too many sad stories, about the growing number of missing Indigenous women and girls. It had been going on for decades. The cycle of poverty, abuse and callous indifference was not unique to Winnipeg, but the city certainly seemed to have more than its share.

I knew the Winnipeg Police Service had a special unit that was dispatched to find young girls who had run, usually away from the care of Child and Family Services, to the lure of the inner city. Time was of the essence. Often these young people were angry, confused and desperate—the perfect ingredients for exploitation. The officers working in these units were exceptional. They gave a damn. It was one of our first stories.

We rode along with a special police unit, searching door to door, from one crack house to another, following trails that led through the sort of poverty and squalor you wouldn't think possible in a country like Canada, chasing down one dubious lead after another, trying to salvage lives, one at a time. Far too often they did not, and the girl wound up on drugs, forced to work the street—or dead.

Then we walked through the fields around Winnipeg with a family who had spent every spare moment they could looking for their daughter's remains. For almost a decade. They had long since given up any hope she would be found alive. Now, they just wanted to bring her home.

Increasingly, the weight of all the misery out there sat heavily on my shoulders. Especially when we journalists, as a profession, tended to want to run with it. An old Detroit radio station was once attributed with coining the phrase, "If it bleeds, it leads." Essentially, it meant the most tragic, horrific stories led the newscast because the thinking inside most newsrooms was that *fear sells*.

To me, it wasn't enough. I wanted to offer more than just a spotlight on carnage and despair. The real questions we needed to ask were: "What is being done about this?" "How can this be changed?" "What can fix this?"

The story from the inner city took us to that next level. It clearly showed what the police department was trying to do about the situation to make a difference. Maybe it was because of all the compelling stories we had told on *Country Canada*, or maybe it was because so little of it was being reported, but I decided to focus on finding stories about the good in this world, and about the honest, hard-working people who were trying to make a difference.

We profiled a non-profit company working in the inner city. The people who ran it weren't just building homes, they were rebuilding lives. They hired people from inside the poverty belt and taught valuable skills, helping them improve their lives and escape desperate situations.

I found another community organization dealing with a growing gang issue in their neighbourhood. They had developed a plan to reach out to those kids through music. They set up a recording studio to give young kids options other than finding trouble on the streets. One of the kids was busted, right there in the drop-in centre, while we were taping. The leaders were concerned about optics. But the incident only made the piece stronger, gave it more relevance, by clearly showing what they were up against every day.

LYNN THE LIONESS

In the fall of 2009 I had the great pleasure of meeting Lynn Thompson, an angel if ever there was one. Lynn was working in the Resource Assistance for Youth Centre, not ten blocks from the CBC. Ten blocks away was a world I knew almost nothing about. It was the one place all street kids could come for a warm coffee and some caring, and it all started with Lynn. Her philosophy was that every conversation should start with a hug and finish with one too. And when Lynn gave you a hug, you could tell she meant it. With her gruff appearance, shock of platinum-blond hair and those sparkling eyes, I could tell from the moment I met her what it was about Lynn. The thing was, she gave a damn.

We stood taping in the middle of a dingy room in a little strip mall just off Broadway downtown, and just observed. It was crammed with teenagers. Lynn approached a young woman who appeared ready to give birth any minute. "How's the baby?" she asked, giving the girl a hug. "You and the baby doing all right, eh?" The girl, obviously shy, just held Lynn's hand. The nearby wall was lined with kids, some eating soup from a huge pot bubbling away in the back, some rummaging through boxes of clothes or trying on donated coats.

These were her children. The food, the clothes—those things helped pull them in, but it was really Lynn who kept them there, because she was someone who didn't judge, who treated them with care. "I don't just go 'hey.' I give good hugs, and they give them back. It's a connection of love, trust and respect, all bottled up. Sometimes that's all they get in a day. Hey, you know, if I can give them that, it helps, and they pass it along." As many as seventy kids a day were washing through there, and Lynn was the woman they all turned to.

"Ninety days clean today," she said to a skinny young fellow. "Good for you, right on." On the big board on the wall she wrote a "90" by his name. "This is our clean-time board," she explained. "It shows the days or weeks that kids have been clean—you know, off the meth, cocaine or other hard drugs. Every success is applauded," she added, "even those who are still trying. They are successful to me too because I don't want anyone to give up."

When she talked, they listened. They knew she knew what she was talking about. Lynn too had grown up on the streets. She had spent over two decades struggling to survive, battling the demons of addiction and physical and sexual abuse, all the while suffering from diabetes, and hovering between jail and death. Anyone could see she truly understood what these kids were going through. "For me, it was hardcore using, living on the streets. [These kids] reflect my former life, dumpster diving, looking for food. When I was in that situation myself, for sure I was using, just trying to exist, to survive—you know?"

Later we followed her home. Her house was full of young people too, dropping by for support or just to say thank you. One of them was a girl named Loni. She said Lynn had literally saved her life, pulling her from the streets and helping her get off drugs. She had been clean for two years and had started her own business. "She's given me the tough love that I didn't always want or think I needed. She was always there pushing, cheering for you. Sometimes when you just needed a hug, she's there for that too."

Lynn had been clean for twelve years. She called it the blessing that gave her a gift: that ability to show kids the way back from the street. Those vibrant young people visiting with Lynn that morning were proof of that.

Another young woman, Sam, had arrived with Loni. Once fighting for her life, in and out of hospital, she was now finishing her undergraduate degree. "My life has just become so amazing. It's not even comparable anymore. I was a lost teenager. I'm going to start crying. I would have been dead. I would have died. I was in a really bad spot. I probably would have ... without this woman, I probably would have been dead two years ago."

Many others said they owed their lives to Lynn Thompson. She was still working on hundreds more. But it was Lynn who insisted she was the one who felt grateful. "I have kids that I help, but they help me, and they love me. It's like a two-way street, you know?"

You could see that too. Her face would light up when she started talking about them. Her own challenges she called "insignificant," but they were not. She was now in a wheelchair and was again fighting for her own life. Her sight was almost gone. Diabetes was taking it, as it had taken her legs and many of her fingers. Then there was the open-heart surgery. After thirty-six years, the disease and the effects of the streets were catching up. "I have lost four, five, six fingers," she said matter-of-factly. "I'm just praying that my thumbs will be okay."

Three days a week, she struggled through hours and hours of dialysis, spending increasing time in the hospital. But she didn't want to talk about that. All she wanted to talk about, all she really thought about, was getting back to "her" kids. "The kids, man, they keep me going. Everybody needs to have a purpose in life. If I can just keep showing up at work, making a difference. You know, I am just so proud of them, I want to encourage them."

We had to stop taping for a couple of days while Lynn received treatment. There was real concern that she would not be able to go on. But after three days she was back on the job, chastising a kid running around in a jean jacket in the middle of winter. "Are you really warm enough in that? Go check out our not-so-cool coats in the back. Not cool," she joked, "but they are warm, hehe." She gave another one a little nudge. "Are you going to stick around for a meeting? That's cool." The kid turned to the camera and said, "It's pretty hard to feel sorry for yourself with her around." They all knew just how sick she was. I think—I know, her illness was pushing them to try harder.

That week Lynn was named Winnipeg's most beautiful woman, a title she brushed off, saying, "It's not about me, it's about them."

When I asked her how long she would keep going, she didn't skip a beat. "Until the day I die," came her reply. Then she spun around on her wheels to give another kid a hug. After the story aired, I heard from former street kids now living across the country. All of them had been touched by her kindness, her trust and respect.

Within a year, Lynn was gone. Her funeral was held in the church not much farther up the street on Broadway from where she had run her own ministry of a sort. There weren't enough chairs to hold all the people who came to pay their respects. Hundreds of us overflowed into the hallway.

I can hear Lynn now: "Come on, people, we can do this. Give each other a hug."

SPRINGTIME IN THE ARCTIC

It was April and spring was in the air, but I was determined to get back up North. Those stories from the days of *Country Canada* still called to me. The opportunity arose when I read of an adventurer who had decided to attempt the longest ice road in the world using a solar car. It was 18°C when we left Winnipeg, but that didn't last long. We landed in a blizzard in Edmonton—blinding snow with wind gusts around one hundred kilometres an hour. We landed, only to have ground crew operations suspended. It wasn't safe for them to work. We sat on the plane, bounced around by the wind for almost another hour. Springtime in Alberta. Yellowknife was sunny, but with another biting wind. Finally, after two wearying days, Inuvik, Northwest Territories!

Before I go any further, if you are wondering what the best airline in Canada is, you need look no further than First Air, "The Airline of the North." Now, this is only my own opinion, but I haven't seen service like that since Wardair disappeared. Friendly, helpful staff, hot towels, lovely food, even warm cookies and complimentary candies, not to mention complimentary wine with your meals.

Flights are expensive, but they are a lovely introduction to the High Arctic.

It's always the wind that reminds you that although it may be spring, you are inside the Arctic Circle. It can send you running for a toque pretty darn fast, especially out on that ice road. I had driven over ice before, in Northern Manitoba, but this was the longest stretch of road over frozen water, both fresh and salt, in the world. It could be a little unsettling to stand there as a big truck passed and have the ice, still several metres thick, crack under every roll of its tires. The slush just off to the sides was water that worked its way up from below the ice and mixed with the snow. As spring approached, it could be a metre deep.

And it was on this road that Toronto-born Marcelo da Luz was determined to drive his solar vehicle, hoping to set a world record. Marcelo, a former airline attendant, had been bitten by the solar bug some years before and had already driven the teardrop solar vehicle he designed himself over thirty-five thousand kilometres. But this was April in the Arctic, and it was still twenty below.

The road runs nearly 180 kilometres from Inuvik to Tuktoyaktuk over frozen fresh water and on the frozen salt water of the Beaufort Sea. Marcelo seemed undeterred, even when his solar vehicle arrived slightly damaged and his high-tech winter clothing didn't arrive at all. A local sympathizer gave him a pair of mukluks to at least keep his feet from turning into blocks of ice during the proposed four-hour journey.

You have just a narrow window of opportunity when your vehicle uses only whatever power it can squeeze from the Arctic sun. The capability of Marcelo's electrical system was a testament to technology. Lithium-ion polymer batteries, charged by 893 solar cells, generated about 900 watts—less than you would use to toast your raisin bread. But would that be enough to push him and his car all the way to the Beaufort Sea? There was also a support team of two volunteers with zero experience—but Marcelo was a dreamer.

However it turned out power wasn't the problem, tires were. The inflatables were smaller than those on a kid's bike, and they easily slipped into the cracks in the ice and deflated, either because of rips or because the ice edge tore them off their rims. It happened again and again and again. His planned four hours on the road went out the window.

When he finally made it onto the saltwater ice, Marcelo had yet another flat, this one coming with a big bang as the car went down in the ice and the impact cracked the housing on the electric motor. This was a big problem. Salt water and electricity are never a good combination. He tried sealing it up with Tuck Tape and it seemed to hold, but then he couldn't get the flat tire off. The nut holding it on was jammed. I had visions of us spending the night out on the frozen Beaufort so I did something I'd never done before: rather than being just an observer, I decided to intervene. Using a metal post to wedge the tire so it wouldn't spin with every wrench turn, I got it off and a new wheel on. The show must go on!

Just over an hour of daylight was left. On we went, spotting pingos—mounds of earth-covered ice unique to the terrain around Tuktoyaktuk—in the distance. Poor Marcelo limped into town on solar fumes, surrounded by the curious on snowmobiles. We were all exhausted and semi-frozen. The trip to the edge of Arctic Canada had wound up taking over nine hours, but Marcelo had made it!

So there we were in Tuktoyaktuk, a 4,628-kilometre drive from Winnipeg, still in Canada, on the edge of the Beaufort Sea. That old joke some folks make about extremely remote areas came to mind: "It's not the end of the earth, but you can see the end from here!" I was thinking exactly that when I heard a voice cry out, "Reg bye, jeez, man, what are you doing up here?" It turned out to be Bob Kelsey, a friend of mine from Newfoundland. He and his wife Mary were spending a year teaching in the tiny hamlet. Now I was thinking about Disney: "It's a Small World (After All)"!

SMOKE 'EM IF YOU GOT 'EM

It was Colorado's first anniversary—of pot. Canada had its own debate raging about the legalization of the herb, so we headed to Denver to see how they were doing the doobie down there. It had been controversial: the police chief, the governor and the military had all been against it. But it came down to a plebiscite and the good people of Colorado had spoken. We want pot, they said.

I thought, "Is it really any surprise?" Have you ever been in downtown Denver? Some of its artwork is quite bizarre, including a statue of a giant blue teddy bear several storeys high (high being the operative word) peeking into office windows. Talk about your Smokey the Bear!

Anyway, as we discovered, mostly the new law worked just fine. Crime was down and the government had lots of new tax revenue to build schools and repair roads. Even the military, which conducted random drug tests on its personnel, discovered that positive test results actually dropped.

The biggest problem for retailers was what to do with all that cash. Because the American federal government still considered pot smoking illegal, the banks wouldn't touch it. It left most pot retailers with huge volumes of cash on hand, along with tons of security to prevent robbery. Some issues also arose with younger kids getting their hands on gummy bears made with THC in them. Colorado has this thing about bears. Making gummy bears laced with dope? Not a good idea. What were those people smoking?

Country Canada was fading into the past, and these new opportunities with *The National* had me feeling more like my old self again. There was always another story to tell!

CHAPTER 17

Making the Story My Own

By now, several themes may be emerging for you from all these tales. First, I love this country. I love its landscape, its people, its nature. I was more than comfortable just telling our story. That foreign correspondent stuff wasn't for me. This was our mandate, and I was happy to keep doing my part to fulfill it.

Second, as the years rolled by, I learned one or two things about the craft of journalism. I was increasingly convinced that, as a journalist, you had to give a little piece of yourself to tell the story. You had to let it touch you. Perhaps that philosophy flew in the face of what, for so many years, had been the standard journalistic stance of objective detachment. But I can tell you this: when you let the story take a little piece of you, your audience will know. There's nothing wrong with appearing human. Emotion is the most powerful thing television and video can deliver. Done right, nothing is more powerful. People are hungry to be moved, to find themselves giving a damn—about the work Lynn the angel was doing, or whether Marcelo would set his record. I didn't mind being their advocate in those circumstances. Stories like that are lifted only when you are on that emotional journey with them. The danger, of course, is that it can take its toll. That emotional weight can reach back and bite you. But it is worth the risk.

Objectivity is always a laudable goal, but the reality is that an audience will interpret what you are telling them as *your* perspective anyway. Every piece leads them to a conclusion, and you are in complete control of that. Be fair, be honest and be prepared to defend your decisions. Some stories, particularly political stories, require balance, but that's not the same thing as objectivity.

The key is in finding the balance. Strong visuals, yes. Compelling characters on a journey, yes. But above all, emotion. It could be fear, anger, joy or sorrow. Whatever trick you need to employ to get it on camera in a raw, untarnished form, the stronger your piece will be. I spoke before about making your subject comfortable enough to be able to tell you how they really feel. Remember when I hid the camera and helped with the dishes while looking out over the field in that Alberta farmhouse?

Increasingly I was asking the camera person to just roll, to be a fly on the wall. I will take a rougher-looking authentic moment caught on camera over polished sequential shooting any day. I was also getting better at being natural in those moments, to show the subject and the audience that I cared too, and to encourage both on the journey.

Back in the edit suite, I would never have someone else transcribe the material we had gathered. I wanted to see every bit of it for myself. It wasn't just *what* my subjects said that was important, but *how* they said it. Going through all that material could be tedious work, but early on I'd learned another valuable lesson: don't do your research on camera. You should try, as best you can, to know the answer to the question before you ask it. When you hear what you need, move on to the next thing. If you later hear a better answer, adjust.

Don't take notes unless you really need to. Record everything, even research interviews. If you are busy writing stuff down while talking to someone, you'll miss things, I guarantee it. That pencil and paper are another wall between you and the person you are talking to. They prevent a certain intimacy, not unlike stick microphones. I avoided those if at all possible. Sticking a microphone into someone's face is the most unnatural thing a journalist can do. Of course, at times that is just the way things are done (such as in a media scrum with dozens of others), but otherwise dump it in favour of a small, less intrusive lapel mic.

Think in pictures. Storyboard. Know as much as possible about how the story is going to go before you even start shooting. But be open to change. If there isn't any, you still have the story. If there is, it could become an even better story. Be flexible and willing to head down another path if it presents itself. Above all, let them know you are human. Let the audience know too. And here's the hardest bit: shut up and listen.

A BREAKNECK PACE

Our little team was making its mark. We were more than quick out of the gate. We were a documentary-producing rocket. If we had to, we could turn around network-quality stories in a day. Jaison Empson and Warren Kay were both great editors, Terry had that professional touch that can only come from experience and we were all damn quick on our feet. Oh yes, we were getting noticed. We were producing one or two features for *The National* almost every week, when other units were taking weeks or even months to produce just one. One week it would be shining a light on racism in Nova Scotia, and the next we were profiling Barbara and Clarence Nepinak, who had been chosen to commentate the Vancouver 2010 Winter Olympics in Ojibway.

In March 2010 we travelled to Hants County, Nova Scotia, where someone had decided to burn a cross on the lawn of a young family just because they were of mixed race. As we scratched deeper, we turned up several disturbing examples of a province still struggling to achieve real equality, and a place where many black people continued to feel marginalized. I found myself thinking about the challenges the good people recorded in the historical *Book of Negroes* had faced in Nova Scotia over two hundred years ago, challenges that apparently had persisted.

In the summer the Truth and Reconciliation Commission, overseen by Justice Murray Sinclair, began its public consultation. The commission had been formed two years before, but internal disputes led to resignations and delays. Finally, people who were forced into the residential school system would get their say. I'd met Murray Sinclair some years before when, as a judge, he oversaw an inquiry examining pediatric cardiac deaths in the Winnipeg health-care system. I found him to be a no-nonsense sort of fellow, and I thought he possessed the right temperament for the job.

By now I had seen all too clearly the horrific impact residential schools had had on huge segments of the Indigenous community. Many of the issues—poverty, social dysfunction, health—had their genesis in a system that tried to systematically eliminate First Nations peoples. It amounted to nothing short of cultural genocide. The first-generation victims were left to their own devices. Many wound up on the streets of Winnipeg and across Western Canada, battling substance abuse or worse. Their children were born into that dysfunction and thus they too suffered consequences. As I have said before, it is the great shame of this nation. As one Indigenous leader once told me, "You spent a hundred years trying to destroy us, and it will take a hundred years to fix this."

Besides Murray Sinclair, I had the privilege of meeting many Indigenous leaders from across Canada. I always found their approach to be honest and genuine, even in the face of seemingly insurmountable odds. The hope was that the Truth and Reconciliation process would be the beginning of a nation's healing and an opportunity to force those who held biases to look past them and see what really happened. To ask the question, "Would any group of people, given what was done to them over generations, have any fewer challenges?" Of course not.

As the public sessions began, I spent time with a young boy who had trained as a traditional hoop dancer. Just ten, he was very skilled, and he had a story of his own to tell. Both his grandparents and great-grandparents had been forced to attend residential schools. His family lived in Winnipeg's north end, not far from the school where he was being taught some traditional ways. The family survived in what were obviously difficult circumstances. I drove to the boy's house to pick him up so we could do some taping with him at the school. I knocked on the door and his mom answered, clearly embarrassed that I would see their living conditions. I assured her we would call when we got to the school.

On the drive over, this young fellow seemed quiet, not the bubbly, bright kid I had met the day before. But at the school his energy seemed to pick up as the camera rolled, even telling us he wanted to be prime minister one day so that he could try to fix "this mess." On the way back home he revealed that he was worried. His older brother had gotten caught up in the Aboriginal gangs that controlled much of the neighbourhood. His brother's thirteenth birthday was today, but his family did not know where he was. He had run away to be with the gang two days ago, and they hadn't heard a word from him. This little boy was clearly lost without his older brother and scared about what might happen. Then he opened the door and was gone. I thought about that little fellow for weeks, even went back and knocked on the door, but the family had moved. I could only hope things with his brother had worked out. All too often in Winnipeg's north end, they did not.

In July I went to Saskatchewan, where a tornado had plowed through the First Nations community of Kawacatoose. It had been a powerful twister, leaving a swath of destruction several kilometres long right through town. Amazingly, nobody was killed.

I had never seen the destruction a tornado could create up close like that before. At one home, nothing was left standing on the foundation. What used to be the house was now a splintered pile of debris sitting in a heap perhaps twenty metres from where it used to rest. It didn't look like a house anymore. In one spot a fridge door stuck out, and in another pile of debris was what resembled a bed, but really it was all just a five-metre-high collection of broken things.

A man was standing nearby with two children, staring down into the now wide-open basement. I wondered if he was still in shock. It would be quite understandable. He spoke quietly, telling me the sky went black just before they saw the tornado heading right for them. He had gathered up his family and they'd huddled under the basement stairs, all ten of them. With heads down and eyes closed, they heard a sound like the roar of a freight train or a jet engine close by. When they looked up, their house was gone.

Nearby, at another ranch-style bungalow, a fellow was out back gathering up cattle. It looked as if someone had sliced through the barn with an enormous jagged knife. One corner of the bungalow appeared to have had a big bite taken out of it. But a strange thing happened there. In between the dining room and living room was one of those partitions with shelves that you could see through from one room to the other. On those shelves stood a delicate blue glass vase with a photograph of a young boy beside it. All around was chaos—the roof was torn off, the kitchen was ripped out, insulation hung from the rafters—but those two items were sitting where they always had been, untouched. Unreal. We taped for about five hours straight, walking from home to destroyed home, talking with people and gathering some of the video they had managed to record on their phones, pictures of this massively destructive act of nature they were lucky to survive. Nobody was angry. Nobody was demanding government help. The band council office had turned into a help centre with food and clothes for those who needed them. Other band councils in the area were sending what they could. Their community was strong.

It was a long seven-hour drive back to Winnipeg. The next night we showed the country this incredible story of destruction, of survival, and of people who were moving forward—together.

THE MISSING McCANNS

In the fall of 2010 we travelled to Alberta and the story of Lyle and Marie McCann. It was news that any family would dread. Back in July, these grandparents, retired and taking trips in their RV, had disappeared while on their way to British Columbia. They were gone without a trace. Days later their empty, burned-out motorhome was discovered deep in the bush. Then the vehicle they had been towing turned up hundreds of kilometres away. The credit card they had last been seen using at a gas station hadn't been used since.

I first spoke to their son Bret on the phone. He was a broken man. There is never a more uncomfortable moment in a journalist's career than when you have to call good people who are in the middle of their grief. I began by telling him how sorry I was that he and his family had found themselves in this circumstance and offered my sincere sympathy. I also told him I would understand completely if he just hung up now. I've never really understood why average folks talk to journalists. I am fairly certain that, under most circumstances, I wouldn't. He said no, that was okay. "It's just that everybody in the house jumps every time the phone rings."

Bret was a soft-spoken gentleman. He thanked me for my concern and asked me how he could help. I explained that I wanted to put a human face on this tragedy, to walk through what details they did know in hopes that someone, somewhere might recall a critical detail. I explained that it would involve coming to meet with him and his wife Mary-Ann and do some taping. I didn't want them to have any surprises. He said yes, please come.

The weekend we arrived, three generations of McCann men were searching using a grid they had drawn on a map, working increasing distances from where the vehicles had been found. Every waking moment, evenings and weekends, they went down another back road in trucks and on ATVs, searching. It was a Herculean task. There were thousands of those back roads. It didn't matter: winter was coming and they had to do something.

When I first met Bret and Mary-Ann in person, they welcomed me as if inviting a distant cousin into their home. They served tea and cookies, but we all knew difficult moments were ahead. Bret admitted he had now arrived at the conclusion that there would not be a happy ending for his dear parents. Something horrible had happened and they were gone. He was sure of it. Now, he just wanted to bring them home. His wife was still not comfortable with this conclusion. She talked about how Marie had been like a mom to her and wanted to believe, against all evidence, that some miracle might occur and they would surface. We all knew it wasn't true, and it broke my heart to sit there and hear her say it out loud.

Online, forty thousand members of the Lyle and Marie McCann information page waited for any little bit of news. Rewards for information were offered. A "leave the light on" campaign, complete with a song, had people across the country leaving their porch lights on all night as a sign of support and respect. In the end the police had their suspicions, which fell on an unlikable character named Travis Edward Vader.

What unfolded next was a tragedy of errors, legal manoeuvres and missteps that continued for almost a decade. Vader was eventually convicted of manslaughter in their deaths but has always denied any involvement and continues to pursue appeals. He's not the only one serving a sentence. That entire family continues to carry the weight of the loss of Lyle and Marie, every single day. Their bodies have never been found. Sometimes there just isn't any justice.

THE LITTLE HOCKEY PLAYER

I can't remember whether the story of little Nathaniel Thorassie even registered with me when it was first reported in December of 2010. I must have seen it in the paper. December 4—just three weeks before Christmas. Some young lads had wandered down to play hockey on the ice on the Red River. The ice broke and one little fellow slipped under the water and was now missing.

Then, in January, we were crossing a bridge over the frozen river when I looked through the van window and saw some bright red tents set up on the surface of the ice and police vehicles parked along the bank. What was going on? I called a fellow I knew at the Winnipeg Police Service, Sergeant Rob Riffel. He was a straight shooter and we had worked together before. The underwater search-and-rescue unit had resumed its search for Nathaniel. I asked if I could go down and talk to them. Rob, who was a member of the team, said sure.

It was a good thirty degrees below zero, a typical Winnipeg January. That didn't stop them. They had cut a hole through the ice in the shape of a triangle. The ice was a good metre thick, and the slush moving in the current under it was another two metres deep. It was pitch dark. Guided only by a donated side-scan sonar, they worked the bottom by hand, investigating each object blinking back on the machine, working the grid they had mapped on the bottom. Sometimes it was a tire or a shopping cart. Sometimes their diving gear became tangled in fishing line. But their motivation was stronger than that. Where was Nathaniel?

The six-year-old had been doing what so many Canadian kids do every day. He'd been outside with his ten-year-old brother playing street hockey. At some point, they had wandered down to the river nearby. A young man driving by in his pickup heard Nathaniel's brother yelling. He grabbed a rope from the back of his truck and managed to save the older boy's life, but little Nathaniel was pulled under the ice by the fast-flowing water.

An initial underwater search turned up no trace. After Christmas the team was determined to search again, farther downstream. Working on a tether in the frigid, dark water, they hoped Nathaniel's body had been snagged by debris on the bottom. A hand would push its way up through the slushy ice in the triangle as one ice-covered diver surfaced, to be pulled out and spelled off by the next guy. It was brutally cold, tough work.

Often when you speak with police officers, their media training kicks in and you get these monosyllabic responses, devoid of opinion or emotion. But these fellows had kids not much different in age than Nathaniel, and this was hitting close to home. In one interview, a burly young officer began to speak but had to stop, his emotions getting the better of him. His daughter was the same age as Nathaniel.

Each day they hoped it would be the day they found that little boy. If not, they were more than prepared to start all over again the next day. Beyond its sadness, the search became a powerful statement about the dedication of those who served, about just how much they were prepared to put on the line. It went on for over three freezing weeks.

It would be in September, many months after they were forced to abandon their winter search, that officers confirmed they had found little Nathaniel's remains, and brought him home from the river so his family could finally rest.

ELECTION 2011

I needed a break. All the sadness was starting to pile up on my shoulders. Of course, you could always count on politics to offer some comic relief. The country's federal political scene was in nothing short of turmoil. The opposition had defeated the budget of Stephen Harper's government, a motion of non-confidence had been pushed through the House of Commons and Canadians were off to the polls. Again. Great. B-roll, B-roll, clip. I had worked on many federal elections, the last time doing reality checks on campaign promises. In my opinion it was dry, borderline boring stuff that rarely achieved a "gotcha" moment.

Then a producer in Toronto, Michael Gruzuk, suggested my little band and I should do something completely different this election. Michael asked us to seek out people who had the same names as the leaders of the various parties and speak with them about the election. I had my doubts, but I also thought it sounded like a hoot, so off we went.

I found an Elizabeth May in Alberta, and a fellow named Jack Leyton (I know, different spelling) was a professional rock guitarist and composer in Ontario. In Toronto I found a baby named Iggy (for Michael Ignatieff), but the most interesting fellow of the bunch was a guy named Stephen Harper who worked as a realtor in Ottawa.

This Stephen was a funny guy. On the pens he handed out to potential buyers, he called himself THE REAL STEPHEN HARPER. He claimed someone close to Harper had given the prime minister one of his pens, and Harper asked for more. He also told people he'd found the gold American Express card the politician used, by the Centennial Flame on Parliament Hill, and it still worked!

But the highlight of the piece was when I persuaded him to plant one of his realtor FOR SALE signs right on the Parliament Hill lawn. Persuading him was easy, but pulling it off—that was no easy task. RCMP officers were posted every ten metres. But somehow, we managed to pull up, plant the sign, get the shots and get out undetected. The symbolism of a FOR SALE sign on the lawn of Parliament, with Stephen Harper's name on it, in the middle of an election was not lost on me. But apparently it was on others.

We got some applause, but mostly people didn't seem to like the series. The election had them in a grumpy mood. Many complained about CBC showing "trivial fluff" (as some called it) instead of hard news coverage. As if there wasn't already plenty of that! Even some of my colleagues thought I had harpooned my own career by fronting the pieces. I thought, "Jeez, people, it's only a bit of fun—lighten up!" If Rick Mercer could do it, why couldn't I? I guess Stephen Harper just wasn't that funny. The real Stephen Harper, I mean, not the realtor. Even so, he wound up winning a majority.

It was certainly a lesson in trying to anticipate viewer interests, and in what to avoid when the federal writ is dropped. It was also a reminder that producers in Toronto too often mean trouble. No joke. Okay, maybe a small one. Hehe.

SOMETHING ABOUT EARL

When I was a kid, my favourite part of *Reader's Digest* was the "Drama in Real Life" section. Now, I decided to return to what I knew people wanted more of—real-life human drama that involved courage and spirit. It came in the form of a young man named Earl.

Earl was in his early twenties when I first met him. To say his life hadn't been easy would be an understatement. Earl Henry Cook had been born prematurely, literally dropped into a toilet by his drug-addicted mom in Winnipeg's notorious inner city. He immediately had to go into detox. Doctors didn't expect him to survive, but he did. He became a ward of Child and Family Services.

Debbie Hopkins first met him years earlier while working as a teacher's assistant. He had been shuffled from foster home to foster home. As we sat at her dining room table, she explained to me that something about this fidgety, undersized Grade 6 kid just made her want to take him home and cuddle him. She decided to pursue adoption. They gave her the list. Fetal alcohol syndrome. Tourette's syndrome. Asperger's syndrome. Pervasive development disorder. ADHD. It didn't matter. He had been with her ever since.

Debbie Hopkins was a woman of no small resolve herself. Her faith was strong, and it had to be. Years before, she had been a young mother with another baby on the way when her husband was in a terrible accident. He would never be the same. Weeks later her daughter, Kelly Lynne, was born, but the baby suffered from a heart defect and lived only a few months. Later Debbie lost her husband in a tragic fire. It was only her son Darby who kept her going. But as he became more independent, she felt a calling to bring Earl home.

She told me that people approached her all the time to say how lucky Earl was that she had adopted him. She didn't see it like that. "You know what? It works both ways, because we're very lucky to have Earl."

I decided the best place to meet Earl would be in his bedroom, although really it was more like a shrine to the Detroit Red Wings. He was without a doubt their biggest fan. Call it his Asperger's obsession. The walls were covered with signed autographs and jerseys. The carpet, the drapes, the bedspread—the entire room was Detroit.

In true Asperger's fashion, he was very direct. If something was on his mind, he said so. "I tell those guys to get their act together," he said of the Red Wings. "I want them to win the cup." But as he was showing me around his Detroit "shrine," it was something else he said that really struck me. "I told my mom that if I ever die, I want to die in this room. She said, 'I don't want you to die in this room.' I said, 'I'll be in Red Wing heaven then.'"

Earl never stopped fighting for his life. At the age of nineteen, he was diagnosed with cancer. They had to remove his leg and half of his pelvis. There wasn't a lot of time to think about it. The cancer was so bad, a huge tumour, that he would not survive if it remained in his body.

It was during those long, difficult hospital days that Earl talked to the head coach of the Detroit Red Wings at the time, Mike Babcock. TSN commentator Darren Dreger had heard about Earl and what he was going through at Mount Sinai Hospital in Toronto, and he went to visit him. When he realized what a big fan Earl was of Detroit, he got Mike on the phone so Earl could talk to him. They had been good friends ever since.

We videotaped Earl at a Detroit game. All the players knew him, and you could tell Mike had a lot of admiration for Earl's spunk. "He's got an infectious personality, he's full of life and I think he's an example to all of us that you play with the hand you're dealt, work as hard as you can with it. You dream, and make things happen for yourself."

When the piece aired, the desk in Toronto called to say there was not a dry eye in the newsroom. Earl—such a brave, funny young man—touched everyone who got to meet him through our profile.

But there would be no happy ending. News came that the cancer was back. It had spread to his kidney and his heart. More treatment was needed. When we went to do some more taping, Earl said he had a motto: "Tough times don't last, tough people do."

He was gone not long after. I attended the NHL Players' Association fall gathering, where Debbie was presented with the Ace Bailey Award of Courage on Earl's behalf. Very appropriate.

CHASING ROYALTY

In the summer of 2011, I was handed an assignment most network journalists would trample over each other to get. The royal superstars were coming to Canada. Prince William and his new wife, Catherine, would fly into Ottawa, head up to Yellowknife, then continue on to Calgary and the stampede, and we would follow them every step of the way. The bigger question was, would anybody care?

My wife Pam is a huge monarchist. Her mom was among the crowd in London, outside Westminster Abbey, for Queen Elizabeth's coronation. I like to tease her about her royal affliction, but Will and Kate had become a very big deal, and we were told to stick to them like glue. Off we went to Ottawa. Security was tight, very tight. Movement was practically impossible. When the tour had been planned over a year earlier, Prince William was still a single man. Now he was arriving with a partner on his arm, and a mob of media trailed behind, ten times more foreign press than during the Queen's tour just a year before.

I was checking things out on Parliament Hill when Paul Harrison, a royal correspondent from Britain's Sky News, stuck a camera in my face. Paul had a bit of a pedigree. Many years earlier, his father John was in Canada covering another royal tour when news came that his wife was about to give birth. In a gracious gesture, Queen Elizabeth offered John a seat on the royal plane so he could hitch a ride back to London and be there for the arrival of his little boy. That little boy was Paul. Now here was Paul, covering a royal tour in Canada himself.

Paul cajoled me into doing a television interview about the popularity of the newlyweds in Canada. Really, it went against CBC protocol and had me straying into the world of commentary a little bit, but what the hell. I said, "You have this mega-popular couple—they're the most popular couple in the world at the moment. But is what we're seeing celebrity interest or star worship, or is it renewed interest in the monarchy? *That* is the real question."

Afterward, I could not believe the number of people I heard from who had seen that clip across the pond in Merrie Olde England. Even the charming and lovely Ann MacMillan, our bureau chief in London at the time, sent me a nice email asking what I was doing cavorting with those British media yobs. Oh, the power of television.

Ottawa was all about parades and flag waving and Canada Day celebrations. We never got within a hundred metres of the royal power couple. But in Yellowknife, they practically landed in my lap. I had just gotten off the elevator in the Explorer Hotel, the same hotel Will and Kate were staying in, when I spotted an RCMP officer I knew from a previous royal visit. He said hello and casually asked me to just stand where I was for a moment. In through the doors they came, looking fresh and relaxed. Will shook a few hands, and I thought, "My God, that woman looks even thinner, if that's possible, in person." Then they quite literally brushed by me and were gone. I'm pretty sure I could have gotten a lock of Kate's lustrous hair had I wanted to.

Then it was off to the Calgary Stampede. After five days of chasing those two from Ontario to the Northwest Territories and Alberta, I thought, "They're going to be doing this for decades. Better them than me!"

A SINKING SHIP

The year 2012 marked the one hundredth anniversary of the most famous marine disaster in history, the sinking of the unsinkable, the *Titanic*. Our family has had a copy of *The Sinking of the Titanic and Great Sea Disasters* for many years. It was written and published in 1912, mere weeks after the disaster unfolded in the icy North Atlantic off the coast of Newfoundland.

Back then, reporters were dispatched to New York to meet the ships carrying survivors. The book was rushed to print, almost like a magazine, as publishers were determined to cash in on the disaster. The front of the book has a short dedication:

> To the 1635 souls who were lost with the ill-fated *Titanic*, and especially those heroic men, who, instead of trying to save themselves, stood aside that women and children might have their chance; of each of them let it be written, as it was written of a Greater One—"He Died That Others Might Live."

A comparison to the sacrifice of Christ himself, no less! So when *The National* decided to make a big production around the hundredth anniversary in mid-April, I said, "Count me in." I also planned to use our family's book as a prop in each piece. I wound up doing three stories altogether, each unique in its own way—stories that would take us right across North America in search of some answers.

TWO GENTLEMEN FROM WINNIPEG

Twenty Canadians were believed to have perished on the *Titanic*'s ill-fated maiden voyage. Among the dead was one fellow from Winnipeg. Among the living was another fellow from Winnipeg. I learned that these gentlemen had lived lives that followed strikingly similar paths. But the outcomes for each that fateful night couldn't have been more different.

Mark Fortune had made exactly that—a fortune—speculating on real estate along Winnipeg's famous Portage Avenue, just as the "Chicago of the North" was booming. He married and built a huge mansion for his wife and family along affluent Wellington Crescent.

Albert Dick, or Bertie, as his friends liked to call him, was also born in Winnipeg, but he ventured farther west in search of his fortune. He found it in Calgary, where he too prospered in real estate, constructing office buildings and putting up the Alexandra Hotel, which in its day was the finest hotel in the city. He also built a mansion, a monument to his success.

Both families decided to embark on world-trekking overseas vacations. While in Egypt, one of Mark Fortune's daughters, Alice, had visited a clairvoyant, who warned her about travel on the water. "You are in danger every time you travel on the sea, for I see you adrift on the ocean in an open boat." It was a bit of a family joke.

Both the Fortune family and the Dicks had booked first-class passage for their return on the finest cruise liner ever built, RMS *Titanic*. The purser looking after the Dicks was quite taken (you might say infatuated) with Bertie's wife, the beautiful young Vera. He made sure to attend to her every need. Those first few days were uneventful, with the families strolling the decks and enjoying the luxurious accommodations and fine dining. The designer of the ship, Thomas Andrews, was along for its maiden voyage, and when he discovered Albert and Vera Dick were married on the very day the *Titanic* was launched (the previous May), he insisted they join him to dine, which they did on the evening of April 14, 1912.

Now, some of these details I learned from research, but the most important details would come from the people interviewed one hundred years ago in that historic book of mine. I also used it to track down their descendants. I found them on opposite ends of the continent.

Bob Rutherford lived on Heckman's Island, Nova Scotia, pretty much as close on land as you could get to the wreckage of the *Titanic* itself. Mark Fortune was his great-grandfather. Bob and his wife were gracious enough to invite us in, insisting we stay for a meal and giving me all the family dirt. All the Fortune women had made it back, but father Mark and son Charles were lost, their bodies never found. Soon, the family fortune was gone too. The stock market crash of 1929 took care of that.

Ironically, Bob Rutherford's father was also lost at sea. A naval officer, his ship was sunk by a German U-boat torpedo back in 1942, not far from where the *Titanic* had gone down. Even more incredible, Bob himself joined the Navy and rose to the rank of commander before retiring. Throughout his career people warned him he was tempting fate, but as he liked to joke, "I guess bad luck doesn't always come in threes."

Fifty-seven hundred kilometres away, in Seattle, Washington, I found Albert Dick's descendants, almost as far from the wreck of the *Titanic* as you could get on this continent. The Dicks may have survived the *Titanic*, but it wound up wrecking their lives anyway. When I first managed to get Bruce Van Norman on the telephone, he didn't really want to talk to me. He was the grandson of Albert Dick, and he said the memories of the *Titanic* and its lifelong impact on his family were better left buried. I must have talked to him four or five times that week. Each time, he took my calls, so I knew I had a chance.

He did not want us videotaping in his house—he was worried the publicity would attract unwanted attention. I said no problem, we would get some scenic visuals down by the water, and any interviews we could do back at our hotel. I asked him if he wanted to bring anyone with him. His daughter Kimberly was interested, and it turned out she had a striking resemblance to her great-grandmother, Vera Dick. The story they told helped me to understand why they preferred to keep their family secrets just that—secret.

After dining with the ship's designer, the Dicks retired to their cabin. Just before midnight they felt the bump of the *Titanic* hitting the massive iceberg. Within minutes, the young purser was knocking at their door, insisting that they head for the lifeboats. There was no real panic, though; nobody, at that point, really believed the *Titanic* was capable of sinking. But as time went on, they put on their lifebelts and the crew started launching lifeboats.

An unwritten code of conduct, "women and children first," was understood. As the story goes, the beautiful young Vera insisted on staying with her husband, even if it meant an icy death in the North Atlantic. She was offered three different lifeboats but refused to get in any of them without him. Suddenly, as she was clinging to Albert, the infatuated purser pushed them both into one of the last lifeboats. As they rowed away, they watched the *Titanic* slip beneath the surface. On the dock in New York, where they were taken by their rescue ship, RMS *Carpathia*, Vera Dick described the scene for a reporter. I had Kimberly read it on camera right from my book.

It was a powerful moment, this young woman who bore such a striking resemblance to her great-grandmother, reading aloud her very words.

Even in Canada, where we have such clear nights ... I have never seen such a clear sky. The stars were very bright and we could see the *Titanic* plainly, like a great hotel on the water. Floor after floor, the lights went out as we watched. It was horrible, horrible. I can't bear to think about it. From the distance, as we rowed away, we could hear the band playing "Nearer My God to Thee."

But when the Dicks returned to Calgary, their rescue haunted them. Rumours persisted that Albert had dressed up like a woman to gain access to a lifeboat. That was false, but people chose to believe otherwise. It began to affect his business, to the point where he was forced to sell his glamorous hotel and eventually his mansion. The Dicks remained in Calgary but became reclusive, rarely even mentioning the *Titanic* again. Bruce Van Norman said it had a huge impact on his grandmother and was a constant source of family tension.

After Bruce and Kimberly told their family story, it was as though a weight had been lifted. They lightened up considerably and decided to let me see the contents of a box they had brought with them, a box that had been sitting undisturbed in their attic for decades. It contained old family photos, ghosts from a different time, but there in the bottom of the box was a photograph of a lifeboat. It was the very lifeboat that had saved Albert and Vera. The picture was taken by a passenger on board the rescue ship *Carpathia* as the couple neared their salvation.

THOSE LITTLE SHOES

In Halifax I found "those little shoes." They were so small you could cradle them in your hand. The worn brown leather, the buttons still shiny on the shoes that held critical clues to one of the saddest mysteries in the tragedy that was the *Titanic*. Who was the unknown child? They were removed from the feet of a small child's body that was found floating in the icy Atlantic.

Producer Catherine Clark found some photographs that really brought the scene on the Halifax docks to life. They showed police officers guarding the bodies that arrived on shore while nearby workers swept up the belongings of the lost, putting them in piles to be burned. One of those officers was Sergeant Clarence Northover of the Halifax Police Department. He had four children of his own, but one had died in infancy. When he saw those little brown shoes, sitting in a pile, he realized he couldn't let them be burned. He tucked them away for safekeeping.

Decades later Clarence's grandson Earle donated them to the Maritime Museum of the Atlantic where, as he told me, he knew they belonged, to help people understand the depth of the tragedy. But what was the name of their owner? The little child had been buried in Halifax with a simple gravestone engraved AN UNKNOWN CHILD.

The new technology of ancient DNA analysis solved an almost hundred-year-old mystery. Dr. Ryan Parr of Thunder Bay was the expert called on to figure it out. Dr. Parr explained that ancient DNA analysis was like reaching back into the past to interview someone who had lived then. There wasn't much to work with. An examination of the unknown child's grave in Halifax had turned up some baby teeth and a fragment of bone. Initial DNA tests first pointed to a young Swedish lad, and then a thirteen-month-old Finnish boy.

But then there were those baby shoes, found on the Halifax pier. Dr. Parr realized the shoes were too big to have stayed on the feet of a thirteen-month-old in the North Atlantic. The initial DNA analysis must have gotten it wrong; the child must have been older. They tried again. This time a dentist was able to extract a better DNA sample from deep inside a molar.

A nineteen-month-old British boy, Sidney Leslie Goodwin, had been travelling in third class with his parents and five siblings, headed for a new life in America. Of the eight, his was the only body recovered. The DNA matched that of other Goodwins who had later emigrated and still lived around Chicago. Carole Goodwin was quite touched when I called and asked to come and interview her.

She was there the morning they reburied Sidney Goodwin's remains on that Halifax hillside. The Goodwin family also decided to keep the stone marking the grave as that of "an unknown child" as a tribute to all the children who lost their lives that fateful night.

WE'RE ON FIRE!

Of all the details surrounding the *Titanic* I discovered, the one I kept going back to was the issue of speed. On the night of April 12, without radar, in what was known to be iceberg-infested waters, RMS *Titanic* was doing over twenty-two knots, close to top speed. This was the largest passenger ship ever built, making it highly unlikely it would be able to respond quickly to oncoming danger. To me, this always begged the question, "Why the hell was the captain pushing the boat so quickly in the middle of the night, when visibility was at it worst?" The more I dug, the more I realized the explanation came down to one word: *fire*. Not "on fire," as most of us would imagine, but on fire deep in the bowels of the ship, where they stored the massive amount of coal required to push a boat of that size and weight through the ocean.

Six hundred and fifty tons of coal a day. That was what it took. Thousands of tons for just a single voyage, all stored in massive bins down along the waterline and below, near gigantic furnaces that converted that coal into steam to power the propellers.

There had been a coal strike in the weeks leading up to the *Titanic*'s departure. It was a predicament that may have led to the fire that sealed the *Titanic*'s fate.

I found a research paper by a gentleman named Robert Essenhigh. Essenhigh was professor emeritus of mechanical and aerospace engineering at Ohio State University, specializing in combustion. He had been asked to investigate the *Titanic*, but his findings were largely ignored. He seemed somewhat surprised that this Canadian journalist was now sitting in his sunroom, enjoying a cup of tea and asking questions about it.

Essenhigh said that in 1912, the owners of White Star Line, the British shipping company that operated the *Titanic*, were worried the strike had made coal so scarce that the *Titanic* would not have enough fuel to cross the Atlantic. They decided to transfer what coal they did have from other ships in their fleet to the *Titanic*. Problem solved? Not really. Under certain conditions, moving coal around can cause it to catch fire; it can spontaneously combust. This wasn't just a theory of Professor Essenhigh's, it was a known fact.

When the coal was moved into the *Titanic*, Essenhigh said, it started to burn in one of the coal bunkers. He showed me a diagram of the ship's hull, outlining where this had happened. The crew had been ordered to keep quiet. Fires in coal bins were not unheard of. Given that the coal was enclosed in a large metal bunker, it remained somewhat contained. The usual way to deal with such fires was to have men simply shovel the burning coal into the furnaces. But on board the *Titanic*, the coal kept burning upward in the bunker and was hard to reach.

Twelve men worked round the clock shovelling, trying to keep the bunker fire under control as the *Titanic* raced through the water. The more they shovelled, the faster the ship went. As the furnaces and boilers created steam, it drove the ship to almost full speed.

Of course, the heat from the fire was also affecting the metal on the side of the ship, the same side that the iceberg struck. This was confirmed by fireman J. Dilley, who survived the sinking and testified during the inquiry conducted by the Committee on Commerce, of the United States Senate. Dilley stated that the metal in the storage bin "glowed red with the heat."

There was my reason. The fire could well have been the reason the *Titanic* was moving at almost top speed, in the middle of the night, through dangerous iceberg alleys. Dilley further testified,

"No sir, we didn't get the fire out." There was talk that "we'd have to put the passengers off in New York and then call on the fire boats there to help us put out the fire."

Other testimony claimed the fire had been put out, but Robert Essenhigh didn't think so. The iceberg made contact on the front side of starboard, where the coal fire had been burning for days.

The Senate inquiry also found the *Titanic*'s speed "excessive" given the ice conditions. Ironically, it was likely the ocean that finally put the fire out as it sent the majestic ship to the bottom.

I turned up one other juicy little tidbit around the fire story. Some conjectured that the fire was the reason American financier J.P. Morgan, who owned the White Star Line, quietly cancelled his ticket on the maiden voyage the night before. It was said he was seen bringing his luggage back to his Rolls-Royce, on the dock at Southampton, and driving away. Of course, separating rumour from fact is never easy when it comes to the *Titanic*.

CHAPTER 18

Digital Demons

Increasingly, just about every story we produced was finding its way online. I say "just about" because the CBC's experimentation on the digital platform was clunky at best. It certainly was in 2012, anyway. It seemed to be madly heading off in all directions with little cohesion. To be fair, it was difficult to know which direction to head in. Build something yourself or attach yourself to something much bigger, like Facebook and YouTube?

Inside the Mother Corp., digital was now referred to as "the third silo" (radio and TV being the other two), and it was quickly becoming the biggest silo the corporation had ever built. It was a silo because, as the other two had historically been, it was not great at playing with the others. Many of the folks being hired had little or no experience in either radio or TV, and some didn't seem concerned with trying to learn. This led to a lot of duplication of effort and flat-out turf protection. The CBC, like every other media outlet, was trying to figure out how to wrestle this digital monster into submission. Meanwhile, digital was gorging itself on resources at both the regional and network levels.

We used to argue that it was far better to get it right than to get it first. That went out the window. Now first was everything.

The more power digital achieved, the cockier that platform became. Youngsters would call up demanding your material so they could remould it for online stories. Digital was a head without a body. They never left the building, but they wanted access to everything gathered by those who did. Management had seen the future and it was digital. CBC.CA was becoming all-powerful. It needed more and more resources. Its appetite was voracious.

And the online platform was starting to creep into editorial decisions. The concept of clickbait—running video of, say, a squirrel on water skis—was becoming a thing. Not just eye candy that folks couldn't resist online, but stuff that was making its way into all the newscasts with regularity. It was the tipping point, where the digital agenda, or what some would call the "dumbing down" of content, took precedence.

Back in 1999, David Bowie commented that we really had no idea where this internet train would take us. No idea. "I think we're actually on the cusp of something exhilarating and terrifying," he said. It was certainly beginning to look that way.

Toronto was on the phone. Serious discussions were underway about whether my unit was needed in Winnipeg anymore. For a while, it looked like my little team and I would be thrown out with the television "bathwater." Ironic, I thought, when we outproduced pretty much anyone else in the system by a long shot. I'm not just blowing smoke here—that was a fact, and we also produced material at a much lower cost than many. But we weren't in Toronto. It's far easier to whack someone when you don't have to look them in the eye. In the end, another intervention by the best management support I had in Toronto, Jonathan Whitten, left Warren and me still standing. Jaison Empson had already been reassigned. Now Terry Stapleton departed to produce the local supper-hour show. It was a big loss, but we were determined to carry on.

I was not immune to reading the tea leaves. I had always known a good story was about great pictures, strong characters and emotion. They had always been good clickbait. The concept of a good story hadn't really changed—yet. Just the delivery system was being adjusted.

And what the internet was great at delivering was more information than any one human could absorb. It made searching out stuff that hadn't really hit mainstream, or certainly not the network, much easier. I went from reading four daily and about twenty-five weekly newspapers to hunting on the internet. The reality was that most of those weeklies had died, early victims in the digital universe, and many dailies were also in trouble or dead. The CBC decided newspapers like *The Globe and Mail* or even the *Winnipeg Free Press* were no longer required reading for a network journalist and stopped buying them. I began buying my own subscriptions.

During the summer I produced a story about trains killing grizzly bears in Banff National Park. The majestic bruins were wandering onto the tracks to eat grain spilled from passing railcars. There was a scramble to fix the grain cars and install systems to scare the bears away. They had limited success.

Next on my agenda was the renewed search for Sir John Franklin's ships, *Erebus* and *Terror*, in the High Arctic, which was attracting a lot of attention. This team had technology on its side and, armed with other knowledge that had always been available, that of Indigenous elders, felt confident about finding the two ships somewhere along the Northwest Passage, where Franklin had died without completing his navigation of it. The team found them.

After that came the Calgary Stampede's one hundredth anniversary. That was a hoot. I spent some time with Bruce Roy, the stampede's longest-serving volunteer. He had started back in 1959, the year I was born. Bruce's passion was the Percheron—or any draft horse. Those gentle giants, which could easily weigh a ton, were descended from the great horses of Flanders, war beasts from medieval times. Bruce was respected across North America. What he didn't know about draft horses wasn't worth knowing.

Then there were the Vaughns, Ed and Dianne. They had met at the stampede and were now celebrating fifty years together. They were great sports in letting me tell the story of their half-century romance.

Finally, I was honoured to meet rancher and businessman Bill Siebens, who gave the Calgary Stampede Foundation the finest gift it had ever received. For the hundredth anniversary, he was handing over thirty-two hundred hectares of some of the most beautiful grazing land in Alberta, $11 million worth, so that it could be enjoyed and protected, unchanged, in perpetuity. Bill made his fortune in oil and gas, but this wasn't about money. This was about two things: protecting the land and building a legacy.

He invited us out to his OH Ranch to shoot some video. My oh my, what a spot—rolling hills and mountains, wildflowers, historic homesteads beside sparkling streams. Then there were the stories, like the one about the Sunshine Kid lying low from the law on the ranch. Bill loved a good story. Bill also owned over thirteen hundred head of cattle. These guys were serious ranchers and did all their work on horseback.

Naturally, I decided I had to ride with Bill. The problem was that the last time I had been on a horse, it wasn't a horse, it was a pony, and I was a kid being led around by a rope attached to the not-so-majestic steed. I casually mentioned to the top ranch hand that I wanted to ride with Bill, but I didn't want to hurt myself or look like an idiot. That sort of imagery could kill you, even before the social media era. Remember the picture of Robert Stanfield fumbling the football, or Gilles Duceppe campaigning in a cheese factory wearing that hairnet? Deadly. Factor in a viral social media disaster—"CBC Reporter Tumbles Off Horse!"—and it could be a career-ending bit of video.

He assured me my horse was used to greenhorns, and as long as he wasn't spooked by, say, a snake, I should be okay. Great. Bill arrived and we were ready to head off for a ride. You don't realize

Philanthropist Bill Siebens and I astride our trusty steeds. I look pretty comfortable in this shot, but you should have seen me trying to get on the darn horse! Warren Kay is manning the camera.

how big a damn horse is until you are beside one, though. The stirrup was a good metre off the ground. It took all my effort, and several tries, just to get in the saddle. But once in there, I could have stayed all day. I jokingly called myself a saltwater cowboy, and yes, the horse did all the work.

Bill was a charming companion, a real gentleman with his respectful demeanour, kind disposition, and that gift that would give so much enjoyment for decades, perhaps centuries, to come. I will remember that perfect day for a long time. It was also the last story we worked on as a team. Afterward, Terry headed off on vacation and then to the local newsroom. He would be missed.

LANDING A BIGGER CATCH

That fall Warren and I decided to go fishing. *The National* and Toronto producer Sheila Rider, a good buddy of mine, had launched a new series called "Canada at Large," and we wanted to own it. The idea was to find tales that reflected the country and the average folks who lived in it. It sounded a lot like *Country Canada*, so I was up for it.

I had always wanted to do a story on the catfish in the Red River, and this was my chance. They were all mud, slime and whiskers, but the hook was that these channel cats were the biggest in the world. I found just the fellow to help us land one. Stu McKay had probably caught more of these monsters than anyone, fishing off his pontoon boat in the turbulent outflow of the Red River near Lockport, Manitoba. England, Germany, Italy, South Africa—Stu had entertained anglers from around the world for over thirty years. And he was a good sport. When I joked that these catfish were dog-ugly, he reminded me that beauty was in the eye of the beholder.

I even managed to haul one massive beast out of the water. Tradition dictated you were supposed to kiss the creature before putting it back in the water. Not one to kiss and tell, I guess I broke with tradition. There was no way in hell those slimy fish lips were touching mine! Stu had so much fun that he wanted us to start a fishing show, catching and cooking fish as we travelled across the country. It was tempting, but I still had a pretty good gig.

Our next chapter in "Canada at Large" was right out of that old American TV sitcom *Green Acres*. Terry and Monique Mierau had been world-class opera singers, performing right across Europe. But the allure of life on the road or in the big city was no longer hitting the sweetest of notes anymore. So they decided to head for farm central—rural Manitoba. Their new life with pigs, chickens, cows and sheep was decidedly less glamorous, but they were confident they could hold this note much longer.

There were the kids with a science project that was carried along on a space shuttle mission, and the fellow who predicted the weather using the spleen of a pig. And there was the young fellow showing his prize cow at Agribition in Regina—but in truth he had his eye on another big-eyed gal, the young lady across the aisle, and romance was in the air! All nice, fluffy potential clickbait. But the assignment for Remembrance Day 2012 was decidedly not.

THE FIRST TO FALL

That fall Michael Gruzuk got in touch. As the senior producer at *The National*, he was also tasked with developing the network's plan to do a full hour of television for November 11. Given my long-standing commitment to chronicling our country's military service, he asked if I wanted to be involved. The idea was to devote the entire hour to the first Canadian woman to be killed in combat. Her name was Nichola Goddard. It would turn out to be one of the toughest stories I have ever had to tell.

The Goddards were now living in Prince Edward Island, but they had literally lived around the world. They were highly educated, thoughtful folks who, I was sure, had their doubts about this media racket, especially when some damn reporter wanted to shine a big bright light on their grief. Little is more difficult than that first call. It's cordial and friendly—small talk and attempts at developing common ground—but everyone knows where it's heading. Can we talk about your first-born, your daughter, now lost? Can we explore the intimate details of her life, her death? Can we record everything and put it on national television?

My position on these delicate matters has never wavered. When approaching people to do interviews, to let you in, you must be 1) professional, 2) truthful and, above all, 3) respectful. I never lie or try to fudge what the call is about. That is pointless, and if you want to know why, I refer you to number 3. If you cannot establish a relationship of trust, trust that you will get it right, trust that you won't blindside them and trust that you will be true—in this case to Nichola Goddard's memory and her family's grief—there will be no respect, and probably no story.

Mom Sally turned out to be a kind and gentle soul. I mentioned I had a daughter of my own, and that I couldn't begin to understand the weight of the grief they were carrying, never mind that in its most raw form it had already been on full display to the entire country. Nichola had been killed six years earlier on tour in Afghanistan. Her funeral had been broadcast live on national television. The Goddards had learned to carry that weight, but it was still a very heavy load.

Sally and her husband Tim agreed I could come and spend some time with them. It was a beautiful fall in Atlantic Canada. Sally and the dog met us at the door and invited us in. I could sense some unease; perhaps they'd had second thoughts about opening everything up again. But over a cup of tea we talked about how I saw the segment going, and I realized it was more of a slow, steady sadness that had settled in around Nichola's memory. I explained that my role was to tell Nichola's story and that of her family. I wanted viewers to know who this brave young woman was, not just from her pictures in uniform and the news reports announcing her death, but through the things her family wanted to say about her character and her motivation. Others would speak with her comrades about that saddest of days, and there would be a segment in which kids from one of the schools named after her would read some of her letters home.

Sally said she had some photos. Photos were always a good start. We spread them out on the dining room table. I took Warren aside and said, "Just start recording, and when I give the nod we'll be into the interview." It was an old technique of mine. Ease them into it. Keep things as relaxed and comfortable as possible. Sometimes the interview could be over before the subject even knew it had begun. Warren was a master at picking up on my signals.

Sally was a little nervous, picking her words carefully. I also realized that she was putting up a wall to protect herself from her emotions. We went through Nichola's breech birth, weighing just four pounds when she arrived in Papua New Guinea, where Tim and Sally had been teaching. She talked about how Nichola fancied herself as the fearless protector of her two younger sisters, Victoria and Kate. We talked about her time in officer training, and her marriage to her husband, Jason Beam.

We hadn't gotten far when Tim arrived home. Tim, a larger-than-life sort of character, gave us a little tour around the house, a museum to their life's work. He proudly showed us his nomadic collection: the war shields and carvings, the caribou drums and birchbark-biting pictures from Saskatchewan, and the many other pieces of art that adorned their lovely home. Right in the middle of it all, a picture of their three daughters, their finest achievements.

In the basement, a different display was tucked away behind the stairs. It was more of a shrine, really, with all the military remembrances, plaques and tokens of grief. A hand-signed note of condolence from the head of the Afghan Army. A shell casing from the last round fired in honour of Nichola. Their Nichola, Captain Nichola Goddard, was dead at the age of twenty-six.

Tim carried his grief in a different way than Sally. He carried it on his sleeve and held nothing back. He laughed as he remembered Nichola as a child of two and a half, when he found her down on the beach with a machete that was almost as big as she was, trying to crack open a coconut.

He also talked about her announcement that she was going to join the military, and his efforts to talk her out of it. Tim, a lifelong educator, believed that knowledge, not violence, changed things. Nichola argued that until peace was established, knowledge had no chance of succeeding. "I do what I do, so you can do what you do," she told her father. He proudly admitted she had won that debate.

Nichola had had options. Near the end of her required duty, she could have walked away. Instead she signed back on and made plans to head with her comrades to Afghanistan. She got her affairs in order. Wrote a will. Tim and Sally

Captain Nichola Goddard, pictured during a tour in Afghanistan, had a beautiful smile, one I unfortunately only ever saw in photographs.

installed phones in every room to make sure they didn't miss a call. They waited and hoped, but mostly they worried.

Tim and I sat in the front room, he in his comfortable chair. I was uncomfortable at best. "There's a certain ... a fear," Tim said. "I wouldn't say I had second sight, that I knew something horrible was going to happen, or anything like that." "But you're uneasy," I said. He replied, "I'm uneasy, yeah. I was uneasy."

I admitted I wasn't sure how to ask about what happened next. About how he found out. He said, "Well, it's easy enough. It was my birthday." At the time, Tim and Sally were both working in Calgary. There had been a phone message from son-in-law Jason. "I just called him back and he said, 'Nichola's been killed.' And, kinda, the roof fell in, right?" He rushed to Sally's school and a certain suspended disbelief settled in.

The plane carrying Nichola's body to CFB Trenton was late arriving. But the nation was intent on grieving with the Goddards. Although it was late at night, all along the Highway of Heroes, from Trenton to Toronto, people stood silently or held up Canadian flags to pay their respects. Nichola's funeral took place on a rainy May morning in the same church in Calgary where she had been married four years before. A nation watched on live television as the Goddards said goodbye to their first-born.

I couldn't imagine having the fortitude to carry myself as they did during those sad, horrible days. I remember sitting in the edit suite going through hours and hours of video material. Sally and Tim at the airport. At the church. At the National Military Cemetery in Ottawa, where Nichola rests. There was nowhere to escape with their grief.

Sally had boxes and boxes of cards, notes and letters sent from across the country and around the world. "We were finding ourselves becoming more and more burdened by memories," Sally remembered. A friend, an elder, gave them some good advice. "She said, 'Nichola needs to know that you're going to be all right. And the only way she's going to know that is if you stop being upset every time you see something. Nichola's got to rest.' And so, we started. We started putting everything in a box."

So many things were done to honour Nichola's memory— schools dedicated, books written and ships launched. It seemed, in some ways, that the Goddards were a little embarrassed by it all, just in the sense of knowing how many other young people had come home from Afghanistan in metal boxes, and *their* loss was barely noted. But they deeply appreciated every gesture, and they and Nichola's sisters worked hard at creating a legacy in Nichola's memory. The Nichola Goddard Foundation funded a program, Light up Papua New Guinea, to bring lights to remote areas. It also funded scholarships at both the University of Calgary and the University of Prince Edward Island.

But perhaps the most poignant tribute came from Tim himself. "I do what I do, so you can do what you do"—that was what Nichola had said to her father. As difficult as it must have been, Tim honoured that rationale by working to help Afghan educators, travelling to the war-torn country to help set up education systems to try, like his daughter, to make a difference. It was a deeply moving expression of love for his daughter and what he could do to honour her life.

KING KWONG

In the spring of 2013, I was contacted by a young man from British Columbia who was possessed by a bit of an obsession. It centred on a gentleman named Larry Kwong. Chad Soon had learned about Larry through his grandpa, and now he was making it his life's work to ensure everybody knew. I was happy to help.

When I first met Larry in Calgary, he walked with two canes. Only later did I learn both his legs had been lost to illness. Walking without them, at almost the age of ninety, was just another challenge to overcome. He still went to the gym three times a week, surrounded by young people who had no idea of the history-making man in their midst.

Larry's thing was hockey, and although he was almost unknown, he held a record nobody else could claim. Larry was one of fifteen kids in an immigrant family from China who lived above their store in Vernon, British Columbia. Every chance he got, Larry had a hockey stick in his hand, along with a dream in his heart to play in the NHL. Only five-foot-six and not 150 pounds, he was still able to help his first organized team, the Vernon Hydrophones, win a provincial championship. He faced all forms of discrimination because he was Chinese. He never told his parents, fearing they would make him stop playing. But Larry proved unstoppable.

During World War II he signed on and played for a demonstration team, travelling around to entertain troops. A scout spotted his talent and said he was good enough to play pro hockey, sending him to the farm team of the New York Rangers. The Rangers were having a terrible year. Larry was called up to play on the NHL team on March 13, 1948. He called it one of the highest and lowest points in his life. This was almost ten years before the Boston Bruins called up Willie O'Ree, who was long considered the first person of colour to play in the NHL. He wasn't. Larry was.

But Larry called his debut a disappointment. They sat him on the bench for the first two periods against the Montreal Canadiens. He played just one shift, just one minute, in the third. It would be the only time he played in the NHL. Still, it was enough for him to hold that record, and nobody can take that from him. He went on to be a scoring sensation in the Quebec Senior Hockey League, winning a Canadian championship. His moment of fame in the NHL was all but forgotten. Larry told me some would joke about it, saying, "You only played a minute." He liked to reply by saying, "It was a minute more than you played!"

Chad Soon continues to be determined to make sure people remember Larry Kwong, writing articles and letters to the editor, teaching his students about him and doing whatever he can to raise awareness about his accomplishments. To Chad, Larry defined what it meant to be Canadian.

He said, "It's that he helped to change the definition of *Canadian*. Today we are proud to be an accepting nation. We realize that our strength is our diversity, and that it's people like Larry who laid down the tracks to get us here."

Larry passed away in 2018 at the age of ninety-four. As I write this, Larry Kwong has still not been inducted into Canada's Hockey Hall of Fame. Someone should be ashamed of themselves.

THE GIMLI GLIDER

Most folks of a certain age know exactly what you mean when you mention the Gimli Glider. The Gimli Glider was the Air Canada jet, the first metric jet in its fleet, that famously ran out of gas and had to make an emergency landing in Gimli, Manitoba.

The summer of 2013 was the thirtieth anniversary of this incredible feat. I was in the local newsroom earlier in the spring when my old buddy, producer Terry Stapleton, suggested I do a story. It was compelling drama, so I thought, "Why not?" Not only that, but because it was Terry's idea in the first place, I managed to persuade the local newsroom to let him work on the project with us.

Between *The National*, a few dollars from what was left of a regional production budget and a top-up from the CBC News Network, I was able to scrape together enough money to try to pull it off. Warren would take the pictures, and we were also lucky enough to get Christine Gurniak, the phenomenal editor who had worked with us for so many years on *Country Canada*, to jump in and sew it all together. The team was reunited

We didn't have long, perhaps a month, to get it done.

Fortunately, many of the key players were easy to find, the biggest being Bob Pearson, the captain himself. He was living not far from Ottawa, and said, "Come on down." Bob's little ranch was near a glider field, which was perfect for the story. You see, it was Bob's training as a glider pilot that probably saved everybody's life. Gregarious and funny, and at seventy-seven still sharp, Bob was more than happy to talk about what had happened and about the way his own company turned its back on him. It was a nasty bit of business, but I'll get to that shortly.

I also found flight attendant Susan Jewett in Ontario, passenger Pearl Dion just outside Vancouver, and Kerry Seabrook, the kid on a bike who almost had a plane land on him!

We talked with Bob about what happened that day, and the mix-up with different fuel measurement systems before they left Ottawa en route to Edmonton. "I remember saying to Maurice [his co-pilot], 'For once everything is working properly,'" Bob said, smiling. "Famous last words."

Pearl Dion had been nervous right from the get-go. She was flying with her husband Rick, himself an Air Canada technician, and their three-year-old son Chris. "When we got to the airport, we were early. Rick pointed out the airplane we were taking and when

I saw it, I had an awful feeling. I didn't know why but I did have that awful feeling."

Susan Jewett had just returned to work. Her new baby girl, eleven-month-old Victoria, was home with her husband. It was supposed to be a quick trip with a great crew, and she was a seasoned professional. Only sixty-one passengers were on board. "It was a very light load, so that was the nice thing about it. For us it's always nice to have a light load, especially in the summer."

Flight 143 was cruising at over eight hundred kilometres an hour over Northwestern Ontario when the fuel pressure gauges started coming on. "There was no thought that we had a fuel problem because we had done all these fuel checks," said Bob. "Our flight management computers are showing we have lots of fuel. We announced to the passengers we had some kind of computer problem and were diverting to Winnipeg, and didn't think any more of it. Little did we know, until the left engine failed."

Things were bad, and quickly becoming worse. "I think it was at twenty-eight thousand feet," Bob remembered, "that the right engine failed. Well, the cockpit went black [and] we lost all our instruments and the lights. I thought, 'What's going on, what's happening here?'" Their brand-new, state-of-the-art Boeing 767 had become a 132-ton glider. With only basic hydraulics left to control the aircraft, Pearson got back on the radio to the Winnipeg tower.

Back in her seat, Pearl Dion panicked a little. "The flight attendants told us to fasten our seatbelts, and I realized something was the matter because they looked grey. They had frightened faces, so I knew from looking at them that something was drastically wrong."

Winnipeg was too far. The tower advised that they were twenty miles closer to Gimli, but it had no emergency equipment and no local control tower. At that point, it didn't matter. Gimli was their one shot to survive.

On the ground in Gimli, the old runway was now a racetrack. Racers had just finished for the day. People were barbecuing, relaxing, having a beer, oblivious to what was about to happen. Young Kerry Seabrook and his buddies decided to take a bike ride up the old runway. He looked up to see this massive aircraft heading right for them.

Bob Pearson had to slow the plane down. He performed an old glider manoeuvre, turning the 132-ton aircraft sideways into the wind to slow it down. It was shaking like crazy. In the back, all Pearl Dion could think about was her little boy. "I just felt so terrible. 'Cause we had brought this little boy into the world and he was going to die. That was the outcome that I expected, that we were going to die."

Flight attendant Susan Jewett recalled, "I'm thinking of my daughter. I'm thinking, she's going to be one year old, and she won't have a mother, and it was very hard on me. I loved my daughter and my husband. I didn't want to be in that situation. I just hoped for the best."

Bob Pearson struggled to maintain control. "I guess that I had tunnel vision. All I could focus on was the airplane, trying to keep it in the air as long as possible, and find a piece of cement to safely put it down on."

Kerry's buddies started hightailing it out of there, but he was frozen. "It's still coming in and getting bigger. I see the wheels touch down on the rear. The front touches, but landing gear gives way. Now there's smoke and spark. It's all coming."

Bob Pearson had gotten the plane on the ground. But then, "I looked up and saw three boys on bicycles. That got the adrenaline really going!" The big plane stopped less than fifty metres in front of Kerry.

Bob made sure everybody was off before jumping down the inflated slide himself. "I can remember one of the passengers coming up to me and saying, 'Captain, that was a bit of a feat. It's the first time back to Gimli since I trained here before going overseas in World War II.'"

It was one hell of a story. Until you do the interviews and hear the emotion in their voices, you never entirely know—but this was gold. Thirty years hadn't affected their memories or their feelings one bit. Just one thing was missing. The Gimli Glider itself. We decided it was worth the money to try to get to it.

I had been on the phone for weeks with a gentleman named Erik Hanvelt from a company called Jet Midwest. The company was now the proud owner of the 767 jet, number 604, formerly of the Air Canada fleet. But dealing with him was a little like something out of a spy novel. After dancing around on the phone for a while, he agreed we could fly out and meet him in a nearby town to further discuss getting access to the old Air Canada plane.

Warren and I flew into Los Angeles, jumped in a van and headed north through fields of rusted wind turbines and out onto the floor of the Mojave Desert. Erik met us in a small town called Tehachapi, and over an ice-cold Corona he explained that he liked Canadians and had relatives up in British Columbia, but a small mountain of clearances were required to get into the secure area were the Gimli Glider was stored.

We had another beer. Told a few jokes. Finally, Erik said, "Screw it, we'll go in tomorrow." We met him in the airport parking lot and threw our gear and ourselves into his old white panel van. He said that if they asked for ID at the security gate, we could be arrested and he could be fired. Great. It was too late to turn back now.

The guy at the gate, who had seen Erik come and go dozens of times, barely grunted. We were in, and Warren and I could stop sweating. Explaining that one to the crowd at CBC Toronto would have been no fun. Stopping sweating proved difficult, though. It was ten in the morning and already 40°C in this place called an aviation boneyard. This was where old workhorses came to die. Hundreds of them baked on the desert floor, the millions of passengers they once carried long gone.

If this was a boneyard, Erik was an aviation gravedigger of sorts. He butchered these carcasses so that others might live, sending hard-to-find parts around the world to aviation technicians looking to get their own planes back in the air. And in the middle of it all, also baking in the mid-morning desert sun, stood the Gimli Glider. After it had outlived its usefulness with Air Canada in 2008, number 604 took one last flight from Montreal to here. It had been here ever since. There was still hope someone would buy it, but the clock was ticking. If a buyer couldn't be found soon, it would be dismantled for parts and scrap.

You don't realize, standing in line at the airport, waiting to walk down the ramp and board, just how big these planes are. But when you're standing underneath one and the front cabin door is five metres over your head, you do. We used an electric hoist to get us up so we could step on board. To say it was eerie would be an understatement. In the cockpit the wool cover on the captain's seat was still there, along with an emergency procedure card. All the seats had been removed except the flight attendant's jump seat back in the galley, where Susan Jewett sat saying her prayers. The window beside it was barely the size of a dessert plate. I realized just how isolated she must have felt during those few terrifying moments.

Then Erik asked if I wanted to open the emergency door and step out on the wing. If I had a dollar for every time I'd listened to a flight attendant recite the emergency procedure for opening the door, I could buy my own plane. Did I want to? You bet! It wasn't as heavy as I thought it would be. I stepped through and onto the massive wing. I tapped my cowboy boot on the surface and said, "It sounds like it's out of gas!" Just a little joke.

Within a few hours we were back on the road, headed for the airport and Winnipeg. I knew we had all the components for a winner.

Of course, we also looked at the inquiry Captain Bob had been subject to. Air Canada was still a Crown corporation then, and it was causing the government no end of grief. A month before the incident in Gimli, an Air Canada DC-9 had been forced to land in Cincinnati with an on-board fire that killed twenty-three of forty-one passengers, including the famous East Coast troubadour Stan Rogers.

Air Canada brass was in full damage control. And Bob knew it. "It was a Crown corporation. They feared for their jobs. So, I guess, what do you do? You blame somebody else. Air Canada put out a press release stating that the fault was the pilots and the mechanics in Montreal and Ottawa. I guess I defended myself and what I did. We were being made scapegoats. I think because I spoke out, the inquiry was called by Minister Lloyd Axworthy at the time."

The federal inquiry exonerated Pearson. Judge George Lockwood found Air Canada at fault for the near disaster and commended Pearson and his crew for the way they had handled a potentially catastrophic situation. In the end, Air Canada was ordered to improve procedures and lines of communication. But Bob Pearson's incredible feat did something else too—it changed jet pilot training around the world. It has even been suggested that those new training regimens contributed to a successful landing when a fuel leak caused an Air Transat jetliner to run out of fuel near the Azores back in 2001, and the more recent "Miracle on the Hudson" in 2009 when Captain Chesley Sullenberger lost both engines because of Canada geese but safely glided onto the water near Manhattan in New York.

There is now a museum of Gimli Glider memorabilia in that small Manitoba town, where you can sit in a seat, just like those in the 767, and watch our documentary for yourself.

I have a few quirky side notes on the Gimli Glider, too. Twenty-five years later, the kid on the bike, Kerry Seabrook, was driving down a Manitoba highway when another plane almost landed on him! And both Susan Jewett and Pearl Dion had children who became jet pilots.

But this one is the best. I talked to a fellow who used to work for Air Canada in Winnipeg at the time. He told me that the next day, an aviation crew jumped in a van to drive up to Gimli. They had been assigned to help assess the damage. Somehow, they took the wrong road. They were turned around, got lost and—wait for it—ran out of gas.

WE WANT MORE!

The CBC's system started pushing for more and more material. The Gimli Glider was a good example. Not only did we produce a one-hour documentary, but shorter versions were prepared for both radio and television, for *The National* and for *The World at Six*. Toronto also needed shorter daily news stories for the regions, for radio and TV, and material to feed the increasing demands from CBC.CA.

It wasn't so bad if, like me, you weren't filing daily and had a chance to develop a roll-out strategy. In daily news it was brutal. I knew people who'd had no time to eat their lunch in months. To be fair, sometimes this business can be like that, but workloads seemed to be increasing and you could see standards slipping. More and more mistakes showed up on the air or online. Not big mistakes, at least not often, but spelling mistakes, grammatical errors, things that slowly chipped away at credibility. And the news across all platforms was becoming increasingly homogenized.

Regionally, the online folks continued to be almost chained to their desks, spitting out every news release that reached the newsroom. It was all about quantity, not necessarily quality, and about speed. Burnout was becoming an issue.

At the network level, you now got *attitude*. As a network journalist of some decades, I felt I was past the stage where I needed to prove myself to anybody. Apparently not. Many of the new people working online did not see it like that. They were busy reinventing the wheel and were often dismissive of any suggestions that might help. Sometimes they wanted your video and your script, and they would use it to make up a story themselves. Sometimes it was just font (words printed on the screen over a video shot) with no voice-over and a bit of added video. That would replace an entire documentary because people reading online "had no time to look at all that."

Sometimes things were taken out of context. Sometimes they were just plain wrong. When you contacted the culprits to point this out, some of them would fight with you, insisting what they wrote was accurate. When you pointed out that you gathered the material, shot the interviews and video, and wrote the original story, it didn't matter. But it did matter. It was a problem.

This sounds like a bit of a rant, and I guess it is. I think the thing that bothered me most about it was the lack of respect. When I was a cub reporter, if someone working on the network contacted me to help me with something or let me know about a mistake, I would be more than grateful. And mortified. Who wants to make a mistake? But this new environment was quickly becoming less respectful, at least when I had to deal with situations like that.

I decided to cut my losses and keep communication to a minimum. I continued looking for stories for *The National* that could be easily expanded into a half-hour or even a one-hour presentation. But it was becoming increasingly difficult to find any small amount of budget to do so.

That spring, *The Gimli Glider: 30 Years Later* was nominated in the best documentary program category at the Canadian Screen Awards. It was a big deal, especially when you consider we had been up against dozens of programs, some costing in excess of $1 million, from right across the country and around the world. Out of dozens, we were one of only five nominated for best documentary. We didn't win—*The Defector: Escape from North Korea* won—but we did prove something. You don't need to spend a million dollars to make something folks want to watch. And if you make it, you own it, which was an important point—at least I thought it was—for a public broadcaster.

In the digital universe, if you don't own anything, what have you got? Not much. Five years earlier, we had produced *The Town at the Top of the World* from the High Arctic. It had now aired six or seven times since, almost every spring. Why did CBC programmers keep using it? They used it because they owned it. It didn't cost anything to rerun it. And each time, it did quite well, and it had a cumulative viewership of around three million. Not bad for a production that cost less than $50,000 to make and was solidly mandate programming. Pretty damn good, in fact. I decided to keep trying to prove my point. As if anyone was listening.

I got back to work. I was now concentrating on three main areas: Canadian history, the environment and human interest. In the summer we travelled to Quebec to catch up with a young couple who had spent six summers canoeing across Canada, even having two children along the way. In my view, the CBC should have been telling those stories, and I had no intention of stopping.

CHAPTER 19

Deadly Ice and Polar Bears

Whatever you may think of the practice of sealing, one hundred years ago it was a vital part of Newfoundland's economy. Not only did it give fishermen an opportunity to get some badly needed cash after a hard winter, but for those youth coming of age, it was also a rite of passage. Often boys who were barely sixteen would walk over a hundred kilometres just to get to St. John's and try to sign on with one of the big sealing ships.

That was the case in the spring of 1914. But before this story ended, many dozens of young men would be dead, frozen to death or lost at sea.

To tell a story that was a hundred years old, I needed some help. I solicited the assistance of four people: an amateur historian, a famous Canadian author, a bronze sculptor and a descendant of someone lost during those few terrible days.

The local historian was Neil Tucker. He lived in Elliston, where many families had lost loved ones that long-ago spring. He explained that life in 1914 Newfoundland could be a brutal existence. It was hard work scraping a subsistence living from the sea. By mid-March, money and food were all but gone. With starvation on the doorstep, the arrival of Arctic ice and the seals offered a chance to make it through. So men signed on for what was nothing short of abuse, working for big merchant ships that would hunt the great seal herds.

The next person I spoke with was award-winning author Michael Crummey, who has set much of his historical fiction in Newfoundland. "It was huge!" Michael said of the hunt. "It was on the calendar of the country. One of the biggest events of the year." (Don't forget that in 1914, Newfoundland was a country.) "The men who became the great sealing captains were looked upon as heroes here, and Abe Kean was the greatest ... he was known as the greatest sealing captain ever."

Abram Kean was also a hard, powerful man who drove his men to exhaustion. The seal hunt was filthy, exhausting, dangerous work. There was little food, and often the drinking water was contaminated with seal fat and blood. Misery from start to finish with the threat of death anytime in between.

"The danger of it was part of what attracted young men to it," said Crummey. "Young men fought to get out there. It was a rite of passage, and they would sign on behind their parents' backs sometimes to get out there." That was exactly what sixteen-year-old Albert John Crewe did.

I found his relative Anne Gosse in Harbour Grace. Anne told me the story that had been passed down through the family. As she recounted, "When Albert John was so excited about going to the ice, his father Reuben said, 'Well, I'm going to have to go with him.'"

Father and son would sail on the SS *Newfoundland*. The oldest steamship in the fleet, it was commanded by Abe Kean's young son Wes. Unlike other ships, it had no means of modern communication—the transceiver had been removed by the owners as a cost-cutting measure. It was a decision that would prove fatal.

Led by Abe Kean in his modern steel ship, the *Stephano*, the ships headed north in search of the great herds. Others, like the *Southern Cross*, sailed for the ice choking the Gulf of St. Lawrence. The older ship, SS *Newfoundland*, was caught fast in the ice. Its young captain could see that his father's ship was among the seals, so he decided to send his men over the side. They would then walk across the ice to his father's ship. It was tough going.

I had acquired a copy of an interview done forty years before with a gentleman named Cecil Mouland. It was some of the most compelling film I had ever seen. Mouland had been an eyewitness to the disaster. "We got on board the *Stephano* and had a mug up, as they called it." Mouland enjoyed his cup of warm tea, but when he finished, rather than offering the men shelter, Captain Kean ordered them off the ship. "Abe Kean was yelling, '*Newfoundland* men over the side!' That was the captain's orders and we had to obey that. It was snowing real bad. We was almost knee deep in snow. Keep the wind in the side of your face and we [would] make it before dark." But the wind was changing. No one even realized they were hopelessly lost.

"Six fellers died the first night," remembered Mouland. "It was vicious then, all that night and all the next day. Wednesday night, that was the last night we were out, that's when most of the men died. I would see them topple over. When they fell they would move no more."

Anne Gosse said that night, Reuben Crewe's wife stirred to find her bedroom bathed in moonlight. "All of a sudden it was like someone touched her. And she woke. And when she woke, she saw Reuben and young Albert John kneeling beside her bed. And she said the image was so clear she could even see the double stitching on their canvas jackets. It was so clear to her she knew right then that something terrible had happened."

Cecil Mouland witnessed their end. "His son lay down to die, and the old man lay down with him. He pulled out his old guernsey, got the boy's head up under the guernsey, hugged the boy to him, and that's the way they froze out there on the ice. It was sad to look at. A lot of fellows were drifted in with the snow—you could see their hair blowing up where they drifted in with the snow."

Mouland stayed on his feet for three days and two freezing nights. By the time the *Newfoundland*'s men were discovered, seventy-eight of them had frozen to death. Thousands gathered and waited for the rescue ship *Bellaventure* to reach St. John's. The survivors were carried off on canvas stretchers, the dead were piled on deck, like cords of wood, frozen the way they fell. As the bodies were identified and the coffins stacked for burial, word came that the sealing ship the *Southern Cross* had also been claimed by the same storm. Another 173 men gone without a trace, lost at sea.

Abram Kean didn't stop hunting seals long enough to respond to accusations that he had caused the disaster. The bodies of Reuben, young Albert John and six others had to be carried home to Elliston by dogsled. The service for the eight dead men was held in the United Church. Ironically, the bell that tolled for them had been donated by Captain Abram Kean some years before.

It was said that Reuben and Albert John Crewe were buried as they were found, still frozen together. I discovered that sculptor Morgan MacDonald was in the final stages of preparing a statue that would be placed on the headland at Elliston. It would be a statue of father and son, clinging together as the life left them. He allowed me to come down to his studio to take some pictures of the clay model before it was fired in bronze. "There's a moment when they lie down to die. I was hoping to capture the emotion of the moment. This is not made up, this is real."

That powerful, sad statue now stands on the headland at Elliston. Facing the sea and the ice that claimed them so many years ago, it's a permanent tribute to those who fell.

TRACKING THE CELEBRITY POLAR BEAR

Sometimes I can be a sucker for punishment, but I just couldn't let it go. Every time I travelled to Churchill, Manitoba, it bothered me. The polar bear industry seemed to be out of control. I had travelled there on various stories four or five times over the years, and the situation appeared to be worsening. Tourists arrived by the plane-load. They arrived by the trainload. They wandered around town, having their pictures taken right by the sign that read, IT'S NOT SAFE TO BE WANDERING AROUND HERE.

They were coming to get perhaps one last look at the most magnificent beasts in Canada, maybe even on the planet, before they disappeared into extinction. Yet Churchill seemed to be over-run with polar bears, and it was no better farther north in Arviat. What was the truth? In my attempt to find out, I produced another one-hour special, one that proved controversial.

We headed up to Churchill just as the big bears and subse-quently the tourists were starting to gather. I thought if anyone knew the truth, it would be Bob Windsor. For years the conserva-tion officer had been at his wits' end trying to keep people safe. Bob had a polar bear jail (holding facility), and he was the sheriff. When we were taping, at least one bear a day was captured, sometimes more. His record was twenty-eight bears in the jail at the same time.

Bob knew what these beasts were capable of. His massive truck had been bounced around like a Tonka toy by one bear. In town, bears had approached people dropping their kids at daycare, been spotted outside the school playground and found literally coming through someone's front porch. And there had been attacks.

The bears Bob captured were in great shape, yet everywhere you looked someone was insisting the polar bear was in grave peril. It had been made the poster child for global warming, and its advo-cates weren't about to give up their star. It might be a bear, but it was also a cash cow. Everyone from the World Wildlife Fund to Coca-Cola was using it to promote products or perspectives.

So were polar bears really in trouble or not? I decided to try to find the truth. Silly me. The truth was that much of the work around polar bear population estimates was flawed, or at the very least confused. I interviewed two scientists. Both, in their day, had been considered experts in the gathering of information on polar bears, conducting extensive fieldwork across the Arctic. But each had completely opposing views on the health of polar bears. In fact, the two were pretty much at war with each other, and the dispute had sunk to the level of character assassination.

Andrew Derocher was a professor who had studied polar bears across Canada's North for decades. And when I met him, he was more outspoken than most about the peril the big bear was in. "Our estimation is that we probably won't have polar bears in Churchill once we get out to mid-century, and it could happen a lot before that as well. ... Our estimations are, if we had a very early melt and a very late freeze, we could see up to 50 per cent mortality in a single year. You put a couple of years like that back to back, and things could happen very quickly."

In as little as two years for some populations? Don't forget, this was back in 2014. It was a startling projection, especially when I looked at what was happening on the ground. In Churchill, the polar bear jail was full. The conservation officers were going flat out. So were the long lines of tourists driven in by the busload to watch the show. Helicopter traffic droned steadily overhead as almost every day another bear was run out of town (okay, flown out of town). Tourists trailed behind in chase helicopters, even posing for pictures with the drugged-up bears.

And it grew even more curious. Online, Environment Canada said of our polar bear population, "The polar bear does not have a small wild population, it does not have a restricted area of distribution and no marked decline has been observed." Experts in Nunavut said the same thing.

Hmm. I found another biologist from Lakehead University in Thunder Bay, Ontario, a fellow named Mitch Taylor. He was initially reluctant to speak with me. His reputation had already taken quite a beating. Over the course of several conversations, he finally agreed to let me come see him. When I asked him the question,

"Are polar bears in trouble or not?" his response was unequivocal. "Not at the present. They don't appear to be declining in any population I'm aware of so far."

For thirty years the scientist had studied polar bears, living in the Arctic, capturing them, advising governments and publishing over fifty scientific, peer-reviewed papers about them. He had even been bitten by one. Taylor had also been a participating member of various international organizations dealing with polar bears. But he said when he started to question whether there was enough solid scientific evidence to suggest polar bears were in immediate peril, he was kicked out.

"I was excluded from the 2009 Polar Bear Specialist Group by the chairman Andy Derocher. I guess, starting with me, there was a decision that only right-thinking people would be included." For years, he said, ensuring that the Inuit hunting of polar bears was sustainable was scientists' primary focus. Then, a few decades ago, the notion that climate change could endanger polar bears started.

"Up until then the focus had really been managing the harvest, and we had been doing a good job on that. There was concern; people were aware that the sea ice was receding. We had seen cyclic events, but the notion that [bears] were jeopardized or this was in some way a threat to them was kind of a new idea, really."

And that new idea, said Taylor, got a lot of traction, for one simple reason: "To start with, the climate is warming. It's very clear. No one that I know seriously doubts that the climate is warmer now than it was ... when the industrial revolution began. Carbon dioxide has increased. We know carbon dioxide is a greenhouse gas, so some fraction of that increase has to be from carbon dioxide and warming does increase warming, so we know that the forcing factor has merit. It is happening. So that's one reason why people find the hypothesis compelling ... it has a good scientific foundation."

But the big problem, Taylor added, was that there continued to be very little research done on the actual size of polar bear populations. Taylor had done some himself but had since realized it was problematic. "When you don't sample the whole area, you underestimate survival, you underestimate population numbers, and in fact the culmination of those biases can result in a scientific estimate that suggests a decline when none exists, and that's the western Hudson Bay scenario."

Taylor also took issue with the projection models for sea-ice changes in the Arctic, projections drawn up by the UN Intergovernmental Panel on Climate Change. In fact, in 2008, he signed the controversial Manhattan Declaration on Climate Change, which argued there was no convincing evidence that CO_2 emissions from modern industrial activity were causing catastrophic climate change. That seemed to be the straw that broke the back of his scientific colleagues. When Taylor made his thoughts known, he expected a free exchange of ideas or at least a healthy scientific debate. Instead he received an email from Andrew Derocher saying he was no longer welcome.

"I've known those guys for, like, twenty years. They know me. They know I would never say or do anything to harm polar bears deliberately. We used to be able to disagree and have a beer and go out and laugh about it. There was room for more than one perspective. It's probably the single biggest disappointment in my career, maybe in my life, that the group had become so intolerant that a diversity of opinion was no longer welcome."

Meanwhile, I found videos online of Andrew Derocher talking about declining polar bear populations. The main reason so many polar bears frequented Churchill, said Derocher, was because they were desperate to find food. "The big problem is hungry bears are much more dangerous. That's one of the real problems going forward."

So, to recap. Churchill was dealing with dangerous, starving bears. Remember conservation officer Bob Windsor, the top bear cop in Churchill? In the past five years he had seen and/or captured hundreds of polar bears. I asked him, "When they're caught, are they assessed for their overall health?" He said yes, they are assessed, weighed, measured and so on. And when I asked him if they appeared healthy, he said, "They've been looking pretty good since I've been here. There was one year where there seemed to be a few skinny bears around. But the last couple of years they've been really good."

Then it surprised me to learn that the estimated global polar bear population (at the time) was between twenty and twenty-five thousand bears, the highest estimate since scientists had been trying to count them. I found another scientist who was using newer techniques and satellite technology to count bears, and he was finding lots of them.

Andrew Derocher was adamant he could see the future. The models that project the loss of sea ice, he told me, spelled disaster. "I mean, I will be fertilizer by the time we really know what happens. But it's going to be. I wish I could believe that I was wrong. I just don't believe that the world's scientists, meteorologists, sea-ice specialists, oceanographers [are wrong]. It's all pointing in the same direction. The body of evidence we have about this issue is absolutely profound."

Mitch Taylor's response? "I somehow wish I had thought of it. Because what could be better than a career where all your projections were, like, not only beyond your career, but your lifespan. How would you ever be held accountable for that? ... In the end nature will speak and it will be clear who knew what they were talking about and who didn't. I'm comfortable with that."

I wrote it all up, and together with the old gang sewed it into a one-hour TV special called *The Politics of Polar Bears: Tracking the Celebrity Bear.* Oh my, what a fuss. I was attacked by animal rights activists, scientists, international organizations and even people I knew!

And even though the piece clearly stated several times that human-caused climate changes were causing havoc, I was also accused of being a climate-change denier. An official complaint was made to the CBC Ombudsman about inaccuracies in the piece. But this wasn't my first rodeo. I had done my homework. I wrote a thirteen-page response challenging every assertion and backing it up with documentation. We never heard back from them.

It was all fascinating and a little sad. All the feedback on all the stories I had done up North about inadequate housing, poverty, social problems, lack of running water for the people living there—all that feedback didn't come close to the traffic generated by one story on polar bears. I'm not sure what that says about us as a community, but I suspect it's not good. The celebrity bear indeed.

CHAPTER 20

Systems Change, Not Storytelling

Facebook. Google. YouTube. Twitter. They had begun to infect everything. Instagram wasn't quite there yet, but it soon would be. Suddenly everything had to be designed around these platforms. You had to tweet about it before you even really had a chance to think about it. All sorts of ideas floated around about the best way to attract eyeballs. Hack it down. Remove the reporter's voice. Put a bunch of printing over the pictures. Nothing longer than a minute. What foolishness.

That old idea that nothing counted but ratings had now exploded, and ratings weren't just determined a few times a season anymore. Ratings were now instantaneous. Things were being judged by the second. It was hard to know what to do for the best. Everyone was looking for stuff that would go viral—as if that would be any reflection of public broadcasting.

I was not immune. I had always taken a more populist approach to story selection. This was just an extension of that. The problem was that my material was taken and used in ways I had zero control over, and little made me more uncomfortable as a journalist. I felt responsible for gathering and presenting information in a fair and balanced way. Now it was becoming out of my control. Unnerving? You bet. But I carried on anyway.

WAVING THE FLAG

It was February 15, 2015, the fiftieth anniversary of the Maple Leaf. Thanks to the vision of Prime Minister Lester B. Pearson and the creative genius of George Stanley, the flag was now half a century old. I knew the idea of making the maple leaf our flag had been contentious, but I hadn't known it was initially so unpopular that it led to near riots, and even death threats.

But George Stanley had a few ideas on the way forward. The dean of arts at the Royal Military College in Kingston laid it all out in a memo. His daughter Della, an accomplished scholar herself and wife of former supreme court justice Thomas Cromwell, was a wonderful host when we visited, showing us some of her father's personal mementos, and was happy to go with us to see his original memo over at the National Archives. She had never seen it and said doing so was on her bucket list. They had a little trouble finding the memo, but it finally emerged, complete with his red-ink sketch depicting what he thought the new flag should look like. A real piece of Canadian history.

And every time I offered up another little chunk, our audience cried out for more. I kept looking for interesting stories, ones with a common theme running through them, topics I could later weave into something else.

So what do the assassination of an American president, an English king who's been dead over five hundred years and Nazi Germany's notorious Buchenwald concentration camp have in common? They all have a Canadian connection. Heading into the spring I decided to do pieces on all three, and then turn them into another one-hour program called *Canadian Connections*. CBC News Network was on side with a little bit of money, and *The National* would pay for the production costs, so away Warren and I went.

The first story dealt with some little-known facts around the assassination of President Abraham Lincoln. Lincoln's murderer John Wilkes Booth used to spend a lot of time around Montreal before committing his terrible deed. He was trying to drum up support for the South and was probably even hiding Confederate money in a Canadian bank account.

In 1863 the not-so-United States of America was busy tearing itself apart. Civil war raged. Many things, including slavery, hung in the balance. Most of those facts are commonly known. But then I discovered a little-known fact about that night, April 14, 1865, when Booth put a bullet in the president. Lincoln died some time later in a room across the street from Ford's Theatre, where he had been shot. And one of the people in the room that night was a Canadian. Not only was Anderson Ruffin Abbott a Canadian, he was the first black doctor to graduate from the University of Toronto.

I found his great-great-granddaughter living in Southern Ontario. Catherine Slaney had a real story to tell, and she had written it all down in a book, *Family Secrets*. She said for generations the black bloodlines running through their family were never talked about. Now that the secret was out, she was happy to talk about her famous relative. Amazingly, she still had her great-great-grandfather's ceremonial dress sabre.

Anderson Ruffin Abbott's father had been badly treated as an American slave, so he escaped to Canada and became a rich property owner in Toronto. When the civil war broke out, his son, Dr. Anderson Abbott, travelled south to support Lincoln. He was one of only eight black doctors in the entire Union Army to achieve the honorary rank of captain, and he oversaw the running of a large hospital in Washington. He also moved in the same circles as Lincoln himself, was good friends with Mary Lincoln's dressmaker and even attended a social event at the White House, one of the first black men to ever do so. The night of the shooting, he rushed to the room where Lincoln lay to be with the president and his wife in Lincoln's last hours.

After Lincoln's funeral, Mary Lincoln gave Dr. Abbott her husband's personal shawl, the very shawl he had worn on the way to his inauguration. I was off to a good start with an incredible and little-known piece of Canadian history.

THE KING IN THE CAR PARK

The second story was taking place on the other side of the pond, in England, but it was very much rooted in Canada as well. The king in the car park had received quite a lot of press. King Richard III's remains had been discovered buried under a parking lot in Leicester, on grounds where a church used to be located. At least it was thought to be him. He had died a particularly nasty death during the War of the Roses, back in 1485, and the exact whereabouts of his remains had proven elusive.

Now experts were almost sure they had the remains of the hunchback king, but it would take DNA analysis to prove it. Well, the expert in ancient DNA analysis was a woman who just happened to be from Canada. Dr. Turi King, genetics specialist at the University of Leicester, had grown up in British Columbia (never mind that her surname happened to be King). When I got in touch with her, she was happy to make time for a Canadian crew, even though she had already been overwhelmed by media attention.

Then the story got even better. They needed a living descendant to make a match with the DNA from one of Richard's back teeth. The king had no descendants, so any match would have to be made from his sister's side of the family. The resourceful Dr. King found just such a person, a furniture craftsman in North London, England. Not only that, but Michael Ibsen was Canadian! His mother's family had descended from Anne of York, and he was a seventeenth-generation nephew. She gave me his contact information and we drove down to meet him. He was a lovely fellow, right down to the Crown Royal whisky sack he used to keep his wood plane in.

And Michael wasn't just a furniture maker. He had also been asked to make the coffin poor old King Richard would be reburied in. When we showed up at his workshop, he had the coffin, constructed from ancient British oak, right there, hidden under some packing blankets. A big British television company had paid a *lot* of money for the exclusive rights to reveal it. I jokingly asked Michael if he would step out for a moment to get a coffee. Not a chance. He did, however, give Warren and me one of the very oak boards he had used to build a king's coffin. Another great story with Canadian connections.

I'M STILL HERE!

The next piece I did also involved death—and one of the darkest chapters in modern history, World War II. I had been contacted by Craig Carter-Edwards, the grandson of a gentleman named Ed Carter-Edwards. Ed was in the Canadian Air Force in the war and had the misfortune of being shot down just outside Paris. Craig had seen other historical pieces I'd produced, and he contacted me to say, "You need to talk to my grandfather. He's about to return to the largest camp in Germany, a place called Buchenwald. That's where he nearly died."

Ed lived outside of Hamilton with his wife of sixty-nine years, Lois. Those two were a hoot. Ed was a little fellow with a big personality and an even bigger heart. They cuddled together on the couch while he told me about being shot out of the sky outside Paris and being handed over to the Gestapo, who refused to believe he was a Canadian airman and sent him to the notorious Buchenwald camp. It was one of the first camps in Germany. It wasn't classified as an extermination camp, but the Nazis did manage to murder over fifty-six thousand people there during its time as a training ground for the brutal Nazi SS.

Ed narrowly escaped death several times before being transferred and eventually set free. Now, at the age of ninety-two, he was returning as a celebrity of sorts, to mark the seventieth anniversary of the liberation of the camp.

Buchenwald was located on a mountain above the beautiful city of Weimar—such a tranquil place to harbour such an ugly past. This was where the Nazi Party was born. Ed was staying at the historic Hotel Elephant downtown. Overlooking the town square, we stood on the balcony where Hitler gave his speeches to the tens of thousands of faithful below. Eight kilometres away, up the hill and through the thick forest, was the end of the rail line. There they unloaded people like cattle, using them as slave labourers or conducting medical experiments on them before killing them and sending them to the ovens.

Not a hundred metres away, SS officers had built a zoo for their children, who lived with their families just outside the camp. On one side of the barbed wire they fed the deer with their Nazi parents, while on the other side prisoners, children too, were being starved and murdered.

And yet this celebration was going on, a celebration of the liberation seventy years earlier. Ed was treated like a star, as were others who showed up dressed in replicas of their old prison uniforms. In town, at the gala, people drank beer and champagne while the band played old war songs. "Boogie Woogie Bugle Boy" indeed. I found it all very troubling.

We took Ed to the camp and recorded him stepping back over seventy years, and it was something I will never forget. It remained a dark, murderous site, and was the most disturbing place I had ever been on this earth. Ed broke down and cried at the rail siding where he was first thrown from the boxcar into the hands of soldiers and faced gun butts and the teeth of German shepherds.

He stared in through the window of the infirmary and was transported back to 1944. Here he had to be hidden by fellow prisoners, hidden from the Nazi doctor who wanted to kill him. It will be etched in my mind forever, watching him shake his fist and say, "You tried to kill me, but I beat you. I'm here today!" To think that such a lovely, sweet man had been put through all that, right on that very ground, was almost too much.

I matched video shots with old black-and-white photos taken around the camp by the liberating Americans. Carts piled high with gaunt, naked bodies, not far from the ovens, their final destination. Near the end they were exterminating as many as four hundred prisoners a day.

The big ceremony was held on a beautiful spring afternoon. Thousands of people had arrived. I spoke with one German gentleman, now living in France, who had come to honour those who had been killed by his relatives. He said he had lived with the shame of it his entire life. And yet others were there, sitting on the lawn nearby, laughing and enjoying a picnic lunch. A picnic at a concentration camp. Unbelievable. It made me forget I was a journalist. It made me angry. It was all I could do not to go over there and say something to them.

But I let it go. If Ed had escaped this horrible place and forgiven, what right did I have to be angry? He'd come home, married Lois and raised a fine family—children, grandchildren and great-grandchildren. He'd lived the good life he never thought he would have. Ed was ninety-four when he passed away in 2017. I was lucky enough to have one more visit with him before he left. I will remember his big baritone voice, and that twinkle in his eye. God rest him.

After the pieces had all aired on *The National*, Warren and I fashioned them together into a one-hour documentary for *Canadian Connections*, which aired on CBC News Network. It was watched by almost two hundred thousand people, a very good number for that channel, especially when you consider how little it cost. It was just me again, trying to make the point that CBC itself, with its own employees, could produce programming that people wanted to watch, that had value. And as I have said before, "It didn't have to cost a million dollars."

This was material that was already paid for, refashioned to enjoy a wider viewership. And on our assignments we shot much more material than we could use in a shorter documentary anyway, or certainly in a news report. For example, around the same time, Nepal experienced a terrible earthquake. CBC had several journalists, cameras and even a drone in the area. I called Toronto and said all the material they gathered should be saved in an electronic file and could easily be turned into a half-hour special. It made such perfect sense to me. It didn't happen.

And of course, in the new digital universe you cannot just set the "tape" aside and collect it later. Even though we used the word *taping*, no tape is used, only computer files on cards. The files are sent to big servers in Toronto. After being in the system for a few days, too often, if they aren't archived, those cards are erased and reused. Very quickly a lot of visual material is gone forever. To be fair, the amount of material gathered every day and the digital space required to store it is enormous. Without ongoing culling, it would collapse under its own weight. But with a little planning, and not much money, the CBC could accomplish so much more wonderful, interesting programming.

FLYING VIRAL

By now I was focused on stories that not only fit into the mandate but might also attract social media attention. In the summer of 2015, I had just come back from vacation when Toronto called and asked if I would mind going to the largest electronic music concert on the continent. Called Shambhala, it was the place where over twenty-five thousand people, most of them quite young, gathered for a week in the British Columbia wilderness to listen to some of the best electronic musicians in the world. It sounded like a modern-day version of Woodstock. Seeing the potential, I said, why not?

A music concert in and of itself was not a story, but what the organizers were doing was. They had banned alcohol and searched every vehicle that came to the concert to remove it. They knew they could not stop drugs, but they also knew how dangerous drugs were becoming. Powerful drugs like fentanyl were killing kids at concerts across the country. Usually they were sold as something else, like ecstasy or molly. Kids not knowing what exactly they were ingesting was a mistake that had already proven fatal far too many times.

And it was something founder Jimmy Bundschuh was determined to try and stop. He had set up the music festival years before on his parents' two-hundred-hectare cattle ranch. So far it had been safe and peaceful. To try to keep it that way, what Jimmy negotiated was unique. Called a "harm reduction tent," it was a free testing site where volunteers who were experts in their field would test drugs to ensure you got what you thought you'd purchased. It was judgement free and sanctioned by the RCMP.

Jimmy was understandably nervous about having a TV crew poking around. We drove up to the hill above the party where his parents' house was located and had a cup of tea with Mom. She knew me from television. After that everything seemed more relaxed.

The night of taping was like nothing I had ever seen. Usually a big concert like that or a sporting event meant a night of drunken louts sticking their faces or other body parts into the camera lens, hassling you or just generally acting like idiots. There was *none* of that. People were courteous, friendly and relaxed—even as many of them were walking around completely naked!

While the music pulsed and pounded away, the RCMP casually wandered about. A long line of party people were waiting to have their drugs tested. It was all so civilized. In eighteen years, the festival had had one drug-related death, and Jimmy did not want another one. "Here, the vibe is different," he explained. "People take care of each other."

When the piece was finished, I tried something I had never tried before. No, I did not start taking ecstasy or walking around naked at concerts (believe me, that would not be entertaining for anyone). But this social media business was starting to fascinate me. In Toronto they had taken to putting certain stories on *The National*'s Facebook page hours before the show even aired. The piece on the festival was one of them.

I contacted Jimmy and asked him if he would tweet a link on Shambhala's Twitter feed. Shambhala had over a hundred thousand followers on Twitter. If they each told three friends, and they each told three friends—you get the picture. He looked at the item and agreed. Before *The National* even aired, the story of Shambhala had already reached over three million people on Facebook and Twitter. That's more than triple the nightly audience *The National* was getting on television. Lesson learned. If you could figure out how to tap into it, an audience beyond our wildest dreams was out there. The trick was figuring out how to build that constituency.

THE DARING YOUNG MAN AND HIS FLYING MACHINE

I have always had a certain fascination with electric vehicles. Over the years I produced documentaries about two different electric cars, an electric truck, and the solar vehicle that set a world record. I also profiled the Gupta family of Mississauga, who had developed a unique lithium-ion battery system, one that was 100 per cent recyclable.

One day in 2015, the light bulb came on for my next one-hour special as I browsed through a magazine, waiting to get my hair cut. A little blurb about a Montrealer who had set a world record with his electric flying machine caught my attention, and I decided to try to get Alexandru Duru on the phone. He was a sharp, funny fellow, and not one to pass up exposure opportunities. After some haggling over what he would and would not show me, I got on a plane with Warren and we headed for Quebec.

Alexandru was holed up in an industrial studio downtown with two other techno-geeks, electronics parts, computers and 3-D printers stacked up around their ears. Dirty dishes were piled high, and an ideas board was covered with formulas.

The flying machine was sitting on the floor over by the wall. It looked like something the Green Goblin flies around on in the movie *Spider-Man*, except this flying machine also had Spider-Man's webbing. Slightly larger than a coffee table, it also appeared to have a set of snowboarding boots in a harness to attach a human being, eight electric motors with lots of batteries, and blades. And to make it all go, it appeared he had rigged up a pair of pliers to use as a hand-held control mechanism.

Without a doubt, Alexandru was flying by the seat of his prototype pants. But make no mistake, this confident, self-assured fellow had designed a flying machine, and it worked! We drove out into the countryside to a friend's retreat to attempt a test flight. His buddy had a large pond on his property, perfect for flying over. If things go bad, landing in water is a lot easier on the bones than solid ground.

A crowd was starting to gather. Turned out his friend did a lot of contract work with Cirque du Soleil. A huge party was getting underway, with good-looking young people emerging from all directions. Alexandru was going to have an audience. The bigger the crowd grew, the more of a showman he became. His mother and father were there too. When I asked them, "Is he super smart, or just a little bit crazy?" Without a pause, his father replied, "I think it's both."

After several hours of pre-flight testing and some trouble for Warren shooting, the young man and his flying machine were ready for takeoff. Mom couldn't watch. Dad was wearing a wetsuit and standing by a canoe. He was the emergency response unit.

We had placed a small GoPro action camera on Alexandru's chest and buried another in the ground right under the machine. Warren was operating what we call the "big" video camera, we had one more locked off on a tripod, and I was also recording with my phone. I think we had it covered.

It was a thing of beauty. He smoothly lifted off the shore and rose immediately to about ten metres in the air. He was moving slowly toward the far side of the pond when suddenly one side lost power to the blades and down he went ... *kersploosh!* Dad was in the water in a flash, grabbing his son, flying apparatus still attached, and dragging him back to shore.

A minor problem, explained Alexandru, a shorted-out wire. Take two. This time he lifted gracefully into the air and moved in a circle around the pond. The crowd gave a collective gasp, then cheered as he swooped, hovered and lightly touched down back on the shore. It was something to behold. He joked that it was my turn, and I replied that I didn't think it had the power to lift my girth. He laughed and said, "No, probably not." It was a powerful, engaging piece that I knew nobody would be able to stop watching.

This time when the piece hit social media, something happened that had never happened before (or has since) in the history of the CBC. The people in Toronto decided to use just the last minute or so of the item (people don't have time to watch the whole thing!) and put it on Facebook. It was the part with him flying around the pond and joking with me after the flight. It went viral. It went beyond viral. Within two days, it had reached well over *three hundred and twenty million people.*

In Toronto, the social media experts, chests puffed out, were willing to tell anyone who would listen how they had achieved this wonderful feat. Some months later I attended the INPUT conference in Calgary, a gathering of producers from around the world. Imagine my surprise when I saw a seminar on the agenda hosted by two CBC social media types explaining their tricks for building a social media audience. My piece was being used as a testament to their success. It was the star of their little show. Nobody had even bothered to tell me it was happening.

You should have seen the looks on their faces when I walked in and sat down. After the audience watched their presentation, their assessment of what they had done to produce this viral master-piece, a question-and-answer session was held. I put my hand up and observed, "To me it looks like you simply chopped the back of my item off—granted, a very compelling chunk of video—and stuck it on Facebook. You didn't change anything or add anything. On any given day, an engaging piece like this can get traction. It did, and then it snowballed. That's all."

Taken aback, they explained that it happened because of their strategy, or some such nonsense. I replied, "If that's so, why have you not been able to replicate it, or anything close to it? Not once since it happened?" They did not have an answer for that.

The simple answer is that it's always about the story, or it should be. All that other stuff, that moving digital target, is just another delivery system. But if you can hit the target, the entire planet is the limit. Nobody has come close to that record. I think it will stand for some time. And thanks to the exposure Alexandru Duru received, the young Canadian inventor began travelling around the globe to give flying demonstrations.

I now had the first piece for my next one-hour special in the bag. The name had a nice ring to it: *Those Amazing Young Canadians*. This time it would be about young Canadian inventors. I went look-ing for and found three more who fit the bill perfectly.

THOSE BIG, BRILLIANT BRAINS!

Ann Makosinski was an engaging young woman with big doe eyes and a vibrant smile who had just started her first year at the University of British Columbia. In her spare time, she liked to invent things. She was pretty darn good at it. In fact, she had done something most young scientists around the world could only dream of—she had won the Google Science Fair. How had she done it? She'd invented a flashlight that could be powered just by the body heat coming from your hand. Very impressive.

When we met at her parents' house in Victoria, she was just putting the finishing touches on her latest invention—a coffee mug that used the heat from your coffee to charge your cellphone. She had an eye for useful gadgets. She was a class act and made a great second segment for the show.

While on the West Coast, I also found Amazing Young Canadian number three, a young man named Austin Wang. About to graduate from high school, the eighteen-year-old had just won the US$75,000 prize at the largest science fair in North America. What had this tall and lanky basketball-loving dude done? It was almost too complicated for this old dog to grasp. Essentially, he had found a way to genetically modify E. coli bacteria to not only clean waste water but to generate huge volumes of electricity at the same time. Not only that, Austin happened to be a pianist and composer who in Grade 10 was one of the winners in an international piano competition, travelling as far as Vienna to perform.

And yet he was simply a humble, extremely nice fellow who seemed more intent on sharing credit for his accomplishments with his teachers and his school. That young man left me feeling optimistic and full of hope for the future.

So did fourteen-year-old Rachel Brouwer from Nova Scotia. She dreamed of clean water in developing countries and, inspired by one of her heroes, Malala Yousafzai, she found a way to do something about it. Using simple materials available in most third-world countries, she invented a way to filter and pasteurize water, making it safe to drink.

She was a really good sport, spending some time with us and showing us how her invention worked. She also showed me the email she had received from Malala. The Nobel Prize–winning young activist had heard about Rachel's work and had written to thank her and to cheer her on.

To me, this was solidly CBC mandate programming. Stories about our youth, their industriousness, the hope they brought to new generations and the way they reflected Canada around the globe. They all left you feeling just a little bit better about things, and it all made for engaging television. I believe *Those Amazing Young Canadians* is still shown in schools across Canada. That I call a public broadcasting success.

BLAST OFF!

The twenty-fifth anniversary of Canada's first woman in space was approaching, and I didn't think Roberta Bondar's huge accomplishment should pass without mention, so I resolved to do something about it. I remembered CBC journalist Eve Savory's wonderful reports back during the original launch in 1992, so I knew there was a ton of material available to us. The bigger issue was getting access to the woman herself.

With persistence and humility, I pestered Ms. Bondar's personal assistant. It paid off. We could come and visit with her at her home in Toronto. She was far too busy for a pre-interview on the phone, though, so I had no opportunity to build a little rapport. Just like a space shuttle launch, there was only one shot at it. I studied everything I could find about her career, her personal interests, her accomplishments. It was a long list. People who possess that kind of intellect, with so much achievement and talent, can be very intimidating. For journalists, they can also be a little hard to handle, especially if they decide you are not worthy and start batting you around like a cat does a mouse.

After the first few moments, when Ms. Bondar realized I had taken the time to do my research, she relaxed and couldn't have been more gracious and accommodating. She told me things she had never revealed publicly before, like the emotional boost she'd felt on her way to the launch pad when she looked up and saw reporter Eve holding a Canadian flag and the Girl Guide trefoil, waving them both and cheering her on.

It was an honour to interview Roberta Bondar, the first Canadian woman in space. For someone who had been partway to the moon, she sure had her feet on the ground!

Or her re-creation of the ending of one of her favourite movies, *2001: A Space Odyssey*. "When I was in the galley area, which was where we dressed as well," she said, "I pulled the louvred curtains around, because I always did that for privacy, and there was a porthole where you could actually see the earth. There was a window right there, and I remember I was changing my clothes. I took all my clothes off, tucked up in a ball without anything touching me, like that embryo at the end of the movie, and I just rotated in full view of the planet. It was my homage to Arthur C. Clarke."

I thought, "Did she just say she mooned the planet Earth from space?" But of course I didn't say it. I wanted to, but I didn't. Later the next day we went with her to a local school where she inspired a large group of students who were, quite simply, in awe. And then she surprised me, insisting that I try on her flight jacket from the *Discovery* mission. We had a great laugh over that. Thank God she didn't try to do it up!

MADLY OFF IN ALL DIRECTIONS

Ms. Bondar's anniversary show, *Canada's First Lady of Space*, also became a half-hour show on the network. I would do another on the attempts by a hardy group of volunteers to save Alberta's wild horses. There was no end to the stories I wanted to tell.

I went hunting for Vikings in Newfoundland with space archaeologist Sarah Parcak. She had attracted worldwide attention by using satellite imaging technology to find ancient Egyptian sites. In Newfoundland she turned her attention to Vikings. For Warren and me, it was to be our first experimentation with drone technology, but we never got off the ground—a strong gale was blowing the whole time. I had visions of the drone landing in Nova Scotia somewhere. Instead, I stuck a GoPro camera on the end of a long pole, swooping it through the grass and out over the cliffs. Nobody knew the difference. The hoped-for new Viking site, however, proved elusive.

We travelled to Germany to profile the Canadian company Electrovaya, which had managed to purchase the largest lithium battery manufacturing plant in Europe. Along the way we dropped into Feldheim, just outside Berlin, to spend some time in the only community in the world completely powered by renewable energy.

In 2016, I'd put together a Christmas special using pieces I'd shot earlier involving an immigrant choir in Newfoundland, a woman from Vancouver Island who was sending food, clothing and money up North to help families cope with the exorbitant cost of living, and telling the story of the folks behind NORAD's Santa Tracker program. Now, approaching Christmas 2017, I heard about Kuldip Sahota of Regina. He and some others had put up a big sign outside their Sikh temple to wish everyone a MERRY CHRISTMAS!

Kuldip said as far as he was concerned, it was important for everyone to celebrate and enjoy their holidays, religious or not. The celebration of the birth of Christ didn't bother him one bit, and he found the expression "Merry Christmas" to be a warm, friendly greeting that should be encouraged—by everyone. I liked the way that man thought. He also sent me a Christmas card!

THE DEVIL'S BREATH

One of the most disturbing stories I ever produced was about a criminal psychiatric facility named Oak Ridge that used to exist in Southern Ontario. The story's genesis came after the telling of another story that was dark enough itself, the story of Dr. John Bradford, who at the time was Canada's top criminal forensic psychiatrist. John had dealt with the worst of the worst—Bernardo, Picton, Russell Williams—before suffering a sort of post-traumatic meltdown of his own. He agreed to speak with me about his difficulties and we developed a rapport. When we were finished taping, he told me about a place he had visited when he first came to Canada. He could not believe what was going on there. He said it needed to be exposed. I could hardly believe the world I was about to step into.

Oak Ridge was like something that a writer for a dark television series would conjure up. Except this story was very real. For over a decade, starting in the 1960s, the Ontario-run facility had conducted a series of bizarre medical experiments on its patients. The experiments involved all manner of drugs, including powerful hallucinogens like LSD and hyoscine (scopolamine). The medical staff employed sensory deprivation techniques and others commonly used in brainwashing. Inmates were physically tethered together, sometimes for weeks on end, or stripped naked, locked together in a sensory deprivation chamber and fed with straws through holes in the walls.

The "doctors" stated their goal was to "cure" psychopaths. The outcome was that many patients with legitimate mental afflictions became worse. Then they were set loose, back into society. I spoke with close to a dozen such people before I found one who was lucid enough to tell me what had happened to him.

Jim Motherall was in Winnipeg, living and working in a halfway house for ex-cons. He felt Oak Ridge had destroyed his life and he wanted to talk about it. He said the place, and what they did to him, made him incapable of functioning in society. What came next was a revolving door in and out of prison until, after attempting to strangle a woman, a complete stranger, in a convenience store, he was locked away in Stony Mountain Penitentiary for the next nineteen years. There Jim finally got the help he needed, and even became the first prisoner at the facility to receive a university degree. When I met him, he was part of a legal action trying to get the Ontario government and the doctors involved to take responsibility for what they had done.

Jim was an engaging fellow, clearly quite bright. I suspect he had a dark side as well, but he never let us see it. We remained friends long after the story aired. I know Jim was hoping it would force people to take responsibility for their actions. It didn't. Jim fell ill and died in the spring of 2018, never seeing the justice or the apology he had so badly wanted.

GETTING CLOSE

Is there anything stronger than two parents' love for their child? I don't think so. The Oake family was proof of that. They were dealing with the loss of their son Bruce. His dad was Scott Oake, an internationally known sportscaster and a friend and colleague of mine, both factors that made me initially reluctant to tell the story. Would it leave the piece open to accusations of bias or favouritism? I did not want to detract from what they were trying to accomplish. But in the end, I decided giving their efforts exposure was more important.

Bruce had died of an overdose after a long struggle with addiction. It had devastated Scott, Bruce's brother Darcy, and his mom, Anne. Now they were willing to put their personal grief on public display if it would help garner support for the Bruce Oake Recovery Centre. In Bruce's memory, they were determined to build a treatment facility that was accessible for anyone fighting to save their own life, fighting to get off drugs. The Oakes' message was powerful, poignant and sad, and I was happy to tell it for them. As I write this, the Bruce Oake Recovery Centre is becoming a reality.

In the fall I was honoured to help another friend, himself a survivor of addiction, who had stepped up to help veterans across Canada. The talented singer-songwriter Séan McCann had battled many demons of his own, mostly during his time with the popular Newfoundland band Great Big Sea. Now recovered, Sean dedicated a lot of his time to various support groups. One of them was VETS Canada, founded by Jim Lowther. Their idea was to help vets through music, teaching them guitar and providing the instruments as a sort of therapy to get many of them past addictions often caused by depression or PTSD. Another great cause I was happy to provide a stage for.

But increasingly, I was thinking about changing course myself. I'd had a few health scares, things that bring your age and how much quality time might be left sharply into focus. That alone wasn't enough to make me step back, but I was also becoming increasingly disillusioned with what I saw happening at the CBC. I had even stopped trying to change anything inside the place. That, to me, was a bad sign.

Some days I told myself, "Just because it's different doesn't mean it's worse. The young people here now don't know what it was like, they've never experienced what you experienced. Maybe it's just time to pass the torch." Some days I thought, "I need to get out of here before I become bitter and twisted." Getting stressed out and bitter could indeed make me sick. I began working on an exit strategy.

Earlier in 2017, I had begun profiling a young woman from Vancouver who was battling brain cancer. The initial idea was to focus on a new technology developed in Winnipeg. It made brain cancer surgery less invasive and offered a higher chance of success. It was being performed in only one place in Canada, Vancouver. I asked Dr. Brian Toyota if he would let me record the surgery, and he agreed. I asked him if he knew of a patient who would agree to be the subject of a documentary. He did. Boy, did he ever.

It would turn out to be the very last story I produced for the CBC.

THERE'S A TUMOUR IN MY BRAIN

She was tall and blond, with intense green eyes and a disarming smile. She had the personality of an angel and the determination of an Olympic athlete. I quickly fell in love with Carling Muir, and before long the country would too.

I didn't set out to meet Carling. It was her doctor I was interested in, and the new technology he was using. It had the promise of offering some hope in the world of brain cancer treatment. But Dr. Brian Toyota thought this courageous young woman should be the face of what he was trying to achieve. I soon realized he was right.

Carling, at age twenty-nine, had already been battling cancer for over a decade. After she collapsed during a college basketball practice, doctors discovered a massive tumour in her head and attempted to remove it. With a big smile she told me, "I remember because I asked, am I going to die?" She certainly could have. Survival involved a large incision, weeks of hospital care and years of rotating chemotherapy to try to keep what they couldn't remove in check.

Then it wasn't working anymore. The tumour was growing again.

But there was something new, something potentially game-changing, available to treat her. Dr. Brian Toyota, her doctor, was the only surgeon in Canada performing operations using the NeuroBlate probe. Instead of a huge incision, the probe could access the tumour through a small hole drilled in her skull. Using a laser probe, guided with a real-time MRI, Dr. Toyota could use heat to try to kill the cancer.

For Carling, letting us hang out was all about helping people at home understand the journey of a cancer victim, about being able to see the process "up close and personal." She had a strength and tenacity about her. A competitor from the get-go, she hadn't asked to play this game, but she had every intention of winning. She had the word *SURVIVOR* tattooed on the inside of her wrist. It was her reminder that cancer didn't get to define who she was, *she* did.

The one time she let just a little of that pressure and stress show was when she spoke about her family. "I worry more, like, about what it does to my family," she said, her voice breaking. "That's the part that gets me. What it does to Andrew, and my parents and brother, all my other family and friends." I reached out to console her, patting her shoulder. "It's okay," she said, smiling that million-watt smile. "I can deal with it myself, but I hate putting them through that. That's what keeps me up at night."

She was about to have brain surgery again in just a few short days, and all she could think about was everyone else. Incredible. Her partner Andrew, her parents Shelley and Grant, and her brother Parker were all walking on this journey with her, every step of the way. But ultimately, this battle was hers and hers alone.

I had recorded surgery before, years ago. It wasn't minor surgery either—it was an open-heart operation—but in that case, I never really knew the patient. This time I did, and it moved the emotion up to another level. Warren had never videotaped in an operating

Warren and I preparing to film a brave young woman having brain surgery. I was more scared than she appeared to be.

theatre before and was, I think, a little concerned about how it was going to make him feel. I had concerns of my own. I'd often said, "Reg Sherren the journalist can do things that Reg Sherren the person probably would not. When you put on that journalist's cape, you become a much braver guy."

Warren recorded the main part of the surgery. I was capturing what I could with the GoPro camera and its super wide-angle lens. First, they placed a guiding mount on Carling's skull, drilling through the bone to provide an entry port for the probe. That was finished in a matter of moments, and they were waking Carling up.

She would remain awake for the next part. The brain doesn't feel pain per se, so they were able to insert the probe, guided by an MRI, and start killing the cancer while Carling remained fully awake. To me it seemed weird and just a little bit creepy, but it didn't faze Carling one little bit—or if it did, she certainly didn't let it show.

But, as can happen with new technology, there was a problem, this time with the software used to run the computer program. Carling was becoming increasingly uncomfortable inside the MRI chamber. Dr. Toyota decided to suspend the procedure until the next day. It was an awkward time for the whole team, especially with the cameras rolling. You could feel the pressure in the room.

Warren and I put Dr. Toyota's focus remained on Carling. The compassion and professionalism he showed were a real testament to the man. I'm sure he wished the camera could forget what it had recorded, but he wouldn't put me in that position. From my perspective, it was a small blip in the scheme of things. Carling seemed fine. We would all regroup in the morning.

The next day, it all went as planned. They placed Carling in the MRI, the probe was inserted in her brain and Dr. Toyota proceeded to guide it, killing the cancer. After about half an hour, he concluded he had done as much as he could reach without potentially harming other parts of her brain.

The probe was withdrawn and Carling, fully conscious through it all, was wheeled into the hallway. That was when she said, "I really have to pee," got up off the gurney and walked to the washroom. This was barely five minutes after they had finished operating on her brain. Unbelievable.

Instead of weeks and even months of recovery, Carling was on her way home barely a day and a half later. As she walked out of Vancouver General, she turned to give a huge smile and wave to the camera. I knew that was how I would end the piece, and that was where even the hardest critics would fall in love with her too.

The piece chewed up over twenty minutes, two entire segments on *The National*. It was one of those rare nights when the ratings for the back half of the show were higher than the front. We heard from people right across Canada and the United States.

"That was amazing! Such a brave young lady!" "Truly a gripping story of this brave young lady who seems more concerned about her family and loved ones than herself." "Brought tears to my eyes when she got up to walk to the washroom. What a brave survivor! Great story ... thank you."

Brave indeed. Warren and I followed Carling through her follow-up chemotherapy, through the hard news of learning the tumour was persisting and her day-to-day struggles to maintain some normalcy. Throughout it all she remained gracious and polite, and as honest and forthright as any person could be.

It would be my last piece to run on the CBC. The half-hour presentation, "There's a Tumour in My Brain," aired Christmas week. I couldn't think of a better way to end a career or a more courageous young Canadian to end it with. I don't like to bother Carling as often as I think about her, but I am still in contact with both her and her parents. The battle continues. The survivor pushes forward.

Who wouldn't love her?

CHAPTER 21

It's Time to Go

Christmas 1975. That was when I'd done my first gig on the radio in Western Labrador. Now, after over forty years of broadcasting, crossing the country and travelling the world, all that was coming to a close. Pushing SEND on this note was one of the hardest things I have ever done:

December 22, 2017

And now, it's come to this. My last day at CBC.

My last piece, accomplished with the stellar work of Mr. Warren Kay, will appear on CBC News Network this Saturday, December 23rd, at 9:30 p.m. Eastern. A shorter version will appear on *The National*, I believe, on Christmas Day. It's a tribute to Carling Muir, the young West Coast woman we have followed through this past year, battling brain cancer. If you have the chance, please check it out. She's quite something.

So many stories told, so many talented people I have had the honour and privilege to walk down this road with. Together, I am proud to say, we have accomplished many things. Stories that changed lives, offered hope, rebuilt homes, found help for those who needed it. Stories that have been raised in the House of Commons, that led to Orders of Canada being awarded, organizations being saved, and statues being erected.

Stories about the wonderful people who make up this country, about our history, about what defines us as Canadian. It's all about the story. The rest of it, the technology, the bells and whistles, that's just the delivery system ... it's ALWAYS about the story.

It's been a great run. Life is too short. On to new things. Thank you, and until next time, take good care of yourself! (old *Country Canada* sign-off)

Yer pal,

Reg

It was done, but somehow it isn't finished. Do I miss the CBC? Well ... I miss the *idea* of the CBC, but then, I had been missing that for some time before I left. What leaving has empowered me to do is share a few observations about the state of public broadcasting in this country.

Survival for any broadcaster in the current environment is a Herculean task. I get that. But it should be much easier for the CBC. For a public broadcaster, content is not supposed to be about ratings. It's supposed to be about mandate, about giving Canadians what they pay for. And what is that exactly?

Blame it on Graham Spry. He was the young Rhodes Scholar with a vision—an argument against the commercialization of our Canadian airwaves—back in the 1930s:

Let the air remain as the prerogative of commercial interests and subject to commercial control, and how free will be the voice, the heart of democracy. The maintenance, the enlargement of freedom, the progress, the purity of education, require the responsibility of broadcasting to the popular will. There can be no liberty complete, no democracy supreme, if the commercial interests dominate the vast, majestic resource of broadcasting.

His Canadian Radio League saw the dangers of large foreign commercial interests, predominantly American, and it appeared Prime Minister R.B. Bennett and his Conservatives agreed, saying a Canadian broadcasting system "controlled and operated by Canadians" was critical.

And now, here we are. In my humble opinion, the voice of the CBC has never been more important than in this age of constant bombardment of information dominated by commercial and foreign interests. Early in 2019, Catherine Tait, sitting at the controls of the Mother Corp., railed against the influences of foreign entities like Netflix.

In the *Toronto Star* on February 4, 2019, columnist Heather Mallick wrote, "All hail CBC president and CEO Catherine Tait for fearlessly standing up for Canada at a parlous time when the American elephant thrashes and trumpets at the rest of the world. Go stomp on someone else was her message, and we should be proud."

But later in the same article, Ms. Mallick wrote, "I tire of *The National* leading with American news, of CBC.CA running American clickbait." Now Ms. Tait wants to reduce CBC's obligation to air Canadian content on television by several hours, promising to make up for it on CBC's digital platform.

I know what the CBC is capable of. When I was a young Canadian, the corporation truly took me under its wing. The imagination, the fearless creativity, the knowledge—it was all there. I grew up with the CBC. I woke up with it and I went to bed with it. I dedicated my professional career to it. I am as thoroughly a child of the CBC universe as you will find. And I think it should be so much more important to so many more Canadians than it appears to be today.

They tell me all the time. My friends, my neighbours, strangers in airports. I'm a bit of a lightning rod for that sort of thing, and happily so. They clearly still love their idea of the CBC, but they say these days, the CBC isn't the same. The stories are more urban based, and the country just isn't being reflected like it used to be on the TV, the internet or even the radio. People pay their taxes. Their taxes pay for the CBC. But as of 2019 you have to pay even more, on top of your taxes, to watch CBC. Watching online means paying for the internet, and if you want to watch CBC's full complement of programming on Gem (CBC's streaming service), commercial free, you have to pay an additional fee on top of everything else. The delivery system is quickly becoming broken.

CBC.CA should decommercialize. It would be a good place to start. Instead of selling advertising, set up a news wire service like Reuters or CP to help the privates survive, or at least transition. The CBC should be the champion of maintaining a diversity of voices in all broadcasting/media communities, not playing a role in their demise. And it should seriously think about ending relationships with entities like Facebook. I think it's the first time in the CBC's history that the corporation has given control of its content to an outside party and retained zero control over what they do with it, what advertisements are placed around it or who even gets to see it.

The legislation is clear. Among other things, it states:

> The Canadian broadcasting system should: (i) serve to safe-guard, enrich and strengthen the cultural, political, social and economic fabric of Canada.

Well then. No mention of ratings in there anywhere. I have watched kids' programs and regional variety, lifestyles and current affairs programming, all of which used to be produced by the CBC's own employees, practically disappear in the last twenty years. The leadership says it's about money. It just isn't.

Each spring CBC radio still offers its employees the opportunity to pitch a summer radio series. If it is deemed to have merit, they produce it. If it enjoys success, it becomes part of regular programming. What a great concept. You can't tell me the CBC cannot do that on the TV side. It can—it just doesn't want to. A recent big programming idea was to get an independent company to produce a Canadian version of the American game show *Family Feud*. Really? That's enriching the fabric of Canada? There is little future in this kind of thinking.

In all programming, stop waiting to see what is trending. Take chances. Don't be afraid of failure. Give the future a chance. Develop shows from the inside. Be the CBC.

Well now, that felt good! Getting a few things off my chest, I mean. And please don't misunderstand me. I love the CBC. I love how it has helped define our nation, and on a personal level I appreciate every opportunity it gave to me and my family. It afforded me the chance to see and learn so many things about Canada and its people. It allowed me to tell you so many important stories (close to five thousand at last count) about who we are and, yes, about the things we need to do better.

The CBC helped me grow as a journalist and as a human being. It gave my family a wonderful life and allowed me to travel the world to bring you stories. Together we explored everything from the best to the worst that Canadians, as a group of people on this planet, have to offer. For that, I will be eternally grateful.

For you younger journalists out there, I think if there's any advice I can offer, it would be this: be true to your dreams and your goals. Don't let anybody bully you into a career path that works better for them than it may for you. Also, remember that the story—and the characters you introduce to tell it—is more important than anything else, more important than the technology, the delivery system and certainly more important than you. Do everything you can to make your characters feel comfortable enough to tell you the real story, the one viewers will remember. Fight for the stories you love. Fight for the stories that are important to you. Fight for the history. You can do it! Don't let *anyone* tell you that you can't.

As for me, after over four decades of playing the most important role in my professional life, I am moving forward now at a new, slower pace. Life is good. In fact, it's great. Pam probably finds me under her feet too much, but I do my best to keep busy. I can almost play the guitar. I've started sketching again, and I still have some more writing in me. I even pick up a camera now and again.

People still come up to me on occasion and say, "Hey, aren't you that fellow from CBC? I love your work!" It's always very gratifying. Often, I don't have the heart to say, "You mean that fellow who used to be on CBC." That's because I remain very proud of my work there, and proud to still be associated with such an important Canadian institution.

If you see me on the street, or maybe in a bookstore, please say hello and tell me a little bit about your story. I've become an excellent listener. Thanks for reading about my journey. It means the world to me.

Acknowledgements

Is there anyone who has more influence on you than family? Of course, I mean the love and support of my wife Pam and our kids, as well as that of my brothers and sisters.

My dad Nelson was my hero. His knowledge and his friendships with so many people never ceased to amaze me. I could travel anywhere in this country and run into someone who knew him. His abiding interest in history often led me to the people or events that help define Canada as a great nation. His love and advice meant the world to me. I miss him everyday.

His mother, my Grandmother Rowena, was a special influence. A lifelong educator, her weekly letters offered comfort and support to a young fellow far from home.

My wife's parents, Phyllis and Minor Tennant, were always ready to step up and help our young family when Dad (me) had to travel somewhere, often on short notice, to chase another tale. I am a lucky guy and have always felt blessed to be part of their family.

And, were it not for my other family—the many colleagues, true professionals all, who I had the honour to work with side by side— Lord knows what would have become of me. The producers, editors, camera ops, sound technicians, librarians, announcers, unit managers ... the list goes on. You number in the hundreds from coast to coast to coast, always ready with advice, support and suggestions, or more importantly, a good laugh to see us through the day! I consider you all friends, and I thank you.

Finally, to the gang at Douglas & McIntyre, thanks for having confidence in me, and for helping with the hard work to make this happen.

About the Author

Reg Sherren is a popular commentator, writer and freelance producer. A two-time Gemini and Canadian Screen Award nominee, Reg has also been the recipient of numerous journalism awards from the New York and Columbus international film and video festivals, as well as the Radio-Television News Directors' Association. He lives in Winnipeg, MB.